Blown Away

BY

A. E. HOTCHNER

A FIRESIDE BOOK

Published by Simon & Schuster
New York London Toronto Sydney Tokyo Singapore

FIRESIDE
Simon & Schuster Building
Rockefeller Center
1230 Avenue of the Americas
New York, New York 10020

First Fireside Edition 1991

FIRESIDE and colophon are registered trademarks
of Simon & Schuster Inc.

Designed by Irving Perkins Assoc.
Manufactured in the United States of America

10 9 8 7 6 5 4 3 2 1

Library of Congress Cataloging in Publication Data

Hotchner, A. E.
   Blown Away
   p.   cm.
   Includes bibliographical references.
1. Rolling Stones. 2. Jones, Brian, d. 1969. 3. Rock musicians—
   England—Biography. I. Title.
   ML421.R64H65   1990
   782.42166'092'2—dc20
   [B]   90-37397
                                                          CIP
                                                          MN

ISBN 0-671-69316-6
ISBN 0-671-74867-X (pbk)

Acknowledgments

The author was admirably assisted by these diligent researchers: Karen Emmons, Teresa Scala, Sally Arnold, Susan Ready, Linda Sykes, Karen Walker, Vicky Hayward, Christine Vincent, and, particularly, Electra May.

The author is also indebted to those people who were intimates of the Rolling Stones and of the sixties, over two hundred in number, and who consented to be interviewed for *Blown Away*. Their memories of events and details are distilled from hundreds of hours of interviews conducted by the author over a five-year span; material from a wealth of published interviews is represented here as well.

This book was written without the approval of the Stones. With the exception of Ian Stewart and Dick Taylor, who consented to interviews, the other Stones did not participate. However, the author wishes to thank the British Broadcasting Corporation for making available to him all of its radio and television transcriptions of interviews with Mick Jagger, Keith Richards and Bill Wyman.

For my friend Cy Coleman,
consummate musician

Contents

PART ONE END OF AN ERA

Chapter 1 Death at Altamont   17
Chapter 2 Death of a Stone   29
Chapter 3 The Faster the Better   36

PART TWO THE RISE

Chapter 4 The Skifflers from Dartford   47
Chapter 5 Down and Out in London   71
Chapter 6 Inventing the Rolling Stones   94
Chapter 7 Flopping in the U.S.A.   111

PART THREE THE CREST

Chapter 8 Marianne Faithfull: The Baroness's Daughter   131
Chapter 9 Success Is the Best Revenge   151
Chapter 10 Ominous Rumblings of Discontent   169
Chapter 11 Glamour, Villainy and Degradation   185
Chapter 12 Acid Dreams and Other Nightmares   207

PART FOUR THE FALL

Chapter 13 The Persecution of the Stones   229
Chapter 14 Anita Pallenberg: Exchanging Allegiances   266
Chapter 15 Who Killed Brian Jones?   289
Chapter 16 The Degradation of Marianne Faithfull   304
Chapter 17 The Long, Ugly Shadow of Altamont   315
Chapter 18 Requiem for the Jagger Generation   331

References   347

CHAPTER 19: CHAPA KILLS Book

Blown Away

You've got to do it all at once—change everything fast—the faster the better. This way each detail of the new life can support other details so one is not constantly reminded of the old ways.

—*Margaret Mead*

PART ONE

End of an Era

CHAPTER ONE

Death at Altamont

Erotic politicians, that's what we are. We're in-
terested in everything about revolt, disorder, and
all activity that appears to have no meaning.

JIM MORRISON
LEAD SINGER, THE DOORS

The Sixties Generation came to an abrupt, tragic end on December 6, 1969, on a desolate, barren field in Livermore, California, with the Rolling Stones presiding over the demise. What had started out, a decade earlier, as a surge of idealistic, carefree young people dedicated to a liberal romanticism and an aggressive idealism, ended up ugly, brutal and bloody, a Hieronymus Bosch madness accompanied by the impotent entreaties of a frustrated Mick Jagger, lead singer of the Stones.

Four months after the joyous love-in at Woodstock where, over one weekend, 500,000 young people had peacefully celebrated the glorious success of their insurgency with the songs of their rock and roll generation, Mick Jagger and the Rolling Stones attracted a throng estimated at 400,000 to the Altamont Speedway and, in the space of a few hours, deep-sixed the spirit of their generation.

Jagger's decision to stage a free concert in California was made impetuously as the Rolling Stones' 1969 tour of the United States was ending. The tour had been hugely successful at the box office, but Jagger had been stung by accusations that they had ripped off promoters and gouged American audiences with their inflated ticket prices. Thus the decision to give a free concert to take the heat off these accusations. A site was selected—the Sears Point Raceway outside San Francisco—the stage was built, lights assembled, when, at the last moment, the deal fell through. In a desperate move to save the event, arrangements were made to switch the event to the Altamont Speedway, some seventy miles away, a grim, remote expanse whose ninety acres were used for stock-car racing. This move meant that the stage and light towers had to be taken down, transported and reassembled within twenty-four hours, and all other arrangements effectuated overnight. The Stones' tour was already being filmed by David and Albert Maysles, who were renowned for their prize-winning documentaries, and they quickly assembled several additional film crews to help them cover the Altamont event. Other basic arrangements, however, such as portable toilets, medical personnel, and security were dealt with haphazardly with no one seemingly in charge.

Out of this confusion, there somehow emerged the notion that the Hell's Angels should be invited, not as bodyguards, but as a peace-keeping force. The suggestion may have come from the Grateful Dead's manager who was helping to plan the event, or from one of the other managers of the various groups scheduled to perform with the Stones. At any event, a number of Hell's Angels' chapters were invited to attend, the reasoning being that it was better to have them there officially than have them come as self-appointed enforcers. Jagger acquiesced but, unfortunately, he was not aware of the difference between the rather harmless biker gangs of Britain and the Hell's Angels, vicious, armed thugs whose criminal escapades even terrorized the police.

The crowd began arriving the night before the concert, lured by invitations going out from rock stations all over northern California. The early arrivals spread their blankets and, to help fend off the cold of that December night, lit fires on the dusty ground littered with the remains of decayed and rusting stock cars abandoned after violent collisions on the dirt tracks. Some of the early arrivals spent the night huddled under blankets inside the abandoned cars.

The Rolling Stones arrived late in the night in limousines to inspect the site. Swathed in a pink cape and matching pink cap, Jagger, followed by a Maysles camera crew, tested the stage and then, along with Keith Richards, visited their disciples at their bonfires, gingerly avoiding the rusty auto parts and the mounds of broken glass, the remains of a thousand demolition crashes. Despite the cold and the depressing nature of their surroundings, the early crowd was good-natured, singing, smoking pot, playing Frisbee by firelight.

Those who arrived the morning of the concert had to park their cars eight miles away from the concert site and hike the rest of the way on foot over rough terrain. In the middle of the morning, the ominous procession of Hell's Angels arrived on their roaring "hogs," dressed in traditional black-studded leather embossed with Nazi insignia, and armed with a variety of lethal weapons. They steered their bikes into the crowd, by now swelled to 200,000, daring them to part and give ground, which they did, enabling the Angels to station themselves directly in front of the stage. Only a few feet off the ground instead of the usual eight or ten feet, the stage allowed easy access to anyone in the audience. Also, unlike the precautions taken at Woodstock, no barrier had been installed in front of the stage to create a buffer zone between the audience and the performers; these two oversights were to contribute greatly to the debacle that occurred later that night.

David and Albert Maysles

THESE ANGELS CAME from neighboring chapters in San Francisco, San Jose, San Bernardino and Oakland, and they were loaded with weapons—knives, chains, lead pipes, tire irons and sawed-off pool cues with lead-weighted ends. The parade of motorbikes was followed by a Hell's Angels' school bus that was stocked with beer, rotgut wine and questionable LSD tabs.

By noon there were many more than the 300,000 that had been expected, but they were not in a very festive mood. One reason was the grubby, desolate nature of the place. Another was that there had not been adequate preparations for a crowd of that size. There were only a few portable toilets, and long lines waited to use them. The medical tents were overrun with kids who had used bad drugs being peddled by syndicate pushers. The weather was gray and chilly, and to top it off, the sound system wasn't working properly so that they couldn't fully enjoy the music they had come to hear. The Hell's Angels had taken up positions on the stage and directly in front of it, obscuring the sight lines of the audience.

There was a negative feeling in the air, a surly something. This was not a huge bunch of carefree kids come to enjoy themselves; no, there definitely was an ominous feeling in the air, something to do with the power of so large a concentration of people—we had no previous conception of the enormous impact of 300,000 people crammed into a single space with the menace of these Hell's Angels hanging over them. And add to that the reputation of the Stones, the reason why everyone had come. Not only were they perceived as rough anti-establishment renegades, but also because so many of their songs (as personified in Mick) had a Satanic aura about them, they saw Mick as Lucifer; so they were awaiting this messenger from hell with these barbarian Hell's Angels as his netherworld entourage.

When the acts began, leading off with Santana and all that brass, the mood got better, some kids began to get up and dance, and we were getting it all with our cameras. But just when Santana and his group were heating up and creating a kind of fiesta mood, the disturbances began. Some kid tried to get near the stage and the wall of Hell's Angels clubbed him down with their pool cues. A naked, obese man, dazed with drugs, wandered around until the Hell's Angels pool cues bludgeoned him. Right in front of us, a photographer taking pictures of this savagery was attacked by the Hell's Angels, who beat him with their cues, kicked him with their studded boots and then jammed his camera into his face, leaving him moaning and bleeding on the ground. There were other pockets of violence out of camera shot, and during Santana's performance unopened beer cans were lobbed from the Hell's Angels school bus, aimed at members of the Santana band.

The Stones' manager, Sam Cutler, tried to calm everything down before the Jefferson Airplane came on with Grace Slick. The Airplane had always been friendly with the Angels, raised money at benefits for them, so we expected Grace to get them under control, but no sooner had she started to sing "We Can Be Together" than the Angels put their pool cues back in action. Grace Slick stopped the music and appealed to the Angels, "Hey, you guys, why are we hurting each other?" Did no good. While the Airplane played their aggressive song, "Volunteers," a group of Angels moved in on a black kid and started to club him mercilessly. One of the members of the band, Marty Balin, jumped off the stage to help the kid but was himself immediately clubbed into unconsciousness by the Angels. When another band member, the lead guitarist, Jorma Kaukonen, announced to the crowd what the Angels had done, a particularly loathsome Angel hulk who was standing on the stage grabbed a mike and yelled, "Fuck you!"

The Stones arrived by helicopter while the Jefferson Airplane was performing. They went immediately to their trailer, which was parked behind the stage. Some kid, high on acid, took a punch at Mick and yelled obscenities at him. Several more acts followed the Airplane, with sporadic clubbings continuing. For some reason, when Crosby, Stills and Nash started to perform, the Angels' violence escalated. They began to beat people for no reason at all, men and women, whoever was in their vicinity. There were bodies all over the ground. Crosby, Stills and Nash grabbed their instruments and bolted to their waiting helicopter. Stretcher-bearers carted off the injured to the overcrowded medical tents.

We don't know if the Stones were told about what was going on. They had brought two bodyguards of their own, but they wouldn't be of much help considering how many and how vicious these Angels were. Sam Cutler tried to get everyone off the stage before the Stones came on, but in response the Angels rode their bikes right through the throng and positioned them in a solid line in front of the stage.

It was dark by now and getting colder. Bonfires appeared as the kids tried to stay warm waiting for the Stones. When Mick left the dressing room, a swarm of uninvited Angels surrounded him and went right up on the stage with him, leaving him little room to perform in. Mick pleaded with them to move aside, and they gave a little but not much.

Then, as soon as the Stones started their first number, the whack of pool cues could be heard just beyond where Mick was performing. Most of the photographers were too frightened to take pictures, having seen what the Angels did to a couple of their colleagues, but for some reason the Angels assigned bodyguards to our camera crews so we were able to keep filming.

And then it happened. Mick wrapped his cloak around him and the band struck up "Sympathy for the Devil," Mick's definitive Satan song, in which he introduced himself as "a man of wealth and taste. . . ." The Angels went berserk, the sickening sound of their smashing pool cues competing with the music. The band stopped. Mick, in a pleading voice: "Brothers and sisters . . . brothers and sisters, come on now! That means *everybody*—just cool out.

21

Just cool out now! We can cool out, everybody. Everybody be cool now, come on . . ."

But no sooner had Mick gone back to the song than the violence erupted again; this time a young girl was clubbed right in front of Mick, who stopped singing again, and rather helplessly said, "Fellas . . . does it take five of you to handle her?" The stage was now overrun with Angels who had unleashed a fierce-looking German shepherd that was focusing its attention on Charlie Watts, the drummer, and Bill Wyman, the bass guitarist.

Keith Richards now reacted to the carnage going on directly in front of him (we have all this on film). "That guy there . . . if he doesn't stop it, man . . ."

"Hey, people . . . who's fighting and what for?" Jagger said. "Hey, peo—ple, why are we fighting? What are we fighting for? We don't want to fight. Come on—do we want—who wants to fight? Hey—I—you know, I swear, like—every other scene has been cool. Like we've gotta stop right now. We've gotta stop them right now. You know . . . we can't . . . there's no point . . ." Nobody was paying any attention to him. The mike could have been turned off for all the effect he was having. "All I can do is ask you . . . *beg* you to keep it together. It's within your power."

We kept our cameras rolling, getting every minute of this bedlam. Mick Taylor, another guitarist, and Bill Wyman were playing some improvised slow chords to try to calm things down but it wasn't working.

A short distance from the stage, there was sudden, violent movement. The mass of people pulled apart, creating a narrow path, and we caught sight of a young black man running frantically toward the stage. There was a blur of activity, his right arm raised up in the air as a second person became involved with him. When we saw this sudden opening in the crowd we turned our camera on it. What were these two people doing? It looked like they were dancing, and then there was a flash of something shiny. The cameraman, his eye to the camera, said, "What the hell goes on, two people dancing with all this shit going on?" The camera was on it but what had happened was too fast for us. As it turned out, the camera had recorded the killing of the black kid. The dance we thought we saw was a dance of death.

□ □ □

A more detailed account of the killing itself was given by a bystander, Paul Cox, who later testified before the grand jury: "An Angel kept looking over at me and I tried to keep ignoring him and I didn't want to look at him at all, because I was very scared of them and seeing what they were doing all day and because he kept trying to cause a fight or something and kept staring at us. He kept on looking over, and the next thing I know he's hassling this Negro boy on the side of me. And I was trying not to look at him, and then he reached over and shook this boy by the side of the head, thinking it was fun, laughing, and I noticed something was going to happen so I kind of backed off.

"The boy yanked away, and when he yanked away, next thing I know he was flying in the air, right on the ground, just like all the other people it happened to. He scrambled to his feet, and he's backing up and trying to run from the Angels, and all these Angels are—a couple jumped off the stage and a couple was running alongside the stage, and his girlfriend was screaming to him not to shoot, because he pulled out his gun. And when he pulled it out, he held it in the air, and his girlfriend is like climbing on him and pushing him back, and he's trying to get away and these Angels are coming at him, and he turns around and starts running. And then some Angel snuck up from right out of the crowd and leaped up and brought this knife down in his back. And then I saw him stab him again, and while he's stabbing him, he's running. This Negro boy is running into the crowd, and you could see him stiffen up when he's being stabbed.

"He came running toward me. I grabbed onto the scaffold, and he came running toward me and fell down on his knees, and the Hell's Angel grabbed onto both of his shoulders and started kicking him in the face about five times or so, and then he let go, and he fell down on his face. And then one of them kicked him in the side, and he rolled over and muttered some words. He said, 'I wasn't going to shoot you.' Those were the last words he muttered.

"If some other people would have jumped in, I would have jumped in. But nobody jumped in, and after he said, 'I wasn't going to shoot you,' one of the Hell's Angels said, 'Why did you have a gun?' He didn't give him time to say anything. He grabbed one of those garbage cans, the cardboard ones with the metal rimming, and he smashed him over the head with it, and then he kicked the garbage can out of the way and started kicking his head in. Five or six of them started kicking his head in. Kicked him all over the place. And then the guy that started the whole thing stood on his head for a minute or so and then walked off. And then the one I was talking about, he wouldn't let us touch him for about two or three minutes. Like, 'Don't touch him, he's going to die anyway, let him die, he's going to die.'

"Chicks were just screaming. It was all confusion. I jumped down anyway to grab him, and some other dude jumped down and grabbed him, and then the Hell's Angel just stood over him for a little bit and then walked away. We turned him over and ripped off his shirt. We rubbed his back up and down to get the blood off so we could see, and there was a big hole in his spine and a big hole on the side and a big hole in his temple. A big open slice. You could see all the way in. You could see inside. You could see at least an inch down. And then there was a big hole right where there's no ribs on his back—and then the side of his head was just sliced open—you couldn't see so far in—it was bleeding quite heavily—but his back wasn't bleeding too heavy after that—there—all of us were drenched in blood.

"I picked up his legs and someone else . . . this guy said he was a doctor or something . . . I don't know who he was . . . he picked up his arms, and he said, 'Got to get him some help because he's going to die. We've got fifteen or twenty minutes, if we can get him some help. . . .' And so we tried to carry him on the stage. Tell Mick Jagger to stop playing so we could get him on the stage and get some attention for him. No one told Jagger that, but someone was trying to tell him to stop, and he kept leaning over and looking out at the crowd like he was paying attention and trying to figure out what was happening. He kept leaning over with his ear trying to hear what somebody was telling him, but he couldn't hear. So they kept on playing and the Hell's Angels wouldn't let us through . . . get on the stage. They kept blocking us, saying go around, go through some other way. They knew he was going to die in a matter of minutes. They wanted him to die probably so he couldn't talk. And so we carried . . . we turned around and went the other way. It took about fifteen minutes to get him behind the stage. We went around that whole thing and got behind where there was a Red Cross truck, something like that. And someone brought out a metal stretcher and laid him on that. Well, first we laid him on the ground. And then we felt his pulse and it was just barely doing it . . . real slow and real weak. His whole mouth and stuff is bashed up into his nose and stuff and he couldn't breathe out of his nose. He was trying to breathe out of his mouth. There really wasn't anything you could do. We carried him over to some station wagon, and then whoever owned the car hopped in and some other people hopped in, and I stayed there. I went over and they had this thing of coffee and I poured it all over to wipe off all the blood."

After Meredith Hunter was taken away on a stretcher, the Hell's Angels' turmoil continued unabated, the Maysles' cameras continuing to record what was happening on the stage. The Stones stopped playing as the stretcher-bearers were lifting the dying black youth off the ground. "Okay, man," Keith said to the crowd, "look, we're splitting, if you cats can't—we're splitting, if those people don't stop beating everybody up in sight—I want them out of the way!"

Mick was trying to peer through the wall of blinding stage lights to determine exactly what was happening in the semi-darkness beyond, but a sense of doom and helplessness seemed to have incapacitated him as a result of the Angels' total disregard of his pleas. "Will you listen to me for a minute—please listen to me just for one second, all right? First of all, everyone is gonna get to the side of the stage who's on it now except for the Stones who are playing. Please, everyone—please, can you get to the side of the stage who's not playing? Right? That's a start. Now, the thing is, I can't see what's going on, who is doing what, it's just a scuffle. All I can ask you, San Francisco, is like the whole thing—this could be the most beautiful evening we've had this winter, we really, you know, why, why don't let's fuck it up, man, come on, let's get it together, everyone, come on now, I can't see you up on the hill-sides, you're probably very cool. Down here we're not so cool, we've got a lot of hassles going on. We can't even see you but I know you're there, you're cool. We're just trying to keep it to-gether. I can't do any more than ask you, *beg* you, just to keep it together. You can do it, it's within your power, everyone, Hell's Angels, everybody. Let's just keep ourselves together. If we are all one, let's fucking well show we're all one. Now there's one thing we need—Sam, we need an ambulance, we need a doctor by that scaffold there, if there's a doctor, can he get to there? Okay, we're gonna . . . we gonna do—I don't know what the fuck we're gonna do. Everyone just sit down. Keep cool. Let's just relax, let's get into a groove. Come on, we can get it together. Come on."

Having given it his best shot, Mick launched the band into a succession of numbers—"Under My Thumb," "Brown Sugar" (in which he sang about whipping women) and "Midnight Rambler" with its macabre lyrics that certainly befitted the occasion, all about a night killer who stalks the corridors with a knife ready to stab a victim. Certainly not words to defuse the rabid bikers with their indiscriminately whacking pool cues.

As the Stones' music escalated so did the carnage of the Hell's Angels. A pathetic fat girl, her breasts exposed, zonked on acid, tried to reach up to Mick only to be seized, pummeled by several Angels and stripped naked; trying to get to her feet, her mouth bloody, eyes unfocused, she was bloodily assaulted right in front of Mick and Keith, her fat body kicked by Angels' boots and pelted with their flailing pool sticks.

"Stop that one!" Keith called out.

"Hey—hey hey hey hey hey!" Mick protested. "One cat can control that chick, you know what I mean? Hey fellows, hey fellows, one of you can control her, man."

The Angels continued to stomp on the girl with their heavy boots as she tumbled back and in so doing toppled some of the people packed in around her.

"Hey, come on fellows," Mick pleaded, "like one of you can control one little girl—come on now, like . . . like . . . just sit down, honey . . ."

The fat girl, her body bleeding, tried to get to her feet, but the Angels beat her back to the ground as Mick continued to plead with them: "Fellows, can you clear . . . she'll . . . let them deal with her . . . they can deal with her . . . fellows, come on fellows, they're all right."

As the Angels began to abate their attack, Mick started to sing "Gimme Shelter," repeating endlessly, "Rape, murder, it's just a shot away," then segued into "Satisfaction" and "Honky Tonk Women." Incredibly, as the song ended, Mick addressed his brutalized audience as if nothing evil had occurred. "We gonna kiss you good-bye, and we leave you to kiss each other good-bye. We're gonna see you, we're gonna see you again, all right? . . . Well, there's been a few hang-ups you know but I mean generally I mean you've been beautiful . . . you have been so groovy . . . Kiss each other good-bye . . . sleep . . . good night . . ."

With that, the Stones bolted from the stage, evading the mass of Angels that surrounded them, and made a frantic dash for a waiting ambulance and limousine, which whisked them to their alerted helicopter, its blades whirling. They hurled themselves aboard, along with some of their terrified staff, fourteen people packed into the eight-seater, which struggled to get off the ground.

The toll they left behind: four dead—one murdered, two run over, one drowned in a drainage ditch—and hundreds injured, some seriously.

The Stones flew back to England on the first available plane without offering any reaction to what had happened—no apology, no explanation, no interest, apparently, in what had actually happened or who had been killed. The indignation over their departure was expressed by Bill Graham, a San Francisco rock promoter who had strongly opposed the Altamont concert when it was first proposed: "I ask you what right you had, Mr. Jagger, in going through with this free festival? You can't tell me you didn't know the way it would come off. What right do you have to leave the way you did, thanking everyone for a wonderful time and the Angels for helping out? What did Jagger leave behind throughout the country? Every gig, he was late. Every fucking gig he made the promoter and the people bleed. What right does this god have to descend on this country this way? But you know what is a great tragedy to me? That cunt is a great entertainer."

Ian Stewart,
ORIGINAL MEMBER OF THE STONES

ALTAMONT WAS the death knell of the sixties. You've got to remember that Brian Jones, who was the one who started the Rolling Stones, was drowned in his swimming pool in July 1969. In August Charles Manson and his crazies, in the name of flower power, slaughtered all those people in Polanski's Beverly Hills mansion. That same month was Woodstock, and then within a year, Janis Joplin, Jimi Hendrix and Alan Wilson of Canned Heat all died bad deaths.

But right in there was the bloodbath that occurred at Altamont, with Mick and Keith like tongue-tied ringmasters at an insane circus.

Rock festivals were never really the same after Altamont, in fact they just about ceased to exist. Flower children, love-ins, acid trips, all that shit, simply disappeared in such a quick and eerie way that you wondered if really they had ever existed at all.

I can honestly tell you that I had a foreboding of disaster for the Stones the day Brian died. If you want to unravel the mystery of what happened to the sixties, start with Brian. I always felt there was something sinister about the way he died.

As Stew had suspected, over the course of the years I have spent researching the Stones and the sixties, I discovered that there was indeed something sinister about Brian's death, but by the time I had uncovered the true circumstances of his bizarre drowning, Stew himself, at the age of forty-seven, had died of a heart attack. What happened to Brian was not dissimilar to what happened at Altamont; in fact, Brian Jones and the sixties experienced their rise and fall in lockstep.

CHAPTER TWO

Death of a Stone

There are some people who you know aren't go-
ing to get old. Brian and I agreed that he, Brian,
wouldn't live very long. I remember saying,
"You'll never make thirty," and he said, "I
know."

—KEITH RICHARDS

Cotchford Farm, an estate located about fifty miles southeast of London, is where A. A. Milne lived when he
wrote his Winnie-the-Pooh stories. The garden of the
ancient house, which traces its ancestry back to William
the Conqueror, is preserved pretty much as Milne left it when he
died. Alongside the main walkway is a life-sized statue of Christopher Robin, and at one end of the swimming pool area there is
a large sundial on which are carved likenesses of Pooh, Eeyore,
Piglet and other characters from the world of Pooh. It is believed
that the original manuscript of the book is buried inside the sundial. A little stream still runs through the property with the bridge
over it, on which Christopher Robin and Pooh participated in the
Pooh sticks game.

It was a most unlikely milieu for Brian Jones, the *enfant terrible*
of the Rolling Stones; however, as a child Brian had loved the
Winnie-the-Pooh stories, knew them by heart, and when the cottage went up for sale in November 1968, Brian snapped it up.
After his years of debauchery, a life consumed with alcohol, drugs
and kinky sex, no one expected Brian to last very long in the
idyllic surroundings of Pooh Corner, but Brian adored the house
and its gardens and immediately began to fix up the deteriorating
cottage and grounds. In his mind he had become a member of the
Pooh family, and caught up in the childlike atmosphere, he turned

away from drugs and cut down considerably on his drinking. Despite the fact that he had recently been traumatized by being excommunicated from the Rolling Stones, he appeared to have found a new lease on his life here at Pooh Corner.

But Brian's lease on life abruptly expired on a warm July night in 1969, nine months after he had purchased Cotchford Farm. His wet body, clad in black swim trunks, lay on the walkway of the swimming pool, illuminated by the lights of an ambulance and a searchlight mounted on a police car. Two medics were desperately trying to revive his unresponsive body.

At the far end of the pool, a police constable was questioning a man and two women near the sundial with the likenesses of Pooh, Eeyore and Piglet. The medics discontinued their grim task with the approach of a lean, brisk man, Dr. R. R. Evans, who, after a brief inspection, pronounced Brian Jones dead; the constable made a dutiful entry in his notebook. Reporters and additional police cars were arriving as the medics placed Brian in a body bag and carried him to the ambulance. The constable led the three people he had been interrogating to his car and drove them to the county police station in East Grinstead. It was, by now, well after midnight.

At the police station, the three people who had been with Brian when he drowned were being interrogated, one after the other, in the office of Detective Chief Inspector Marshall, a stenographer transcribing their statements. The first person questioned was Anna Wohlin, a twenty-two-year-old Swedish beauty who had been living at Cotchford with Brian for about six weeks. She stated that Brian and she had been watching television when, about 10:15, he suggested they go for a swim with Frank Thorogood and Janet Lawson. Frank had been living in a flat over the garage for the past eight months. Janet was a nurse who sometimes came to stay with Frank for a few days at a time.

Anna stated that the men had sat around having drinks for a while before they got into the pool. Anna said that she was the first one into the water, and that when the two men came to the pool they were both a bit drunk. Janet did not go in the water. After a while, Anna said, she got out of the pool and went up to her room to dry off and dress, leaving the men in the water, with

Janet sitting beside the pool. While Anna was in the house, the phone rang. She answered it, and the call was for her. Anna said she heard Frank come into the house, and he picked up the phone in the kitchen. Anna told him the call was for her. The next thing she knew, she heard Janet shout that "something has happened to Brian!"

Anna said she rushed out of the house about the same time as Frank, that Janet was standing there looking at Brian, who was lying facedown on the bottom of the pool in the deep water. Anna said she dived in and got Brian off the bottom, and then Frank jumped in to help her pull him out as Janet ran into the house to phone for help. After they got Brian out, Anna and Janet applied artificial respiration, and Anna said that while they were doing this, "I felt Brian's hand grip mine." They were still trying to revive Brian when the ambulance men arrived to take over. Then the doctor came and told them that Brian was dead.

Frank Thorogood was next. He stated that they had been watching "Rowan and Martin's Laugh-In" on television and had had "quite enough to drink" by the time it ended at 9:50 P.M. "Brian was staggering, but I was not too concerned because I had seen him in worse condition and he was able to swim safely. He was a good swimmer, but he was an asthmatic and used an inhaler. He had some difficulty in balancing on the diving board and I helped to steady him, but this was not unusual for him. He went in off the board, and I went in the shallow end. He was swimming quite normally. Anna was in the pool with us for some of the time, then she went indoors, leaving us in the pool. Janet also went indoors.

"After we had been in the pool for about twenty minutes or so, I got out and went to the house for a cigarette, leaving Brian in the pool.

"I got a cigarette and lit it, and when I went back to the pool, Anna appeared from the house about the same time. She said to me, 'He is laying on the bottom' or something like that. I saw Brian facedown in the deep end on the bottom of the pool. Anna and I got in the water and after a struggle got him out. His body was limp, and as we got him to the side, Janet joined us and helped get him out. Janet said that she had had difficulty with the phone, and I went to the house and dialed 999.

"I returned to the pool and the girls were trying to revive him.

When the ambulance men came, they took over. The doctor came and said he was dead."

Janet Lawson mentioned nothing about watching television but said she didn't join the others to swim because she felt that Frank and Brian were in no fit condition to be in the water. After watching them for a while, she said she returned to the house and went to the music room to play the guitar. She heard Anna come in and go upstairs to her room. "About ten minutes later Frank returned to the house and asked for a towel. I went out to the pool and on the bottom I saw Brian. He was facedown in the deep end. He was motionless and I sensed the worst straightaway.

"I shouted under the open window of the bedroom to Anna, who was speaking on the telephone. I ran into the house and shouted to Frank. Both joined me—I was by then in the water but realized I couldn't manage him alone, and I shouted to Frank to get into the pool to get Brian out. I returned to the house to use the phone, but I had difficulty as the line was engaged and there were several telephones in the house but I was not sure of the location of them all.

"I returned to the pool to get Frank to use the phone, and he and Anna were struggling to get Brian out of the water. I helped and we eventually got him out. He lay on his back, and as Frank went to the house to phone, I turned the body over and attempted to pump the water out of him. It was obvious to me he was dead, but I turned the body back and I told Anna how to apply mouth-to-mouth resuscitation as I applied external cardiac massage. I carried on for at least fifteen minutes but there was no pulse."

These somewhat conflicting statements aroused my curiosity about Brian's death, especially in light of Ian Stewart's feeling that there was something "sinister" about it. I contacted the Eastbourne coroner's office and requested permission to inspect the 1969 inquest file on Brian. The coroner who conducted the hearing at the time, Angus Sommerville, was no longer in office, but his successor, E. N. Grace, granted my request. The file included the signed statements of the witnesses, the police, Brian's father, and Tom Keylock, who, according to his statement, "looked after [Brian's] interests," plus the autopsy findings and the reports from three pathologists.

On the train returning to London, I began to read the copies I had made of these various official documents and was shocked by what I read. The London newspapers had attributed Brian's drowning to a variety of causes—an asthma attack, an overdose of drugs, a heart attack, intoxication—but the pathology reports that I was reading did not confirm any of these. Pathologist A. Sachs of the Queen Victoria Hospital reported that his postmortem examination disclosed no evidence of an attack of asthma. Another detailed postmortem report from the Queen Victoria Hospital showed no evidence of a heart attack, although they found alcohol and some amphetamine-like substance in Brian's body. The autopsies revealed some liver dysfunction due to fatty degeneration and the ingestion of alcohol and drugs, but none of the reports established this dysfunction as the cause of Brian's abrupt death.

The inquest had been held in the magistrate court in East Grinstead before coroner Sommerville, five days after Brian's death. The file I received from the coroner contains no indication that the three witnesses who gave statements to the police were actually called to the inquest. Apparently, the coroner simply accepted the written statements of Janet Lawson, Frank Thorogood and Anna Wohlin, along with written statements made by Tom Keylock and by Brian's father to the effect that the last time he saw Brian he seemed "very fit and well," that he hadn't had an asthma attack "for many years," and that he had always been "a very keen swimmer." Even if coroner Sommerville had wanted to interrogate one of the three people who had been with Brian on that fateful evening, perhaps he would have been unable to. According to one account, Anna Wohlin had been moved out of the country and told to say nothing.

After entering these reports in his file, Sommerville concluded that Brian Jones had died as a result of "drowning whilst swimming under the influence of alcohol and drugs: misadventure."

The media were all too ready to report that Brian's life of debauchery had suddenly caught up with him at age twenty-seven and left him spread-eagled dead on the bottom of his pool, itself a symbol of the high-flying existence he had led.

But as I carefully read the witnesses' signed statements, some variations presented themselves. Anna said that she had been watching television with Brian, who afterward went to get Frank and Janet to swim. Frank said that after he and Janet returned to the farmhouse with Brian, they had been watching "Laugh-In," which ended at 9:50. Janet mentions no television.

Frank stated that he left the pool to get a cigarette, lit it and returned to the pool; Anna says Frank came into the house and picked up the phone; Janet says he came into the house and asked for a towel. (Frank had no recollection of asking Janet for a towel.)

Frank said that he left the house with Anna, who claimed that Brian was lying on the bottom of the pool. Janet stated that she returned to the pool, discovered Brian and shouted to Anna and Frank. Anna said she rushed out of the house with Frank. Anna reported that when she ran out, she found Janet standing pool-side and looking at the body, and that she, Anna, dived in and tried to raise Brian, and Frank joined her to help. Janet indicated that she was the first one to dive in and that she shouted to Frank for help. Frank stated that he and Anna dived in together and that Janet *then* helped them get Brian out.

In addition to these differences, there is a time discrepancy. Frank Thorogood said that Brian came to the flat at 9:30 or "nearer 10 P.M.," and yet Frank goes on to say that they returned to the farmhouse with Brian, had some drinks, and *then* watched the "Laugh-In" program, which he claims ended at 9:50. After that, they put on their swimsuits and went into the pool. He stated that they swam for about twenty minutes. That would indicate that it was around 10:30 when Brian drowned, and yet Janet claims that Brian did not *arrive* at the flat until 10:30. The police listed the time they went to the farmhouse as 12:10 A.M. What happened during that unaccounted-for time?

There is still another disturbing factor: Frank Thorogood stated that Brian was "swimming quite normally" when Frank went into the house for a cigarette, which he lit, and then returned to the pool. Forensic experts told me that in the absence of a sudden trauma, such as a heart attack, a swimmer could not possibly ingest enough water to be weighted to the bottom in such a short time.

It should be noted that these were immediate recollections taken while the evening's events were fresh in the witnesses' minds and not affected by the distortions of time lapse.

The question remains, then, all these years later—what really took place at Cotchford Farm the night Brian Jones drowned? The answer is inextricably intertwined with what happened in the years of the decade that preceded Brian's death. For the truth is that Brian Jones was a victim of the sixties, not of drugs and alcohol as were Janis Joplin, Jim Morrison, Jimi Hendrix and many others, but he was done in by forces spawned in that decade, the very forces that had propelled him from the lower-middle-class neighborhood of his adolescence into the world's limelight.

On the basis of the evidence I will produce, it is my view that Brian Jones was probably killed, not accidentally drowned, and we have to understand the sixties to understand why he was killed, and who did it. With that as my objective, over the past five years I have interviewed hundreds of people who were at the heart of the sixties: musicians, actors, writers, dress and hair mavens, rock impresarios, money men, groupies, rock wives and girl friends, drug dealers, addicts, film stars, dancers, politicians and historians, artists, photographers, criminals, prosecutors and lawyers, professors, bodyguards, hustlers and prostitutes, and, of course, the rock stars themselves, with particular emphasis on Brian Jones and the Rolling Stones.

All their voices will appear in this book, as I let these people speak for themselves about their memories and interpretations of what happened during those intriguing years, revealing special moments, secrets, animosities, fears and ambitions, and reliving what were, for most of them, the best days of their lives.

What happened to the joyous King's Road revelers, to the Tiananmen-like teenage insurgency that pathetically bled out on a desolate field at Altamont? Why did a talented kid from dreary Cheltenham, whose musical talent and zestful originality brought him superstardom and fortune, meet his own Altamont, doing a dead man's float on the bottom of his swimming pool? Their lives were intertwined, in fact synonymous, Brian Jones and the sixties: They began with such bright promise but wound up on a tragic slag heap. Why?

CHAPTER THREE
The Faster the Better

You can build a wall to stop people, but eventually, the music will cross that wall. That's the beautiful thing about music—there's no defense against it. I mean, look at Joshua and fucking Jericho—made mincemeat of that joint. A few trumpets, you know?

KEITH RICHARDS

In 1968 I lived for a while in the London town house of a friend. It was not until I arrived there that I discovered that his place on Royal Avenue, a tranquil street of polite houses, was only a few steps away from King's Road, which was anything but tranquil since it was, at that time, the appropriated preserve of hordes of parading, carousing, uninhibited teenagers who had been carried there on the tidal wave of the sixties that had swept Britain.

During the ensuing weeks, although I was not a part of their generation, they tolerated my presence in their midst at Aretusa, Alvaro's, Granny Takes a Trip, Hung on You, and other King's Road haunts. I still have an extra-wide ostrich belt with an outsized brass buckle that I bought at Granny Takes a Trip, and there hangs in the back of my closet, like a Madame Tussaud relic, an electric-blue silk dress shirt with ornately ruffled cuffs and bib that came from Mr. Fish.

After my King's Road indoctrination, I remained fascinated with the escalating excesses of the sixties, and with the often (to my ears) baffling new music. When I went to Paris, the rock concerts were just as riotous, and the teenagers just as rabidly devoted to upending the establishment. In New York their rebellion seemed even more strident, their behavior more outrageous, ranging as it did from the pacifism of bare feet, daisies and finger cymbals to the anarchistic battles at the university barricades. In Hollywood the concentration of robed and beaded hippies thronging the sidewalks along Sunset Boulevard seemed peculiarly disjointed and devoid of the boldness that had brought them there. A pall of pot smoke hung over Beverly Hills, and despite police prodding, at night the parks filled with recumbent figures smoking pot and strumming guitars that accompanied the songs of Bob Dylan and Joan Baez.

Now, armed with twenty-five years of hindsight, it seems to me that apart from the two world wars, the sixties was the most cataclysmic period of this century. In retrospect, those King's Road swingers, the Haight-Ashbury flower kids, the Carnaby Street hipsters, the acidheads and the groupies, were merely surface manifestations of a deep undercurrent of rebellion that struck relentlessly against the universities, Vietnam, the cops, the political establishment, the dress code, the sex code, the language code—name it, the youth of the world was turbulently aroused against all the cherished traditions. The generation of the sixties was, adamantly, the first generation that refused to inherit the earth.

At the heart of this rebellion, fueling its drive, goading its ambition, was the new, contagious rock music. First the Beatles, then the Rolling Stones, singing songs that gave the kids their catchwords, pounding out new rhythms that furnished the beat for a generation that marched in cacophonous stride to new and different drummers. And of all the sixties musical groups that came into being, none was more representative of those times than the Rolling Stones. The very nature of the group—its irreverent appearance and mocking behavior—was appealingly antiestablishment, and the music it played underscored the mood of the times.

From what I saw of the demonstrations opposing the Vietnam War, espousing civil rights, stumping for more idealism and less commercialism, proselytizing for the legalization of dope, although they were part of the sixties rebellion, what really was the driving force behind all of it was the music. That's what united this rebellious generation—rock and roll. And as the sixties gathered momentum, the Stones increasingly became the symbol of the nonconformity, vulgarity, creativity, waywardness, antiestablishment bravado, rampant sexuality and drug experimentation of that contumacious generation. Whether the Stones' lives actually encompassed all these elements is not relevant. That was their perceived image, fostered by the media.

At the time, Mick Jagger said he felt a great deal of danger in the air. "I feel that teenagers are not screaming over pop music any more, they're screaming for much deeper reasons. We're only serving as a means of giving them an outlet. Pop music is just the superficial issue. When I'm on that stage, I sense that the teenagers are trying to communicate to me, like by telepathy, a message of some urgency. I interpret it as their demonstration against society and its sick attitudes. Teenagers the world over are weary of being pushed around by half-witted politicians who attempt to dominate their way of thinking and set a code for their living. This is a protest against the system. And I see a lot of trouble coming in the dawn."

Although these rebellious teenagers had at first fastened their allegiance onto the Beatles, they reluctantly began to desert them when their parents began to share their enthusiasm for the Fab Four, an unexpected development that blunted the edge of their rebelliousness. It was this ironic twist that induced teenagers to turn to the gamy newcomers, the Stones, of whom their parents would never approve. In fact, parents angrily disapproved and the more the Stones were reviled—the more they were busted for drugs and enmeshed in unsavory scandals—the more parents were outraged by them, and the better the kids liked them. "They are denounced as subversive, immoral, filthy," the director Peter Hall said. "It's all terribly healthy."

In reflecting upon the phenomenon of the British rock and roll bands that gave birth to this startling new music, basically derived from the rhythm and blues of celebrated American black performers like Bo Diddley and Muddy Waters, but nonetheless original, I pondered what had brought about this sudden emergence of groups of English boys who furnished the driving cadence for the eruptions of the sixties. How did it happen that in stodgy old tradition-ridden Britain, where in modern times there had never been much originality, nor any leniency toward sex or censorship or mores, that all this took place virtually overnight, as mysterious as a new crop of mushrooms? The fashions of Carnaby Street and Mary Quant became the fashions of the world. Vidal Sassoon universally invaded the barbershops and beauty salons. English pop artists set off pop art everywhere. Uninhibited sex, drugs, language, in film and books as well as everyday living, were copied from Stockholm to Tokyo. And most of all, the music.

It was that music which linked the youth of the world, a universal language they all understood, a musical badge of their brotherhood. It was the music that goaded them into their excesses, their indifference to consequences, their insistence that their lives were to be lived as swiftly as possible. Driven by an insistent force they didn't understand, nor question, they were eager to gobble up their lifetime allotment of fun at one sitting. "The nightlife is just a symptom," the *Weekend Telegraph* observed, "the outer and visible froth, of an inner, far deeper turbulence that boiled up in Britain around 1960. In that period youth captured this ancient island and took command in a country where youth had always before been kept properly in its place. Suddenly, the young own the town."

In 1962 a teenage girl told a reporter for *Queen* magazine, "I expect I'll be dead by the time I'm thirty. We all will. It's the strain, you know."

The origin of the electrifying events of the sixties can be traced to stirrings in the forties, which intensified in the fifties and eventually erupted into the turbulent events of the sixties: Kennedy elected president, de Gaulle's assuming power in France, the Bay of Pigs fiasco, the Profumo sex scandal, Macmillan's resignation, Harold Wilson's ascendancy to prime minister, the Kennedy-Khrushchev summit, the great train robbery, race riots in Watts, Cleveland, Chicago, New York City, the assassinations of President Kennedy, Martin Luther King, Bobby Kennedy and Malcolm X, the Vietnam War, Johnson's withdrawal from the presidency, Nixon's election, astronaut Neil Armstrong's walking on the moon, the enactment of stringent apartheid laws in South Africa, the first skyjacking, John and Yoko's bed-ins for peace, Russia's invasion of Czechoslovakia, Chappaquiddick, the Castro takeover in Cuba, Hemingway's suicide, the Manson murders. And accompanying all of this, the rhythmic blare of rock and roll.

Astride the rampaging teenagers, holding rein over them, was a new breed of colossus—the rock superstar. Displacing the movie star, the matinee idol, the titled aristocrat, were scruffy boys from Merseyside and Tottenham and Liverpool who, without warning, were rocketed to tempestuous fame for which they were totally unprepared. But they made brave attempts to try to understand what had happened to them. "I'm not only part of the establishment," Pete Townshend of the Who said, "I *am* the establishment."

"Of course, we're subversive," Keith Richards admitted. "But if they really believe that we can start a revolution with a record, they're wrong. I wish we could. We're more subversive at live appearances."

Jagger tried to downplay his importance. "I think rock and roll is all frivolity," he said. "I wear pink satin suits and white socks because that's all rock is. We know a lot of people don't like us because they say we're scruffy and don't wash. So what! They don't have to come and look at us, do they? If they don't like me, they can keep away."

But from the flood of money rolling in, the Rolls-Royces, the chartered planes, the town houses, the overwhelmingly willing girls, the adulatory invitations from the powerful, the rich and the titled, Mick and Keith and the others certainly knew that they had become a rare breed apart. "We're more popular than Jesus now," John Lennon declared.

"Wait till you see the Stones!" enthused Baby Jane Holzer, a New York socialite. "They're so sexy! They're pure sex! They're *divine*! When Mick Jagger comes into the Ad Lib in London—I mean there's nothing like the Ad Lib in New York. You can go into the Ad Lib and everyone is there. They're all young and they're taking over, it's like a whole revolution, I mean, it's exciting, they're from the lower classes, East End sort of thing. There's nobody exciting from the upper classes anymore."

It seems to me that the story of the Rolling Stones is, in effect, the story of the sixties. What happened to them was, to a lesser degree, happening to all kids their age. More than any other rock group, the Stones were a product of their times, and from boyhood on they were shaped by what was occurring around them.

Although most of the Stones' publicity has been focused on Mick and Keith, the fact is that Brian Jones was the soul of the Stones. It was Brian who put the band together, named it, found its musical identity, and who was the only true original musician in the group. It was also Brian who was in many ways the Pied Piper of the sixties, leading the way with his outlandish look, his hairstyle, his sexual exploits, his addictions, his eager willingness to experiment with any and every new drug, his profligacy, his devotion to music. His life and death are a metaphor for the life and death of the sixties.

The sixties should be viewed as a gay and wonderful party that really got up to speed around 1964 and got madder and gayer, everybody going faster and faster until—as parties will, when the dawn comes—everybody wound down and the festivities ended. The revelers all took off their funny hats and went home. But it was a hell of a good party while it lasted. As is always the case, however, when the party's over, you sweep the floor, clean the ashtrays, pitch all the paper plates and noisemakers and plastic glasses, all the discarded costumes, and when you look around the next morning, it seems as if nobody had been there. No signs of the marvelous party of the night before, no trace at all.

And yet, even though the vestiges of the party have disappeared, not so the memories of the partygoers. Indelibly implanted are daring escapades, camaraderie, confrontations won and lost, virginal sacrifices to sex and drugs, the religion of love, peace and meditation, a suspicion of the body politic, a celebration of one's entity, and the power and immortality of rock, the new universal language.

This nostalgia has recently manifested itself in the resurgence of the music of the sixties, and, after a hiatus, the triumphal, lucrative tours of the Grateful Dead, the Who, and, particularly, the Rolling Stones, whose audiences are now largely composed of middle-aged supplicants reviving youthful memories of what for them—rock and the sixties—was the highlight of their lives.

I had been coming to England since World War II when I was a captain attached to the Eighth Air Force, and I was well aware of the conditions that prevailed prior to the sixties. It's hard to imagine it now but basic commodities like food, clothes and gasoline continued in short supply right up to the sixties. England was a nation of shortages—housing, food, clothes, cash in the bank, all the basics were in short supply. People queued interminably for everything, and the ration book with its hoarded coupons ruled the land. Every indication was that hidebound old England would be a long time recovering from the stultifying effects of the war. But virtually overnight something happened that ignited the young Brits, roused them from the national lethargy and gave them an impetus that carried their elders with them. What happened was that America elected John F. Kennedy as president.

I asked Tony Palmer, who is a distinguished academician, music critic and rock authority, for his evaluation of the conditions that prevailed in Britain as it entered the sixties.

Tony Palmer

KENNEDY'S MARVELOUS speeches came across to Britain as a rallying call. Our teen generation seemed to sit up and say, Hey, wait a minute, why should we live in a world of scarcity? Why shouldn't we have greater goals than our parents, who had suffered so greatly during the war? And this generation, suddenly, for the first time, thought: We've got to get off our behinds and do something. Now the question was, what?

Everybody thought, Well, there are no rules, let's make our own. In Britain, until the sixties, people led formula lives—children went to the school that the parents wanted, learned a craft, got their qualifications. They went off and became assistant bank clerks and gradually moved up to being bank manager. And at the end of the road there was a pension; you retired at sixty. Ever since the industrial revolution, for the last hundred years, that's what the pattern of life was. But now, for the first time, partly because of these speeches that Kennedy was making, this generation didn't want to follow that pattern. They wanted to make their own rules, their own music, their own art. They seemed determined to create their own way of life. I think that philosophical background is really the clue to everything that happened in the sixties.

I remember one particular place in London around 1965, which was the Roundhouse—it's still there. I remember one Sunday watching, absolutely fascinated, as secretary after secretary came in, clearly after spending Sunday lunch with their parents, and these girls were all conventionally dressed. And they carried a paper bag. In that paper bag was *the gear*. They all went straight to the ladies' room, and they'd change into the most extraordinary clothes, put on Indian makeup, emerge as startling birds. There was a sense that once you got inside that building, you were absolutely inside your own world. And drugs became a part of that world.

Christopher Booker, a trenchant observer of the sixties and the first editor of England's *Private Eye* magazine, has written that "in President Kennedy, all that longing for youth, for toughness, for efficiency, for nonconformity and for excitement, [which] since the middle fifties had been welling up in the collective subconscious of America, Britain and Europe at last found its focus. Not since the youthful Napoleon had any man so captured the dreams of half the world.

"The influence of the Kennedy 'image' and of the trappings of Kennedyism on the climate of British politics was to be enormous. Within weeks of his election, an opinion poll showed that this fresh wind blowing from across the Atlantic had almost erased the general anti-American feeling that, only two months before, had been expressed by forty-seven percent of the British people."

PART TWO

The Rise

CHAPTER FOUR

The Skifflers from Dartford

*For most people the fantasy is driving around in
a big car, having all the chicks you want and
being able to pay for it. It always has been, still
is and always will be. And anyone who says it
isn't is talking bullshit.*

MICK JAGGER

England is scattered with a succession of dreary places—
Liverpool, Tewkesbury, Bromley, Cheltenham, Dartford
—with their monotonous row houses, unexciting shops
and stodgy mores, and suburbs like Sidcup and Richmond, just far enough away from central London to keep them
isolated. These were the very places where the teenagers who
fomented the revolution of the sixties were spawned.

Perhaps it was the mounting pressure of wanting to escape
these deadly towns that motivated their young people to turn to
one of the few avenues that afforded them a way out—music.
Otherwise, they were trapped in a system that apprenticed teenagers to the work their fathers performed—generations of tradition dictated that a bricklayer's son became a bricklayer, a
railway worker's son went to work for the railway. For the most
part, the only hope of escape was either professional soccer or
what was destined to become rock music. And, of course, there
was crime, which required less talent and had much better odds
for success.

In the town of Cheltenham, where conformity and tradition
were bywords, many of the teenagers were expressing a newfound defiance in their obsession with a new kind of developing
music of which their elders vehemently disapproved. Brian Jones
was one of the most irrepressible of these teens. His father was a

straitlaced aeronautical engineer, his mother taught piano, and until he was twelve, Brian was a model Cheltenhamian who excelled at the piano and played the recorder and clarinet as well. He had an excellent record at Cheltenham Grammar, particularly in science and languages, he played on the cricket and swimming teams, and he was a clarinetist in the band. His parents fully expected him to pursue a career in classical music, but when he turned thirteen, Brian developed a sudden, consuming interest in jazz, taught himself to play the saxophone, and he not only renounced classical music but also began to rebel at the strictures of his life at school and at home.

Mick Jagger, Keith Richards and Dick Taylor, destined to join Brian as original Rolling Stones, all lived in the town of Dartford, even drearier and more hidebound than Cheltenham. They were childhood friends, and all three followed pretty much the same pattern as Brian—admirable conformity until thirteen, and then escalating rebellion with music as the catalyst.

This rebellion cut across all lines of British society, even the previously inviolate class demarcations. I discussed this with my friend Michael Prowdlock, a member of the upper classes who was expensively and privately educated. After attending Eton, he spent five years in Paris, without much purpose, which was what upper-class gentlemen traditionally did, but then he returned to London in the early sixties. Today he is co-proprietor of a fashionable London restaurant, Fox Trot Oscar's, drives a Rolls-Royce, and is currently restoring a stately mansion outside London.

Michael Prowdlock

ETON PEOPLE LIKE myself were totally geared to the sixties, which was never a class thing at all. It transcended all classes. In the sixties it didn't matter whether you were born in the gutter or in a stately home. You all mucked in together. But to my mind, what Eton taught me was two things: One was how to get the most result with the least effort. If you were doing your Latin or Greek, there was always one person who would actually do the work. The rest of us would go in ten minutes before, he would take you through it, you'd bung him a milkshake once a week, and you'd invariably score

48

much better than he did. So that was the first thing it taught you. And the second thing it taught you, when you were punished, you were only punished for being caught, not for doing something wrong.

When my father's generation turned eighteen, they went straight off to the Second World War. My father's father's generation went straight into the First World War. Going into the army at eighteen had always been a young Englishman's rite of passage. You grow up fast in the army, especially in combat. But the young men of the sixties were the first generation that did not get called up at eighteen for compulsory military service, which had finally been abolished. So the sixties itself became the substitute rite of passage. With the Labour government in power, jobs became plentiful, the kids had money in their pockets, and credit cards were being distributed for the first time, setting off an unprecedented buying binge.

And everybody let their hair grow long as a sort of rebellious celebration at not having to have an army haircut. And the new clothes—all that outlandish getup—was a kind of rebellion against all those years of necktie conformity. My parents were very upset about my hair, which was down to my shoulders. But it made me feel good—like I was part of a special new world, and I wouldn't have had it cut off for anything.

So there was a kind of erasure of lines during the sixties. Shopkeepers' sons could mingle with the sons of the stately homes, and you've got this wonderful mingling of boys from the East End, Cockney, of course—your David Baileys, your Michael Caines, your rock stars, all these sorts of people.

It wasn't enough just to wear the clothes or drive the cars or have the hairstyle, you actually had to ape the accents, and really do everything the rock groups were doing, even though they were from a much lower socioeconomic group than these upper-class people. The Beatles started it and the Stones carried their accents to outrageous extremes. Mick Jagger can speak perfectly acceptable English, but he chooses to speak with a Cockney accent he has invented. In the sixties everything emanated from the rock groups. How they spoke, what they wore, where they went, every facet of their lives came under scrutiny and was mimicked.

Mark Birley, another member of the upper class, also discussed this class-busting phenomenon of the sixties with me, as I sat in his office above Annabel's, the ultra-snobby London supper club and disco. "When I opened Annabel's in 1963," Birley said, "I didn't self-consciously try to give it an upper-class aura, but as the club evolved, along with the landed aristocracy came a new kind of aristocracy—super-rock figures who were sought after by aristocrats. Photographers like David Bailey and rock stars like Jagger assumed godlike qualities; they were sort of center court; they added a tempestuous, threatening element to the scene. All that led to a social revolution, and it was a very good thing that it did, because otherwise there would have been complete social stagnation."

This, then, was the climate in Britain when the country was quite suddenly overwhelmed by teenage boys trying to master home-made guitars and drum kits and form skiffle bands, the progenitors of what would be rock groups. Mick Jagger was one of those teen boys. He had started performing when he was about fourteen, but his interest in rhythm and blues long pre-dated that. "Keith and I went to school together," he has recalled, "when we were about seven. We lived in the same block. We weren't great friends, but we knew each other. We also knew each other when we left school. I went to grammar school while Keith went to another school in the same village, so I used to see him riding to school on his bike. Then I saw him again when he used to catch the train to get to school and I was on the same train to attend college.

"When I was thirteen the first person I really admired was Little Richard. I wasn't particularly fond of Elvis or Bill Haley—they were very good, but for some reason they didn't appeal to me. I was more into Jerry Lee Lewis, Chuck Berry and, a bit later, Buddy Holly.

"I never got to have a raving adolescence between the ages of twelve to fifteen, because I was concentrating on my studies, but then studying is what I wanted to do and I enjoyed it. I was very emotional as a teenager but then most adolescents are.

"I started performing when I was about fourteen in front of my mother's family; they're a working-class family, and in England working-class people sit around and play and sing and carry on.

My aunts and uncles would do the popular musical songs of their youth.

"Though my dad was a physical training teacher, his job didn't really rub off on me. I didn't believe in running if there was a chance of walking. So, naturally, organized games weren't my cup of tea. Even now, you couldn't catch me going to watch a football match.

"When I couldn't get out of it, I resigned myself to playing a game. But I soon found out that if you kept out of the way of the ball, you couldn't get too much harm. So I'd appear to be running all over the place, getting puffed out and so on, but really I wasn't. While other boys on my side would call for the ball, I'd just keep quiet. It was a real drag when it was passed to me.

"Now I didn't really mind having a go at basketball. For a start I was pretty tall and that helped in grabbing the ball, but there was also the little matter of tackling in rugby football. Enough, I reckon, is enough. Rugger [rugby] is a pretty tough sport, and in most games I played somebody would get bashed around. I honestly hated it."

I asked Chris Jagger, Mick's younger brother, to give me his impression of teenage Mick. Chris bears a striking resemblance to Mick, only more handsome. He is married to a famous model of the sixties, has four children, scrapes the barrel bottom to make ends meet. He has tried his hand at a variety of jobs—most recently making guitars. Mick has never given him a job with the Stones' organization.

Chris Jagger

AS A BOY, Mick had no interest in music. He didn't take piano lessons or anything like that. I was four years younger so I was just a punching bag as far as Mick was concerned. There wasn't much music around our house. We didn't own a record player, and about all we had was a cheap tape deck but not enough money to buy many tapes.

My memory of Mick is how much time he spent studying, always with his books. I really think he wanted to be a businessman. I think Mick's main ambition as a boy was to be rich. Money meant a lot to him.

Our father had a lot of sports equipment in the backyard but the only sport Mick liked was basketball, which wasn't very popular in England then. As a teenager, I don't think Mick had many friends—certainly not girl friends. He didn't go out very often and nobody much came around the house. Not until Mick began to play with a skiffle group. Then they'd come to rehearse once in a while but mostly Mick went to their houses.

☐ ☐ ☐

Keith Richards also came from a working-class family. "I was once a choirboy—Westminster Abbey, soloist," he has said. "Then my voice broke. That was my first training in show business; my voice broke and suddenly it was, 'Sorry, son, we can't use you anymore.' I was a soprano. It was a school choir—the weirdest part of it was that me and the other two guys who were the soloists, we were the three biggest hoods in the school, and there we were, singing like angels down at Westminster Abbey at Christmas, with our tight jeans underneath the surplices.

"My parents weren't musical but my grandfather was. He used to have a dance band in the thirties. Played the sax. My father had a variety of professions. He was a baker for a while. I know he got shot up in the First World War. Gassed or something. I was working class. English working class, struggling, thinking they were middle class. Moved into a tough neighborhood when I was about ten. I used to be with Mick before that . . . we used to live close together. Then I moved to what they'd call in the States a housing project. Just been built. Thousands and thousands of houses, everyone wondering what the fuck was going on. Everyone was displaced. They were still building it, and there were gangs everywhere. Coming to teddy boys. Just before rock and roll hit England. But they were all waiting for it. They were practicing.

"Rock and roll got me into being one of the boys. Before that I just got me ass kicked all over the place. Learned how to ride a punch.

"It's strange, 'cause I knew Mick when I was really young . . . five, six, seven. We used to hang out together. Then I moved and didn't see him for a long time. I once met him selling ice creams outside the public library. I bought one. He was trying to make extra money.

"I went to art school. Suburban art school. In England art school

52

is where they put you if you can't even qualify for a technical school because you can't saw wood straight or file metal. It's where they sent me to learn graphic design because I happened to be good at drawing apples or something. I was there for three years, and meanwhile I learned how to play guitar. Lotta guitar players in art school. A lot of terrible artists, too. But there were skiffle groups all over the place, and I played in a lot of them."

Not only Keith Richards, but almost all the performers who became the rock stars of the sixties got their start as skifflers—the Beatles, the Stones, the Pretty Things, most of them initially performed as skiffle groups that played in living rooms, basements, attics—just about anywhere their noise was tolerated.

Harold Pendleton, who is president of the National Jazz Federation of England, runs London's Marquee Club, where many of the sixties rock groups, including the Stones, got their start. Over drinks in his office above the Marquee, Pendleton, a silver-haired, elegantly tailored gentleman, reminisced about his jazz-band background and how skiffling was rather accidentally invented.

Harold Pendleton

I HAD FORMED a jazz band with a young chap named Chris Barber, who was as nuts about jazz as I was. He had a wonderful collection of records of the great American jazz bands and blues performers, and assembling a British jazz band had long been a dream of his. But we discovered that our trumpet player, Ken Colyer, had a weak lip, which gave out on him, so he needed an occasional rest.

As a solution, Chris devised a little four-piece band within his band to perform as a novelty respite while Ken's lips recovered. This little band was composed of a crude guitar, a homemade bass, a suitcase that was played on with whisk brooms and a washboard strummed with thimbles. Chris called it his skiffle group. He got this name from having read about the rent parties that used to be given in poor, Negro quarters to raise rent money—the blacks of New Orleans called them skiffle parties. Of course, none of those poor blacks owned any real instruments, so the instruments of those skiffle bands had to be kazoos, papers and combs, whisk brooms on suitcases, dustbin basses, homemade guitars with strings on a board—like that. That's how the skiffle group came to be invented in England, and it caught on like wildfire. Skiffle bands sprung up everywhere because the kids didn't have to learn how to play difficult instruments like the trombone or trumpet or clarinet. Anybody could skiffle. Every house had a washboard and thimbles—in fact, the skiffle craze caused a run on washboards and the factories had to work overtime turning them out. And then there was the tea chest. England was full of tea chests, and all you needed to do was to take a piece of string, knot it under the lid, put a hole in the lid, run it tight over a brush, and you could thud away, bum bum bum, on the one string—totally unmusical but you could establish a rhythm with it. There were other kinds of skiffle instruments of this order.

Out of this skiffle craze, the new rock groups like the Beatles began to emerge. The Beatles began as a skiffle group—so did the early Rolling Stones when they were known as Little Boy Blue and the Blue Boys. So you could say the Beatles and the Stones owed their existence to Ken Colyer's weak lip.

□ □ □

Dick Taylor

I WENT TO grammar school in the town of Dartford with Mick. I occasionally saw Keith Richards, who also lived in Dartford, but we weren't pals the way I was with Mick. The big thing between Mick and me was music—jazz, I'm talking about, especially rhythm and blues. My sisters and cousins had some Big Bill Broonzy records and that's what first got me hooked. With Mick, it was Bo Diddley records. At any rate, we were all into skiffle, in fact I was in a skiffle group that played on the radio.

I liked jazz more than Mick did—he was more into rhythm and blues, even then, as a boy. Mick was much more of a doer than I was. He sent off for record catalogues from Sue Records in the States, and from Chess Records in Chicago, and then he'd order from them and get them sent over. We'd all sit around and listen to Mick's records, and then our little skiffle group would try to imitate what we were hearing.

Before the guitar, I used to bang drums for a little school group that Jagger had organized. At first I bashed around on an old drum that belonged to my granddad, but I was never even pass-

54

ably good at it. I had a few lessons on the trumpet, but I really didn't get involved until I got a guitar for Christmas from my mum and dad. I was fourteen then. It was not much of a guitar, I guess, but for me, at that time, it was the answer to my dreams. After I got the guitar I began to teach myself how to play it—an instruction book came with it that showed the basic chords, and that's how I learned. There were a couple of kids at school who took lessons and they were very good, but they looked down their noses at our kind of music and only participated in "respectable" things. But all the kids I knew who played guitar, picked it up from instruction booklets and listening to records.

Mick wanted to have a regular group, so he organized a little band with two kids from Dartford Grammar, Bob Beckwith, Alan Etherington and me. We called ourselves Little Boy Blue and the Blue Boys, and we tried to play rhythm and blues the way we heard it on Chuck Berry records, Jimmy Reed records and other records of black blues performers. We were a group for about two years, and we took turns practicing at one another's houses.

Keith wasn't with us at the beginning. He lived on the other side of Dartford. His father worked a long factory shift in Hammersmith, and his mother worked in a bakery. Keith was always in trouble at school, but his mother let him get away with murder. Keith's record at school was riddled with truancy and other scholastic misdemeanors, and by the time he was thirteen he was relegated to the Dartford Technical School, but he didn't last there very long, either. His mother, who really doted on him, had bought him a cheap guitar for a few pounds, and once he got his hands on it, he never put it down.

After Keith got expelled from Dartford Technical, he wound up, as a last resort, at Sidcup Art College, and by then, that's where I was also enrolled. All they taught there were graphic design and technical drawing. Keith and I were doing graphics, but we didn't work very hard at it. There was a lot of music being played at Sidcup because nobody took the art part seriously, and we'd go into empty classrooms and fool around with our guitars. I sometimes played with Keith in one of those classrooms, but it never occurred to me that he'd be interested in playing with our group. Mick was now attending the London School of Economics, which sounds grander than it was, but we still got together three, four times a week with Beckwith and Etherington in my mum's back room.

In order to stay up late with our music and still get to Sidcup in the morning, Keith and I were on a pretty steady diet of pep pills, which not only kept us awake but gave us a high. We took all kinds of things—pills girls took for menstruation, inhalers like Nostrilene, and other stuff. Nothing serious, just those kinds of drugstore things but, for Keith, it was the beginning of what turned out to be a lifelong addiction to "taking things."

After Mick invited Keith to join our Blue Boys group, we took on a better sound because, with Keith on guitar, I was able to switch to bass. It was hard to find a bass player—everybody wanted to play guitar because it was more glamorous. I also played a little drums. We had all gone beyond skiffle instruments by now. Mick sang—he hadn't tried to play guitar at that point—Bob Beckwith played guitar, and Alan Etherington sort of waved maracas around, did some singing, filled in at this and that, but we never played any place except my mum's back room. She liked watching us, especially Jagger. She'd poke her head 'round the door and watch him dancing while he sang—he had all those moves even then. She really enjoyed watching Mick and thought he was something special.

Once Keith became established with our group, a bond grew between him and Mick. Mick liked Keith's laid-back quality, his tough stance, his obsession with the guitar, and Keith was attracted to Mick's intelligence, his dramatic flair, his streak of ambition. Even then, I feel, they were experiencing the beginning rapport that would be so important to their future.

□ □ □

Sidcup professor Brian Yates

THE ART SCHOOLS were the breeding and fermenting grounds for groups of students who were more into music than art. They went to classes and went through the motions of learning graphics or whatever, but most of their attention was focused on their music sessions held extemporaneously in empty classrooms, the corridors, the basement, all over the place. The Who, the Stones, the Beatles, the Yardbirds, the Kinks—all were bands that started in art schools.

Young people who went to art school rarely finished their courses—they were sort of seduced away by more immediate distractions. I can assure you that virtually nobody went home after classes—that's when the groups got together and really got into their music. You can't imagine the cacophony. And what made it so easy to form these groups was skiffling. Some of the students had guitars, but most of them played with skiffle instruments.

Before World War II, there would not have been so large an enrollment at art school, nor so many dropouts, because young people would have been hostage to the apprentice system. That was the custom. As soon as you finished school, you joined a trade or occupation as an apprentice at virtually no salary, which meant that during your apprenticeship—and many of them stretched out for many years—you lived at home or in drab company quarters, had very little money to spend and no way to change your destiny. But the war drastically altered that. Adults emerged from the war *expecting* change. I think that's why Winston Churchill and the Conservatives were voted out in the first postwar election in 1945. People wanted social change, to do away with some of the traditional hardships, like people on the bread line, the dole, things like that. Also, the class structure, sacrosanct in Britain, suffered a severe pummeling. The concept that each person "knew his place" went by the boards. I myself changed from becoming an engineer to being an art student. My family expected me to go into engineering, which was the family business, but I happened to draw well, and although before the war it had never occurred to me to go to art school, afterwards I felt I could do what I wanted and my family didn't seem to mind.

So that would partly explain the permissive atmosphere at Sidcup. I had Keith Richards in a couple of my classes. He was studying technical illustration but his work was perfunctory since his primary interest was in getting out of class and into the cloakroom to practice on his guitar. If only he had worked as hard on his artwork as he did on the guitar, he would have been a brilliant student.

Dick Taylor was also in those classes, but he was a more serious musician than Keith, and from what I heard of their music, his playing was superior to Keith's. He had better technique, and their sessions often consisted of Dick showing Keith how to do certain things on the guitar. I was amazed, one day, when Dick came to school with a Stockhausen record. All the kids brought records—jazz, blues, that ilk—but Dick was the only one who was interested in orchestral music.

Certainly Sidcup was where Keith Richards began to learn how to play his guitar.

☐ ☐ ☐

Besides being a breeding ground for rock groups, art schools also provided a fertile atmosphere for students with other interests. Ossie Clark, one of the pioneers of the fashion revolution of the sixties who probably had the most influence over the decade's styles, was one of the art school renegades.

Ossie Clark

IN THE LATE fifties when I finished school, with compulsory military service eliminated, there were a lot of people like myself who were kind of misfits. The majority of misfits went to the art schools if they had any talent at all. That's what I did. I went to Manchester Art School. And from feeling that I was the only person like that, a freak, I met other people who were on the same wavelength.

For poor kids like myself, it was the only escape because you could get a grant, which took the financial burden off your parents. And it was something to do. The art schools had a rather loose curriculum so there was a lot of time on one's hands, and you met many students who were also kind of drifting around.

Now, until the war, school life was predictable—homosexuality was rife and there was a lot of pedagogic brutality. And before the war there was a terrific suppression of anything that smacked of individuality. But after the war, individual expression became much easier. The men at art school, for example, wore jeans, which was also unheard of. Jeans were only for weekend casual wear and for mending the car. At art school everyone wore jeans; going to and from school, these students were seen on the street, in the buses and the tube, and other kids began to pick up on it. And then there was the shoe business, those very pointed shoes. I owned a pair. Tight trousers seemed wrong with them, so that's how bell-bottoms evolved, to fit over these pointed shoes. When I was at art school in Manchester, I invented bell-bottoms by buying a huge pair of trousers meant for a man with a forty-inch waist— that gave me the width at the bottom, and then I remade them so that they fitted my waist at the top.

Thanks to one of my teachers, I was able to go to art school specifically to design clothes. This teacher was a frustrated dress designer, and somehow he'd ended up teaching boys in a secondary technical school. Somehow, because of this teacher's influence, I was channeled into the art-school system to study dress design. I learned the art of dressmaking and how to make patterns and how to tailor clothes, and we all went to Paris to study the collections.

It certainly was quite a contrast, all that Paris chic and our group of bedraggled art students with their miniskirts and bell-bottom trousers. Women wearing trousers then was outrageous, very daring. I went to Paris with Celia, the woman I eventually married, and there were women actually laughing out of windows as we walked by. Simply because she was wearing trousers. And yet, twenty years before, Chanel had done it and Dietrich had done it. But the difference was that back then only show-business celebrities wore such risqué costumes.

When I finally graduated from the Royal College, I knew very definitely what I wanted to do, and it was quite easy to do it, really, because at that time, there was very little that was made specifically for young people. So I began by making really feminine clothes for the young girls using fabrics that weren't about at that time, like satin, lace and stuff. You couldn't buy that really, and I sold it in my shop on King's Road called "Quorum." At first, it was derided by the press. They thought it was a joke. It wasn't until people came along and started to wear them that they took it seriously and began to accept skirts up to here, and snakeskin jackets and all my things, which were very different from everyone else's. Also, I used a lot of crepe that was kind of "drapey" and very nice. I did just about anything to be different, just simply to be different. That was half the motivation. We all had this feeling that youth could do anything. And I think at the time that anyone with a good idea could get the money for it quite easily.

It was the first time that England was becoming a fashion center. Until that moment, England was just for cashmeres, tartans and raincoats. For fashion, Americans had looked to France. The recognition of England began about the same time as I began.

Richard Hattrell spent time in Cheltenham as a teenager and became friendly with Brian Jones. A small, cheerful man, Hattrell has been a bartender for the past twenty years.

Richard Hattrell

BRIAN AND I had the same proper family backgrounds, the same obsession with music and we suffered the same fate of being banished from our houses as teenagers. My father was a small-town lawyer. My mother belonged to garden clubs, that kind of thing. We were middle-class people. I took piano lessons, and when I was fourteen or so, and got swept up by the jazz craze like everyone else, I began taking double-bass and big-bass lessons. It seems that all the kids my age suddenly got hooked by jazz as I did. I suppose it was because life was very, very dull for a teenager in Tewkesbury, and music furnished the only possible excitement. Everybody listened to blues records, and I was particularly devoted to a British big band led by Ted Heath, who patterned himself after Stan Kenton's band. If Ted Heath's band was playing anywhere within fifty miles of Tewkesbury, I'd hitchhike there and back again after the performance.

I also became obsessively interested in pure New Orleans jazz, the kind of music that drove my father up the wall. He wanted me to listen to Gilbert and Sullivan, that was his idea of "good music." So there was that friction between us.

The other thing I did that nicked it with my father was that on Saturday night a group of us kids would hitchhike into London—a hundred miles away—to hear Ken Colyer's band perform an all-night jazz session that began at midnight and ended at seven o'clock in the morning. We'd stay up all night, have breakfast at a J. Lyons tearoom and hitch back home. Then we'd sleep all day to catch up. This really riled my father, who had a very strict upbringing—his father was a Baptist minister—and from his point of view I was sleeping off my all-night jazz orgy when I should have been in church.

So eventually he said, "Richard, you're a dear lad, we've got nothing against you. But we're living in a small town, the people here are narrow-minded, and in all fairness to both of us, if you want to continue to carry on the life that you are leading, I think you'd better go and live somewhere else."

So that was my choice, give up my musical ways or leave home—without giving it a second thought, I left home and went to Cheltenham, which was the neighboring town. I knew a woman there named Mrs. Filby, whose daughters ran a jazz club in the basement of their house. I often went there to listen to jazz, so I sought out Mrs. Filby and asked her if she could put me up for a while. She said, "Certainly, I've got one room available. There's four or five young people in there already, but I'm sure I could squeeze in another bed for you."

So I wound up at Mrs. Filby's sleeping in a room with five other kids who had all been kicked out of their homes. Their fathers were engineers, accountants, businessmen, all from good backgrounds, some of them from good private schools, and all of us willingly having renounced our middle-class lives for the pursuit of jazz, by which I include blues, rhythm and blues, all that. We all played in different little groups that were forming in the neighborhoods, and I think most of us had dropped out of schools.

It was at this time that I met Brian Jones, who sought me out because he'd heard I had a collection of Muddy Waters records, which I had. He was absorbed by the Muddy Waters type rhythm and blues as I was, and he was having the same kind of trouble at home as I had had. His father was as straitlaced as mine. His mother gave piano lessons and taught Brian from the age of six—so he had a solid musical foundation. He could also play the clarinet and saxophone, and he was better on the guitar than any of the kids I knew. He was already playing in a local jazz band.

As long as Brian was playing classical music on the piano and clarinet, he had no problems at home. But his father loathed the sound of jazz, and by the time Brian was thirteen he had renounced classical music and only played jazz, to the consternation of his father, who told Brian he didn't want "that music" in the house. Brian defied him, bought a secondhand saxophone and began teaching himself to play it in the manner of the great Charlie Parker, but, of course, he was far off that mark.

Brian had a much more serious problem with his father. Brian attended the Cheltenham Grammar School where he was often in hot water, because of his clothes, his hair, drinking ale at lunch, missing classes and so forth. But the capper was when a fourteen-year-old girl got pregnant and identified Brian as the culprit. News of the event spread around the town and even got written up in a Sunday tabloid. Of course, Brian's parents were mortified.

The baby was put up for adoption and, to be expected, Brian was kicked out of school. He went to work after that, at all kinds of jobs, and that's when I met him. We decided to get a flat together, and Brian left home. Our flat wasn't much of a place but it was much better than the six-bed room I was living in.

We had become really good friends by now, despite the fact that our personalities couldn't have been further apart. Whereas Brian was totally extroverted, given to impulsive outrages, disdainful of rules and regulations, I was rather shy and introverted, rather unimaginative, an appreciator rather than an innovator like Brian. But the one thing that bound us, the common interest that made us friends, was jazz. That's what we did ninety percent of the time—listened to, talked about and tried to imitate jazz, particularly New Orleans jazz.

☐ ☐ ☐

Harold Pendleton

TO UNDERSTAND THE music revolution of the sixties, why the Beatles, Stones and the others rocked the world with their "new" music, one must backtrack to the forties when jazz first got its foothold in Britain. In 1940 the first jazz bands were formed—there was a Dixieland band in Southport, the Dave Wilson Dixielanders, that tried to copy the Muggsy Spanier Ragtime Band (which they had only heard on records), and in southeast London there was the George Webb Dixielanders. There was one other band in Liverpool that called itself the Merseysippi Jazz Band, which was a pun on Mississippi because the river Mersey runs alongside Liverpool.

They were all playing imitative jazz music. The word "imitative" is the key word there. If you look at the actual history of jazz itself, every so-called style was a failed attempt to copy the previous style. In other words, New Orleans jazz went up the river to Chicago, and the so-called Chicago style was simply the Chicago musicians trying to play New Orleans style, and failing. Therefore, they created the Chicago style. Then the New York musicians tried to copy the Chicago style, failed, and that became the New

York style. And when the British musicians tried to copy the U.S. bands and failed, they produced the British style. At the beginning of their careers, all artists inevitably copy somebody because that's how they learn to play. They have their favorites, but after they fail to produce an accurate copy, they become themselves. So, I have always been amused when people talk derogatorily about imitation, because virtually everybody starts by copying somebody. It's the most logical thing to do, but out of failure emerges a brand-new style.

I belonged to the Southport rhythm club or jazz club, so I grew up being very interested in jazz, knowing very little about it, buying anything that I could get my hands on that was about jazz. In fact, during the war, I used to ask people who were in the merchant navy and were sailing the Atlantic, and who occasionally got back if they weren't torpedoed, to bring back American jazz records for me. I can remember the excitement of getting my first Commodore record with Wild Bill Davison, George Brunis, Pee Wee Russell, and all those wonderful musicians. I'd never heard them before. I wore the damned record out on the gramophone listening to it over and over.

Later on, when I went to London, I first met Chris Barber, who was an absolute nut about jazz. He had a wonderful collection of blues records, and there wasn't much Chris didn't know about jazz records and the great American jazz artists. Because of Chris, I abandoned my career as an accountant and began to manage jazz bands, which were starting to perform in cellars all over the place. In 1951 we staged two big jazz concerts in the Royal Festival Hall, with Her Royal Highness, Princess Elizabeth—now Queen Elizabeth—in the royal box. Well, this caused a furor around the country because up till then we were having trouble with the Watch Committees and all that—oh, we don't allow this dreadful jazz music in here—but now they're fucked because the royal family has been at the concert. Jazz became respectable.

□ □ □

Ahmet Ertegun, the head of Atlantic Records, is a student of jazz and the ramifications it has had in the music world. For fifteen years his label distributed all the Rolling Stones records, and in addition he has written songs for Ray Charles, Joe Turner and other Atlantic recording artists.

Ahmet Ertegun

THERE HAD ALWAYS been music companies in England who were interested in jazz and blues. They'd compile records by Tampa Red, Washboard Sam, Big Bill Broonzy and the rest, so that English kids heard not only the music of Chuck Berry, but a lot of the early blues. And their main inspiration came from those old early blues: Robert Johnson was the main inspiration for Eric Clapton, Mick Jagger, Robert Plant and Jimmy Page, and these kids had complete collections of all those blues musicians. White Southerners had heard these black singers all their lives, but for the English it was something new and exciting. The Southerners would say, What's new about these guys—nigger music, man. But Jagger, Pete Townshend, McCartney, Lennon, were all intellectual appreciators of this foreign form—in a sense they were appreciating something the Americans did not value. The Brits took it much more seriously and were trying to be authentic in reproducing this music they loved. Imitating it, yes, but at the same time trying to get the true feeling of it. Blues music is a kind of folk music, and you have to understand how it's generated; these English boys were trying to divine the key that would enable them to generate this kind of music. They knew that the key was to get it right emotionally, and to get it inside in order to play it naturally, spontaneously, but they found this to be very difficult.

So there was a constant attempt to find out how to play like a black person. But no matter how they tried, it came out English, but it came out like the real thing, too. I think the key group was Cream—Eric Clapton was the center of it. And *the* person who really got this the best was Stevie Winwood who, at age sixteen or seventeen, was singing and playing very black. Amazingly so. The Beatles veered off it very quickly and became more and more anglicized. The Beatles had it in the beginning. They really had it—their first records were Chuck Berry songs; they sounded pretty ratty as a band, but that black influence came through very strongly. However, the natural bent of the Beatles was lyrical and poetic, so they moved away from Berry and into their own thing very quickly, and that's what gave them their huge fame.

The Rolling Stones were rougher, tougher, and in certain ways, better. They were tighter knit than the Beatles and kept very close to the basic black music that had motivated them. They refused to slip into something much more commercial. The Who did both—Pete Townshend, on the one hand very intellectual, but on the other hand very natural in his playing and singing, and even in his latest record, he sounds very black.

☐ ☐ ☐

Harold Pendleton

CHRIS BARBER AND I had started to bring in American musicians to play with our band, and one of them was Muddy Waters, who came from the South Side of Chicago. To the absolute horror of the London critics, Muddy came out on stage and played an *electric* guitar. This was the first electric guitar anyone in Britain had ever seen and Waters was lambasted for defiling the purity of jazz with his guitar.

But Chris and I were captivated by the Muddy Waters music, which came to be known as rhythm and blues. When we opened the Marquee Club in 1960, skiffle was on the way out, so we were able to occasionally feature a rhythm and blues group, and slowly, very slowly, audiences began to accept it. But what I discovered was that no matter what the music—jazz, blues, rhythm and blues, rock, whatever—it's basically all the same music, for it all comes from the same source. All this music comes from the circumstance that when the Africans were shipped to America, they superimposed the African five-note scale on the European diatonic scale, which buggers up the thirds and sevenths, and that's what makes what were called blue notes.

The Africans created the blues because they tried but failed to copy European music. The origin of jazz can be traced back to the end of the Civil War when the Confederate Army disbanded. The countryside was littered with Confederate band instruments that had been abandoned—trumpets, trombones, clarinets—which became the basic jazz instruments. The Negroes of the South accumulated these abandoned instruments, and they tried to play European music on them but they couldn't get it right. They had no instruction, and how they played was the result of their teaching themselves to play those instruments. When they began to form little bands of their own, they tried to sound like bands they had heard but they couldn't. That's why, at first, white people refused to listen to jazz—their ears were accustomed to something

65

else. But I believe change in music is always based on failure: As far as I've been able to determine, nobody who deliberately set out to invent a new kind of music ever succeeded.

□ □ □

Brian Jones was at the Marquee Club on the night Muddy Waters first performed with his electric guitar, and it had a profound effect on Brian.

Richard Hattrell

AFTER THAT NIGHT, it was as if Brian had found his mission in life. He got himself electrified and he never stopped practicing, hours and hours at a stretch. I was quite amazed by the sound he was getting from his guitar—the Muddy Waters style. I was also amazed when he brought a girl named Pat Andrews, whom he'd been seeing, into our tiny flat one day and announced that she was going to live with us. She was quite obviously pregnant, and after the baby was born, we all of us lived there, cramped together though we were. Brian named the baby Julian, designating Julian "Cannonball" Adderley, the great jazz saxophonist, as his namesake. Brian made plans to marry Pat, to placate her, but he kept procrastinating and the wedding never occurred. Pat worked in a chemist shop and brought home her wages, which is basically what we lived on since Brian and I only got work sporadically.

But we did organize rent parties every week. Brian got to know jazz musicians who would come by the flat and play—word got around and people would come from all over to hear the jazz jam sessions. There was a bowl at the door for them to drop money into as contributions to us. Also, they'd bring drinks and leave the bottles behind when they left. The following day we'd take all the empties back and get the deposits. That was our bread money, and as time went on our rent parties got more and more popular. Jazz musicians enjoy getting together to have a jam session—it's traditional—so even great American black musicians like Sonny Boy Williamson and Chuck Berry, Bo Diddley, even the great Muddy Waters himself, they'd drop in when they were performing nearby. The night Muddy Waters showed up, I thought Brian was going to pass out with excitement. Then, when Muddy invited

66

Brian to join him in a number—well, that was almost too much for Brian. Brian played quite often during these rent parties, and he seemed to learn a lot playing with those big names.

□ □ □

Phil May,
FOUNDER AND LEADER OF THE PRETTY THINGS

I ATTENDED THE Sidcup School of Art with Keith Richards and Dick Taylor, and I formed a group, same as they did. They called theirs Little Boy Blue and the Blue Boys, and I called mine the Pretty Things. What we were into, all of us, was traditional jazz. New Orleans stuff. Most of our early gigs also came from art schools. We played for fairs at the art school, dances, as amateurs, of course. No pay, just playing for the sake of playing. There were three or four art schools around us so we had plenty of playing dates. Sometimes Keith and Dick and I went to hear the few bands that were playing rhythm and blues— Johnny Kidd and the Pirates, and Screaming Lord Sutch.

The Stones first started to perform, really, in Dick's back room, and I went there a few times. It was just sort of getting together, plugging your guitar into a record player and sitting around playing, not only listening to the music, but then learning the songs on guitars. We'd build up a sort of repertoire by listening to those tapes and learning the music. This was the only way to learn to play rhythm and blues because you never heard it on the radio, and you certainly didn't hear it in any public place you went to. So we started to make our own music, really. What I'm trying to say is, it was the kind of music that pulled this sort of musician thing out of people. The furthest thing from my mind was being a professional musician. I don't think that deep down in their souls Jagger and Richards felt they were going to be professional entertainers.

There was never a thought that this music would suddenly take off. Because for a long time, the Pretty Things and the Rolling Stones were only playing little clubs to thirty, forty people, little jazz clubs located in the backs of neighborhood pubs, without pay. When we played rhythm and blues for the art-school dances, it worked great, but we couldn't even get bookings at local dance halls. When I started the Pretty Things at art school, we audi-tioned for the local dance hall but we didn't get the gig because we didn't have the right clothes. We were wearing jeans and jean jackets at the audition, and the owner said, "Okay, you can do Sunday afternoon, but don't forget to bring your suits." We said, "We're wearing them." And he said, "No, I mean the proper suits." And we said, "We haven't got any." So he said, "You're fired." So we had the job for about three minutes. They wouldn't let you into those places unless you conformed.

☐ ☐ ☐

Although the "new" music of the Blue Boys and the Pretty Things was not attracting an audience, traditional jazz had more audience than it could handle, and its popularity paved the way for other activities that highlighted the sixties.

One of the young men who was swept up in the jazz fervor was John Dunbar, who was a student at Cambridge. He now lives in a narrow rickety house in an unfashionable part of the Maida Vale sector off Edgware Road. He is married to a young, pretty woman who stands on the first landing holding their bare-bottomed in-fant son. Dunbar's Dickensian study on the top floor is awash with spilling books and untidy mounds of pamphlets and yellowed manuscript pages. He sips white wine, smokes a joint while think-ing back to the best time of his life.

John Dunbar

THE FIRST BIG jazz festival in England was Lord Montagu's joint down south on the seaside. We all turned out, hitchhiked and stuff. They were called beatniks in those days. That was in the art-school period. They had long hair and were sort of rough. This was before they turned into hippies. Also at the festival were the teddy boys, and it turned into a big riot. There was a beer tent, so they were all pissed, and it just turned into a really amazing riot. I have never seen anything like it. They had TV cameras there, and the kids climbed up on the masts, the scaf-folding for the lights, and one of these huge masts just caved right over, spilling kids everywhere. It was total, absolute chaos. No one was prepared for this response. This was round about 1960. I was still at school. It was school holiday or something. For me, in a way, that's where I first became aware of the sort of power, the kind of mass lunacy that music concerts could generate.

There was a similar big event in the Albert Hall that got out of hand—"Beat Poetry in the Albert Hall" with Allen Ginsberg. Six thousand people came and watched it. And I thought, well, if six thousand people can watch this, you can probably do a book shop and gallery. That's how come I started my bookstore. Thousands of people just wanted to have a good time. It was nothing else. They were all on the street—what I had was a combination book-store and art gallery. It became a great hangout for the writers and pop artists of the sixties. The art I exhibited was pretty weird—moving things, undulating sculptures, op art of all kinds. Yoko Ono doing her sort of things. In fact, I introduced Yoko to John Lennon. Lennon used to come into the gallery quite often— he was a pal—I knew him from around the clubs, the Ad Lib and these funny odd places. Yoko was one of the artists I exhibited. Icky stuff—a frame on the ceiling with a stepladder. That kind of thing. I thought John would like her so I invited him to one of her openings and got them together. I don't think he liked any of her stuff but he bought one anyway.

□ □ □

Dunbar became cofounder of the Indica Gallery in London, a celebrated trysting place devoted to new painters and sculptors, whose bookstore was dedicated to the new radical literature later identified as the "underground." When his girl friend, Marianne Faithfull, became pregnant he decided to marry her, but eventu-ally Marianne was destined to leave John and the child in favor of a life with Mick Jagger.

Having exhausted their musical apprenticeship and with just enough confidence in themselves to risk it, the three boys of Dartford—Mick, Keith and Dick Taylor—set their sights on Lon-don, as did Brian Jones of Cheltenham and his chum, Dick Hat-trell. They were without funds or jobs and with no prospects of either. But so great was the lure of performing in London that without hope or common sense, they left the security of their little towns to brave the uncertainties of the big city.

Looking back on that period, Keith Richards still feels the seis-mic impact of the rock and roll quake. Although Richards has the face of a man who has died and gone on, his eyes hollow, his cheeks deeply sunken, mummified by the years of drugs coursing through his body, his skin a bleached parchment, his teeth nicotined and haglike, his hair an uncombed tangle, nonetheless when he speaks, an animation struggles to his surface; his speech is stylish, his recall peppery and his basic life attitude unperturbed: "In England, when rock and roll happened," he has observed, "it was different than it was in the States, where you had all the ingredients if you wanted to find them. They were already there. You could hear the rock and roll ingredients in the twenties and thirties, and more so in the forties and early fifties. But in England, it just suddenly—Boom!—one minute it wasn't there and suddenly it was Little Richard and Elvis and Chuck Berry. In the space of a few months, all this music suddenly arrived. Elvis was selling millions of records. And suddenly rock and roll in England appeared as if it were dropped out of the sky. We'd never heard anything like it before."

CHAPTER FIVE

Down and Out in London

*Obviously, being in a rock band makes you more
adolescent than if you worked in an IBM company and really had to worry about your future.
I don't worry about the future. I'm living out my
adolescent dreams perpetually. My mother has
always been unhappy with what I do. She would
much rather I do something nicer, like be a bricklayer.*

MICK JAGGER

It was meeting some of the great black jazz musicians who
came to his rent party jam sessions that emboldened Brian
Jones to move away from Cheltenham and go to London,
according to Richard Hattrell. "Brian hated Cheltenham,
despised it, felt that he was suffocating there, all the Victorian do's
and don'ts, and especially his family, he loathed his family and the
way they nagged him all the time and tried to tell him how to
behave and stop him from listening to his music. That was the
worst part, his father always turning off his tape or his record
because he said the music gave him a migraine."

Not only had Brian outgrown the provincialism of Cheltenham,
Richard thinks, but he also wanted to rid himself of Pat Andrews
and the baby. Brian liked to have a variety of girls, and he resented being tied down to Pat. So without telling her, Brian took
off for London with Richard and found a small, badly furnished
flat in Notting Hill. Brian got himself a job selling appliances at
Whiteley's department store, and Richard was in and out, mostly
out, of various pickup jobs.

71

Richard Hattrell

THE MOVE TO London inspired Brian to try to sit in with some of the London bands. Having had all those great blues players coming to our flat for the rent parties, and letting Brian play with them, is really what built up his confidence. There was one jazz club where we were already known, since we used to hitchhike there when we lived in Cheltenham. It was called the Ealing Club and was the only one of London's many jazz clubs that permitted electric guitars in the band. Blues Incorporated was the name of the band that allowed Brian to sit in for his debut. He played an Elmore James song, "Dust My Broom," using the same slide technique that James had used on his recording. Slide guitar was virtually unknown at that time so Brian's appearance made quite an impression.

After that, Brian sat in quite often at the Ealing, not only showing off his slide guitar but also his mastery of the harmonica. After getting this taste of band life, Brian decided that the time had come for him to form his own band, a rhythm and blues band, so he put an advertisement in a music newspaper called *Jazz News*, asking for interested musicians to come to the back room of a pub he had found on Broadwick Street, to audition for his new band.

Brian had been writing to Pat, telling her of his struggles, promising to send for her and the baby as soon as he could, but in fact he had several girls he was seeing and he had no intention of having any more involvement with Pat and Julian. Pat finally sensed this and showed up at our London door one day with the baby in her arms. The flat was barely large enough to accommodate Brian and me, and now it really became a squeeze—and Brian didn't fancy having a crying baby around. Pat got a job in a laundry, cleaned the flat and cooked, but Brian didn't come to the flat for days on end. Pat was a plain-looking, rather frumpy girl, and now that he was performing, Brian had access to a lot of pretty, sexy girls who showed up at the Ealing Club. He was also totally absorbed with plans he was making for this new band of his.

□ □ □

Ian Stewart was the first one to answer Brian Jones's notice in the *Jazz News*. He drove a motorcycle in those days, and since he was on his lunch break he brought his lunch with him to the audition. He was working then as a shipping clerk at Imperial Chemical. Ian was a squarely built Scotsman with a conventional haircut and a rock-ribbed jutted jaw that commanded his face. He played an extraordinary piano and keyboard, but it's hard to imagine anyone who looked less like a rock musician.

Ian Stewart

THAT AD THAT Brian put in the *Jazz News,* as far as I know, was the first time anyone attempted to organize a band in the rhythm and blues style. That's what interested me, and why I went to the Bricklayer's Arms. I had played a lot of jazz piano—when I played with skiffle groups, the piano had to be the rhythm section. Mostly the left hand, like a bass player. Sometimes I'd play banjo. There were pubs all over London with jazz groups playing in the back rooms and I played piano in some of those pub rooms. We didn't get paid—just fooled around.

At the audition, I played a little barroom ragtime on the pub's piano, and then Brian took his guitar and we jammed together and I could tell right off that Brian was a talent—he knew his rhythm and blues and he could really handle his slide guitar. The slide guitar was brand-new back then, and that time at the Bricklayer's Arms was the first time I'd ever played piano to a slide guitar. When I discovered Brian could also play saxophone, harmonica, clarinet, just about every band instrument, I was certainly impressed with his musical abilities.

Mick Jagger and Keith Richards showed up at the audition together. We had all seen one another at the Ealing Club, which is where Blues Incorporated played. That was Alexis Korner's club. Alexis was one of the great jazz impresarios. We not only went to the Ealing to hear the music, but the policy there was to let performers in the audience come on for a turn with the band. I'd seen Brian perform, and I had been impressed with how much self-assurance he had when he played. He knew how to arouse the audience, doing many of the little sexy things that Jagger picked up and ran with later on. Richards and Jagger also had performed a few times at the Ealing—of course, all of it for nothing more than a free beer—but I didn't think either of them was anything to write home about. Mick sang off-key and was rather self-conscious, but he had enough of his raw moves to get a good reaction from the audience. Keith was stiff but had a good grasp of his guitar.

But to tell the truth, I sure as hell wasn't impressed with these guys. It was obvious that Brian was a flake from the things he said, Mick and Keith looked like a couple of Piccadilly panhandlers, both skinny and undernourished, Keith with his red nose and pimples, Mick all bones and always talking about food, which obviously was in short supply. In fact, they looked like they were both going to starve to death. Neither had a shilling to his name—all Mick had to live on was a seven-pounds-a-week student grant, and Keith was totally dependent on what he could cadge off his mother. The less said about their clothes the better—every day they wore the same stuff, which they probably slept in. But the raunchiest one of the lot was Brian's buddy, Dick Hattrell, who had the pasty face of a sewer worker. And clothes to match. He was always around even though he didn't play, and when these guys all got together in the closed confines of that rehearsal room, believe me, it was a pretty gamy place.

The only really good musician who auditioned for Brian was a pal of mine, Geoff Bradford, a guitarist who could play mean Muddy Waters. And another fellow who auditioned was Dick Taylor, whom I had also seen at the Ealing a couple of times, playing bass. Of course, I'd gone on with the Ealing band once or twice myself.

So, me, Jagger, Richards, Geoff and Dick—we were Brian's original band, plus a drummer named Mick Avory, who acted like he was doing us a favor. Brian arranged for us to have our first rehearsal in a room above the Bricklayer's Arms, and he had a name for us: the Rolling Stones, which he had copped from Muddy Waters's song, "Rollin' Stone Blues." I thought it was an awful name and I told Brian so. People would expect to see a group of Irish acrobats, I told him. The others didn't seem to care one way or another. Of course, a name's not important until you start to get booked—and we were a long, long way from that. Speaking for myself, I looked on the band as a way to practice and I never seriously considered that we'd ever actually get to perform anywhere.

□ □ □

Dick Taylor

I THINK WE all decided to throw in our lot with Brian because he was the most experienced; he was musically the most competent. But as far as being a leader, Brian was too introverted, and although we were in awe of him musically, he was just too nervous, too moody, too unpredictable to inspire confidence. At times he was quite optimistic and ebullient. His clothes were already a little strange, and his hair was cut in a way it came over his forehead and touched his eyebrows.

But in those beginning rehearsals, Brian did hold us together. He knew how to use what little equipment we had—Brian had a crude, cheap amp that he and I shared, and Keith had an amp called a Mighty Midget, and we scraped along with those. One day Brian showed up with a couple of Harmony amplifiers, and that helped us get the right sound, but it was all incredibly crude equipment. Not long after Brian appeared with those Harmony amps, he got sacked from his job at Whiteley's for pilfering from the till—I guess that's how we got the Harmonies.

□ □ □

Richard Hattrell

WHEN BRIAN WAS auditioning for the band, he had a talk with me over drinks and explained that I played bass okay but not at the level he was looking for—that he needed a bass player with more feel for the music. He was right—I loved the music but I really didn't measure up to these other fellows. The feel you have inside for this music is one thing, but to get that feeling to come out in the way you play, that's what's difficult.

But Brian was very considerate and said, "But listen, Dick, I want you to be part of the band—you can be the road manager, set things up for our gigs." I jumped at the chance. Trouble was, of course, we didn't have any gigs for a long time, but it didn't matter to me—I belonged and I was at rehearsals and I was in on everything.

Brian somehow managed to get a free room at the back of a pub at the bottom of the King's Road—the Weatherby Arms—where the band could practice. They got together as often as they could, and in the beginning Brian would simply put on a record or a tape of Bo Diddley or whomever, and all of them would sit there for six or seven hours listening to the music, not playing anything, just listening to it over and over and over again, letting it seep into their systems.

Later on, when they did start to play, Brian would sometimes change some of the chords around, write them down on a scrap of paper or the back of a cigarette packet, but mostly they were just trying to play the music the way they heard it, and Jagger tried to sing the way the black men did. None of the music was put on paper—no one except Brian could read notes anyway—but what came out was an approximation of what they had been listening to.

Of course, these rehearsals were being squeezed into what everyone was doing—Jagger was still a student at the London School of Economics, Keith and Dick Taylor were studying at Sidcup Art College, Stew was a shipping clerk at Imperial Chemical, Brian had a job in the sports department at Whiteley's in Bayswater (until he got sacked), and Hattrell logged some time with the army reserve.

Richard Hattrell

BRIAN DECIDED HE had to get away from Pat and the baby, so at the start of 1963, he and I took a flat in Edith Grove, in Chelsea, the only place we could afford. Moving out without notice was Brian's way of trying to discourage Pat and convince her to go back home without having to have a tearful row with her. But moving to that flat in Edith Grove was a hell of a sacrifice because it was the worst place imaginable. It's a wonder it hadn't been condemned by the Greater London Council or whoever shuts down places like that. It was filthy, unpainted, wallpaper peeling off the walls, two small rooms, plaster off the ceilings, chairs with busted springs, tattered filthy curtain, the toilet halfway up the outer hallway, the only heat a one-bar electric heater that was coin operated. There was only one light bulb hanging from the ceiling, for the rest of the place it was matches and candles. Brian and I had to wear all the clothes and coats we owned to keep warm, but I was the only one who owned an overcoat—it was my father's army overcoat, and we took turns wearing it. There were mice and rats and God knows what else. The rugs were in dirty strips and most of the dishes were cracked or broken. What looked like generations of flies and roaches had been squished against the walls and their smudges left there like grave markers.

□ □ □

As awful as Edith Grove was, it didn't discourage Keith and Mick from moving in. Mick continued to go to school, but he just had to get out of his house and away from his nagging father, who was giving him a perpetual hard time. Keith had left the Sidcup Art School but seemed to have no interest in getting a job.

As bad luck would have it, it was one of the coldest London winters in anyone's memory. On the coldest nights, Brian, Keith and Mick slept three in the bed for warmth, and Hattrell slept on the couch wearing his overcoat. It was so cold that the water pipes froze and they couldn't use the toilet or get any water from the tap in the kitchen.

After Brian got sacked from Whiteley's, he and Keith found themselves sitting around that grubby, frozen flat all day with nothing to do but play their guitars. They often didn't have a coin to put in the electric meter—not that it gave off *that* much heat— so it's a wonder they were able to move their frozen fingers on their guitars. But they did. For hours and hours and hours, they'd sit there facing each other, playing endlessly, beginning to develop a style of playing together, taking turns at lead guitar. Being shut up in that terrible flat for all of that freezing winter was fortuitous for the future of the Rolling Stones because Keith and Brian developed a style of playing together that never would have materialized if they had only played in practice sessions at the Wetherby Arms.

"It's winter, it's like the worst winter ever," Keith Richards has recalled. "Brian and me sitting around this electric heater, wondering where to get the next shilling to put in it to keep it going. Collecting beer bottles and selling them back to pubs, getting like three shillings, and going to pads where we knew there'd been parties going on, walking in saying, 'Hello, how nice, we'll help you clean up,' and we'd steal the bottles and whatever food we could find lying around the kitchen and run for it. It's getting really sick, down to picking people's pockets. That winter, Mick

went through his first camp period. He started wandering round
the flat in a blue linen housecoat, wavin' his hands everywhere—
'Oh! Don't!' A real King's Road queen for about six months, and
Brian and I used to kid the piss out of him. But Mick stayed on
that queen kick."

Ian Stewart

THE FIRST TIME I walked into that
Edith Grove flat, the stink almost
knocked me over. There was rotting food
and old cigarette butts all over the place,
dirty clothes flung around, but that disgusting smell, like rotting
cabbages, I couldn't imagine anybody living there. You had to
pick your way through the room, stepping over all the guck that
covered the floors.

It was amazing to me that Keith and Brian could sit around
there all day, working their guitars. What they worked out was a
synchronization of playing that the guitarists in other bands didn't
have. Instead of one guitar playing lead and the other a rhythm
guitar underneath him, which was the usual way, Keith and Brian
were more of a piece, alternating as leads, taking turns soloing,
blending. During this period, Keith and Brian developed a relationship as close as their guitar playing, and I sensed that Jagger
was beginning to feel left out, jealous, resentful of Brian. Mick
didn't have much to contribute, since his guitar playing and his
attempts at the harmonica were pretty feeble, but he had a lot of
ambition and vanity and he was damn smart, and I could see him
looking at Brian in a way that was a little bit menacing. I could
sense back then the beginning of Mick's desire to distance Keith
from Brian, and much later on it didn't surprise me one bit when
Mick began plotting to ease Brian out of the band.

As a matter of fact, Mick flashed his hostility toward Brian in an
incident involving Pat Andrews, who had not gone home with the
baby but was still living in the London flat. Even though he had
moved to Edith Grove, Brian continued to see her and sometimes
spent the night with her. Well, one afternoon Jagger came to the
flat looking for Brian who wasn't there. So Mick hung around,
eventually got Pat to get into bed with him and knocked her off.
Brian found out about it, of course, and from then on it was a thorn
in his relationship with Mick—which, I guess, is what Mick inten-

ded. There were plenty of ready and willing girls Mick knew from the Ealing Club and the Marquee, so I figure the only reason he balled Pat, who was certainly not very attractive, was to get at Brian.

□   □   □

Dick Taylor

AFTER WE HAD only had a few rehearsals, it became apparent that Geoff Bradford and Keith were not going to get along together. Geoff was a good sound musician but he was a blues purist and unbending about accommodating Keith's rhythm and blues approach. They had a couple of bloody awful rows during rehearsals, and finally Geoff just banged out of there one day, and frankly nobody regretted seeing him go.

□   □   □

Harold Pendleton

THE FIRST TIME the Rolling Stones played in public was on my bandstand at the Marquee. It came about this way: The band that was playing rhythm and blues at the Marquee that summer of 1962 was Alexis Korner's Blues Incorporated. Thursday night was set aside for rhythm and blues, and Blues Incorporated was the regular Thursday night band, but on July 12th Korner's group had been booked for a BBC program, "Jazz Club," so I filled their spot with the small band that regularly played during intermission. I now needed a group to replace them as the intermission band. I knew about the group that had been rehearsing at the Wetherby Arms, so I got in touch with Ian Stewart, whom I knew, and gave him the booking.

That's how it happened that the Stones, six in number then, made their debut at the Marquee—Jagger, Jones, Stew, Keith, Dick Taylor and Mick Avory on the drums. They wore a ragtag assortment of clothes, ranging from Jagger's colorful pullover to Richards's necktie and banker's suit. As they mounted the bandstand, a gasp arose from the jazz-blues regulars in the audience when they saw Dick Taylor's bass guitar, which was as big as a bass fiddle. The Stones' playing elicited some derisive comments from the jazz regulars, but also present was an even more animated group that supported rhythm and blues. This clash brought a certain electricity to the occasion—the jeers of the jazz buffs, the applause of the R and B devotees. If I had known that Jagger and Company were going to play R and B the way they did—like nothing we had heard quite like it at the Marquee before—I would never have booked them because the Marquee was essentially a jazz club, pure jazz and blues, and I didn't want to go as far off our base as they went.

But I kept them on for a while, in the Thursday spot, because R and B was becoming more and more popular, displacing jazz. As a matter of fact, we started evolving our own bands at the Marquee and produced quite a lot of them. We needed a Tuesday band so we assembled a group that first was called the High Numbers. Later on they changed their name to the Who. I gave them a lot of publicity and eventually they became the star attraction on Tuesday night.

The Stones, meanwhile, were doing their Muddy Waters type music on Thursday, but they were not really a very good band because they didn't have a decent drummer. You can really divvy the whole of jazz from the whole of rock just by listening to the drums. The rock beat is: da da da DUM—it's triplets, whereas the jazz beat is: dum ticka dum ticka dum—it's four-four, whatever. The Stones' drummer couldn't keep the triplets beat. The best drummer around played for Alexis Korner—his name was Charlie Watts and he could do solid triplets all night long.

□　□　□

Ian Stewart

I MUST CONFESS, I never liked the Who very much. Largely because they had such a bad drummer. The Who were really all flash. I mean, they could play all right, but there was never any good time thing there. I quite liked the Animals from Newcastle. They could play nicely. There were a lot of good groups in Liverpool, but they weren't players, they were singers. I've never yet heard a musician who came out of Liverpool who would actually make you want to stand still and listen to him. Including the Beatles. That's the one thing I had against them. They couldn't play. They wrote pretty little songs and they were pretty little boys and they could play just the way they wanted to the songs that they wrote. But the trouble was that Liverpool was never much of a jazz scene—that's what it really comes down to—whereas London and Newcastle and Manchester were. Most of the groups that were around in London at the time had a lot of jazz influence in them. There were people like Graham Bond and Jack Bruce and the guys that played with Alexis Korner. When they played, there was a lot of things to listen to, a lot of things going on that were very interesting, the creativity of good musicians. But the out-and-out pop groups never did anything different; no originality.

To me, the Hollies were better than the Beatles. They had a good drummer and they had some sort of feel to them. There was one or two good groups. There was a group called the Charts, which nobody ever heard of, they were brilliant, wonderful singers. But they never got anywhere—it was just Beatles, Beatles and more Beatles. I was so disappointed when I first went to Liverpool because we'd heard so much about Liverpool, the great place for R and B, all these fantastic groups, but the truth was that all the groups we heard were terrible, absolutely awful. Terrible drummers, and as far as I'm concerned, no group is any better than its drummer, who is the heartbeat of a good group.

That was the basic problem with the Stones—we had no real drummer. We kept changing, trying to find a guy who could give us the beat that would hold us together, but the only drummer I knew who could fill the bill was Charlie Watts, and he worked regularly with Alexis Korner so we knew there was no sense asking him to throw in with a group of guys who didn't know where their next meal was coming from.

At that time, if you had asked me what my goal was for the Rolling Stones, I would have said, "Maybe some day, with a good drummer, we could get bookings to play in the back of pubs"—what are called club dates. With Mick's thin voice and the musicians we had, I never dreamed we'd catch on. Never, never, never.

While the Stones were struggling with the vagaries of the rock and roll establishment, a young woman their age named Mary Quant was having an equally difficult struggle trying to make her name in the world of fashion. And just as Mick and Brian had to overcome resistance to the then strange beat of their rhythm and blues rock, so, too, Mary had to dislodge long-established British traditional dress with her revolutionary new look. As much as anyone, it was she who opened the floodgates that engulfed Carnaby Street and King's Road, eventually spilling over into American shops. Amazingly, today she looks exactly as she did in the sixties. Her distinctive hairdo, her little-girl figure, her enthusiasm—all intact. And her dress business thrives, although her styles are but variations of her sixties' concepts.

Mary Quant

I GREW UP making my own clothes because I didn't like clothes the way they were. My clothes were very much dance-school clothes, things like black tights, leotards and tops, and then circular skirts with flat shoes. I had a very strong idea of how I wanted to look. An innocent, child look—that's what it was.

I didn't like the shock, the change that happened to girls when they grew up. In the late fifties, when I started, girls didn't have jobs, didn't have their own money. As a result, all their lives, they were dressing for somebody else. They grew up with their father paying for their clothes and had to look the way he wanted. When they got married, they had to play the wife and dress in a way to please the husband. Women just didn't ever have a look that was themselves, it was a look for somebody else, for the men in their lives. I inherited clothes from my cousins, but already when I was five years old I knew they weren't me, they weren't my clothes. I disliked wearing them, and I began trying to make my own clothes at the ludicrous age of five or six.

Until the sixties, fashion was dictated by Paris—expensive originals, cheap copies—but these frilly Paris fashions seemed to kids like us perfectly irrelevant to the life we inherited after the war. Those dresses were okay for duchesses and film stars and people who lived in Chantilly, but those dresses didn't have anything to do with the reality of our lives.

There was a very big gap between the people who'd been adults during the war, and the next generation that came along, who had been children during the war. Not only had most of those children not suffered during the war, but, in fact, they had rather enjoyed the war. Being a child in the war was quite fun, from the child's point of view—there was a sense of excitement, inventing things, strange foods, ersatz shoes, whatever, a source of adventure that children actually love. They moved around the countryside, there was less schooling, all sorts of things like that. The Battle of Britain, that stuff, was full of all kinds of theater, tremendous excitement, and when those children became teenagers they continued wanting that kind of life. When I came to London, having been evacuated during most of the war, I was terribly excited, for I had heard my parents talk about the glamorous life before the war, but there wasn't any left. London was a place of despair, a great heap of ruins. Of course there were places like the Savoy and the Dorchester, but young people couldn't afford to go there and nothing existed for people with little money.

A few people like myself started saying, "We've got to create our own fun," that the clothes were wrong, the music was wrong, the whole way of life was downbeat, dismal. The first break through this stodgy wall was the advent of the teddy boys and their Edwardian costumes. It was an inspired and exciting contribution because it was the first sign of the craziness that was going to inundate the sixties.

When I started, I simply wanted to design for people like myself—skinny sweaters, black leotards, black patent leather shoes or tap-dancing shoes with white ankle socks—that getup transfixed me. I was struck by the drama of dressing like that. The kids in art schools liked the look—it was all right in art school to wear that sort of thing. But other people didn't dress like that, nor have a bobbed haircut as I did—it was very much a child's look as compared to things then. I wore circle skirts, or an elongated man's cardigan worn over tights and leotards—it was really a dancing-class look, especially with a child's haircut.

We opened our first shop—my husband, Alexander Plunkett, and I—in the late fifties when I was twenty. We thought we were elite, that our clothes were for art students and our friends, for sculptors, a few tarts, but what took us by surprise was that the entire younger generation wanted this sort of look, and that the elitist concept was quite wrong. We were flooded with massive orders from America, from Germany, Australia and South Africa. Our shop, Bazaar, became a social salon for photographers, playwrights, painters and musicians. The Beatles brought their girl friends, and it was really the beginning of the two sexes wearing the same clothes. Vidal Sassoon created a hairstyle for me that went with my clothes and pretty soon the Sassoon cut became as popular as my dresses.

We were so excited about the enormous success of the whole thing that we used to forget about shutting up the shop. We would stay open until we were absolutely out on our feet. It was a madness, hysterical. But people loved it. They loved coming up to the shop with husbands and boyfriends late at night after a good dinner and looking through our things and trying on the dresses they liked and buying them. It was because of all this that the shop developed such a marvelous character of its own. All sorts of exciting people used to come; interesting people who were really something. They would just strip off the dress they were wearing in the middle of the room and try on others.

Over and over again I was told I was responsible for the offbeat clothes that became known as the Chelsea Look. I heard my clothes described as dishy, kinky, mod, poove and all the rest of it. People either loved or hated them. But, in fact, no one designer is ever responsible for such a revolution. All a designer can do is to anticipate a mood before people realize that they are bored with what they have already got. It is simply a question of who gets bored first. Fortunately I am apt to get bored pretty quickly. Perhaps this is the essence of designing.

Good designers know that to have any influence they must keep in step with public needs and that intangible "something in the air." They must catch the spirit of the day and interpret it in clothes before other designers begin to twitch at the nerve ends.

I just happened to start when that something in the air was coming to a boil. The clothes I made happened to fit in exactly with the teenage trend, with pop records and espresso bars and jazz clubs. The rejuvenated *Queen* magazine, *Beyond the Fringe*, *Private Eye*, the discotheques and "That Was the Week That Was" were all born on the same wavelength.

I never knew when or where inspiration would come. When I saw Rudolf Nureyev—dashing, sweatered, very Russian-looking— he made me want to toss out every one of the lean, mean things I had in my collections. Suddenly I was sick of them all. I wanted a great, husky, generous shape . . . a big top with a short, straight skirt . . . a kind of offstage Nureyev look.

I found inspiration in *Goldfinger,* too, Shirley Eaton sparked off the idea. Seeing her, I realized how terribly sexy the allover pale-gold look was—just the thing for girls out for a quick killing.

One day I pulled on an eight-year-old boy's sweater for fun, was enchanted with the result. And, in six months, all the birds were wearing the skinny-ribs that resulted.

It was the same thing with string tops. As a joke I put a man's string vest over the dark dress I was wearing. The effect was electric. I bought up all the string vests I could put my hands on and had them dyed in the colors of the year. Fashion became a thing of tangled textures and stringy shapes, of hole-peppered stockings, crochet tops and fishnet gloves. I loved the look.

I think the sum total of what happened in the sixties is that whereas before everything started with the rich and trickled down to ordinary people, now groups like the Beatles and the Rolling Stones wrote and performed music directly for the masses and not just for cafe society. I think that I broke the couture stranglehold that Chanel, Dior and the others had had on fashion, when I created styles at the working-girl level. It all added up to a democratization of fashion and entertainment, and that included, of course, the proliferation of inexpensive bistro-like restaurants.

It was very gratifying to see that not only did the mods of the sixties want my clothes, but so did the grandees and the millionaires. They had everything else—all the minks and ball gowns they could use; the silk shirts and the silk trousers; the stretch pants and the leopard tops. But they hadn't any fun clothes. This was something quite new to them and I had no idea to what extent this look was to grip people's imagination and how popular it was to become.

The girls of the sixties were curiously feminine but their femininity lay in their attitude rather than in their appearance. They might be dukes' daughters, doctors' daughters or dockers' daughters. They were not interested in status symbols. They didn't worry about accents or class; they were neither determinedly country nor working class. They were scornful of pretense of any kind.

There was a time when clothes were a sure sign of a woman's social position and income group. Not anymore. Snobbery went out of fashion, and in the shops you found duchesses jostling with typists to buy the same dresses. Fashion had become the great leveler.

Rock music was also destined to become another great leveler but the Stones were finding it difficult to emerge from the bleak obscurity of the back room at the Wetherby Arms.

Dick Taylor

ALL WE DID was rehearse, rehearse, rehearse. Our only gigs were the few Thursday nights when Harold Pendleton booked us as intermission band at the Marquee. But even there, the going was rough. Pendleton only liked jazz and he was always disparaging our rhythm and blues music. One Thursday night we were to do the intermissions for Cyril Davies's band—Cyril had previously been a booster of ours. This particular Thursday he was churlish, and when we came on the bandstand to play he told us to fuck off, that we were bloody awful and we were not going to stink up his bandstand. Pendleton enjoyed our getting publicly sacked like that, and Keith picked up his guitar by the throat and took a vicious swing at Pendleton's head. We all felt awful having to pack up our stuff and troop out to the alley where Ian's battered old van was parked.

So there went our only gig, but we continued to rehearse at the Wetherby Arms. Sometimes we sounded good when a drummer we knew, Charlie Watts, who was with Giorgio Gomelsky's band, sat in with us, because he really had the R and B beat. But the other drummers who came around, like Tony Chapman, didn't have a good, reliable beat and, besides, they couldn't be counted on to show up at rehearsals.

I was trying to get into the Royal College of Art, but I was finding it really hard keeping up with my schoolwork and rehearsing. Also, I was getting a bit fed up playing the bass. I really wanted to play the guitar because I liked playing lead guitar best, but, of course, Keith and Brian were on the guitars. I knew Phil May wanted me for a new band he planned to start, the Pretty Things, and that I could play lead guitar with him. At that time, the bass guitarist was just a plodder, playing simple bass riffs, boring and unrewarding musically.

My decision to leave the Stones was definitely a hard one, because I certainly did think we had a pretty good potential. Of course, I was far from realizing that one day they were going to become a super-band of world renown. But one night, after one of our long rehearsals, I just said that I'd had enough and I was cutting out. Tony Chapman had a friend who was a bass player, Bill Wyman, and he was brought in to replace me. With Bill, the Stones got their first decent amplifiers—Bill even had a spare Vox 850.

Once I left the Stones, I was able to concentrate on getting into the Royal College, but the sad fact was I didn't get accepted. So if I had stayed with the Stones I could've been a millionaire or flat on my face at the bottom of a swimming pool—that's what I always say. But looking back on it, no doubt I made a wrong decision, not because of the money and the fame, but because it was what I really wanted to do. But I kind of sidetracked myself into thinking that I wanted to be a graphic artist. I guess I just didn't really know my own mind. After all, I was pretty young. But over the years I've had my regrets, and sometimes, when I'm driving around in my lorry, making deliveries, I think about what might have been.

□ ⬚ □

"I was in a small rock group in South London that had been going for about a year," Bill Wyman has said, "just to play some fun music and earn a little bit of cash, because money was pretty scarce. I had a baby just born, in the beginning of '62, I'd only been married about two years, I had to go to work at six o'clock in the morning, and I was earning only eight or nine pounds a week, which was about eighteen dollars. After my payments on the furniture and all that, we finished up with about four pounds a week for food. We couldn't possibly exist on that, so I used to play occasionally at the local social club with a piano player and a drummer. We would get two pounds each for that and all we wanted to eat and drink. So that added another twenty-five percent on my original wage, tax-free, of course.

"But anyway, we jogged along for about a year like that, and it was a terrible struggle. Brian Jones had put an ad in *Jazz News* for a drummer, and my drummer went to be interviewed. He went uptown and played, and when he came back he had a tape with him of some real blues—slow, Muddy Waters. And I said, 'Wow, that's really slow stuff, it's so simple, right?' Dummy me. It's slow, and there's not much being played, so it's simple, right? And he said, 'But they haven't got a bass player, why don't you come up?

I told them that I knew one.' So I did, and we went up to the next rehearsal in this pub, and they took us. But a month later they fired him, because he really wasn't a very good drummer.

"They liked me straightaway because I had more amplifiers than the band had at that time, bigger and better. So I guess what they really hired were my amplifiers."

With the addition of Bill Wyman and his big amps, the Stones improved their sound but they were still handicapped by the lack of a good drummer; without a drummer who could give them the right beat, they couldn't perform anywhere but the back room of pubs.

"We didn't dare try to book a gig," Richards has recalled. "We were constantly rehearsing drummers. Mick Avory came by, the drummer of the Kinks. He was terrible then. Couldn't find that off-beat. One day we picked up a drummer called Tony Chapman who was our first regular drummer. Terrible. One of the worst. Cat would start a number and end up either four times as fast as he started it or three times as slow. But never stay the same."

After getting bounced from the Marquee, and without a reliable drummer, there was nothing for the Stones to do but spend the endless days and nights in the grotty Edith Grove flat in Chelsea, playing their instruments. Mick had never learned to play anything, but in this period Brian, who played brilliant harmonica, gave Mick lessons in how to play the harmonica with a blues feel, what they call, technically, "flattening the notes," giving the notes more soul. Mick couldn't get the hang of it at first, but Brian coached him along and helped him get to the point where he could play acceptably on stage, although he never approached Brian's musicianship.

Richard Hattrell

WE SOMEHOW MANAGED to scrape together enough money to pay the paltry rent, but the fact was we were all starving. I'm not being overly dramatic about that, we were literally starving. That's when my health started to fail. We simply had nothing to eat, no money to buy food of any kind. Our big treat was every second or third day we'd go to the all-night Wimpy bar next to the tube station in Earl's Court and treat ourselves to a hamburger. That's all we had to eat, umpteen cups of tea and coffee and a twice-a-week Wimpy.

So we were getting in a pretty shocking state of health. Mick was eating more than the rest of us because his girl friend was Chrissie Shrimpton and she'd invite him to her family home for weekends and he could store up the eats for the coming week. For a while Keith's mother used to send him money to buy food, but Keith used the money to buy records and strings for his guitar. When Keith's mother found out about this, however, she began sending food parcels instead of giving Keith money, and we used to devour the contents of those food packets ravenously. My family didn't help me at all—neither with money nor food parcels. They were hoping I'd get starved out and be forced to go home.

What really compounded our troubles was the severity of that winter. It was a pisser—paralyzing amounts of snow, the temperatures constantly below zero that froze all the water pipes in our flat, thereby cutting off the sink and toilet. Against that kind of cold, that little one-bar electric heater we had was a joke, even when we had the coins to operate it.

What food we had, we nicked from food shops along the nearby Fulham Road. Keith or Brian would be asking questions of the shopkeeper and distracting him, while I stuffed whatever I could, like a few potatoes and turnips, up under my big overcoat. And we all kept a sharp eye on the flats in our building, locating those that were giving a party, and then checking their garbage the next morning for leftover bread and whatnot that looked edible. One of my regular duties was to go out early in the morning, half past five or so, and nick a couple of bottles of milk off the milkman's float so that we could have milk in our tea.

Keith's responsibility was getting the coins to feed the electric heater. He wasn't very conscientious, and we'd usually run out of coins and *really* freeze, but the way he got hold of coins, when he remembered, was to go around the hallways of our building and collect all the empty bottles that had been put out and take them back to the stores for the deposit money. Looking back on it, we were really like some kind of outlaw band out of Dickens.

But despite these terrible hard times, Brian Jones and I managed to get hold of a bottle of brandy and a bottle of whiskey every day, and Brian would polish off his daily brandy and I would drink my bottle of Teacher's or bottle of Bell's. We'd just carry them around in our pockets and drink from the bottles. It kept us warm, God knows, and it was a kind of food, even though the wrong kind. I was getting a small stipend from the army—I had done two years in the national service, and continued to do a fortnight's camp in the summer and two weekends in the winter, and this army money was just enough to pay for the daily fifth of booze.

Brian was subject to wild swings of mood. Most often he'd be seized by a kind of madness and he'd turn on me. One night when the snow was really falling and it was freezing cold, he asked me to go get some cigarettes, but when I came back he had locked the door and wouldn't let me in. Keith and Mick were there, and they were enjoying it. When Brian was depressed or bored he'd have to invent excitement. I thought he'd keep me out in the cold for only a short while and then relent, but, no, I was locked out until morning and I damn near froze to death.

There was another night he did something similar. He had some live-end wires coming out of a big amp. I don't know if they had juice or not, but he chased me outside with them and then locked the door on me. Again, he had Keith and Mick as an audience—I think Ian Stewart was also there. It was snowing like crazy that night and I thought I'd get pneumonia for sure. But this time Brian relented and after several hours let me back in.

Brian did have this incredible cruelty in him—a raging temper, beating up his girl friends—but he could also be a good friend and very considerate. I understood about his temperament and was willing to take the bad and the good. I could appreciate how hard it was on him to sit around day after day with nothing to do but rehearse with Keith.

□ □ □

In the cold of that winter, sleeping three to the bed, hungry and disillusioned, there developed between the trio of Mick, Keith and Brian the basic ties and antagonisms that were to dominate their lives in the prosperous years to come. The fact that Keith and Brian spent their days alone in the cold flat, endlessly and relentlessly playing their guitars, scrounging for food, drink and cigarettes, sharing their struggle, united them in a way that excluded Mick, who spent his days at school. Mick came to resent their relationship, in fact, became jealous of Brian, both for his rapport with Keith and for his superior musicianship, which gave him dominance over the band.

This was also the period when Mick's sexual personality manifested itself. He became very camp, mincing about in a lavender robe and a hair net, giving full rein to the female part of his makeup, and the more camp he became, the more Keith and Brian accentuated their maleness, so it was a very strange trio, indeed, who slept in that bed. "Brian and I immediately went enormously butch," Keith says, "sort of laughing at Mick. That terrible thing . . . that switching-around confusion of roles that still goes on."

It was that dual sexuality that was to emerge later on when Mick performed with the band, and it probably accounted for the fact that Mick became a sexual turn-on for both the female and male members of the audience.

As for the fortunes of the band, under the circumstances it would have been easy to become demoralized and disband, but Brian somehow managed to keep them together and make them believe that they were going somewhere, that the bands then getting all the attention were out of sync with the future, and that gigs and recognition for the Stones' brand of rhythm and blues were just around the corner.

They turned that corner on the night they finally got the drummer they had so desperately sought. They were playing one of the infrequent dates they had managed to book in a little out-of-the-way club, alternating with another band that played rhythm and blues, which was still not very popular. The other band's drummer was Charlie Watts, whom the Stones knew about and coveted but had never approached because they had so little to offer him in the way of play dates and remuneration. But on this occasion, after Charlie heard the sound the Stones were creating, he quit his band right then and there and threw in his lot with the Stones. They could now attain the complete sound they had been aiming for, the full-bodied R and B that was to become their hallmark.

Brian was the only one of the Stones who went around soliciting clubs for playing dates. One of his contacts was a well-known jazz promoter named Giorgio Gomelsky who had tried to promote a jazz club called the Piccadilly, which had failed, and now he was opening another club called the Crawdaddy, which only operated for a few hours every Sunday evening at the Station Hotel in Richmond. When the band he had booked couldn't make it one Sunday because of the snow, he gave the Stones a chance. Since Brian had made Hattrell the road manager, it was his job to map the way there by tube and bus, lugging the musical instruments with them because Stew's old van was in for repairs.

This was the Stones' first public appearance with Charlie Watts on the drums, and with Brian playing blues harmonica and guitar. They put on a good show, but there were only twenty people in the audience. Giorgio liked what he heard, however, and he booked them again for the following Sunday. Within three weeks, they were playing to packed houses—the word about the Stones had got around, and since the kids in the outskirts towns of Richmond, Twickenham and Surbiton had very little to do on a Sunday evening, the Crawdaddy became the place to go.

The first night the Stones played at the Crawdaddy, Giorgio paid them one pound apiece, but after that he split the gate receipts with them; admission to the Crawdaddy was a rather paltry amount, however, so the Stones' take didn't amount to much. They also got bookings at a couple of other minor clubs, Studio 51 and the Ealing Club, where they were paid little more than their expenses and some free beer.

Phil May

IT WAS THE lack of gigs that forced new groups to seek places where they would be accepted. Hamburg was certainly the most important of these places. Everybody did three months in Hamburg, working six shows a night, for coolie wages. Hamburg had an incredible group of jazz clubs—the Star Club, the Top Twenty, the Storyville, lots of clubs. Some fly-by-night agent in London would book you to go there and promise you a decent fee. But the German owners didn't pay, and you'd be so broke you'd have to stay there and keep working because you couldn't buy the tickets to get home. We all hated Hamburg, hated the Germans, but had to hang on. We were doing eight shows, half an hour off and an hour on. So we used to hang around in the bars with the whores because we didn't finish till four, and you started again at one the next day. So we'd be having breakfast about six or seven in the morning. I think that's what caused the ingredient of drugs to be added to the music. It was the necessity of having to stay awake for such long periods of time. You took upper pills, prellios, and other things to stay awake for eighteen, nineteen hours a day. The Beatles were trapped there, broke, hating the Germans, but it helped forge their band into the successful unit they became.

The Stones didn't play Hamburg but they were playing the dingy clubs and had the same problems. The Stones were working third-rate road shows, but working just as hard. Bands tended to have residencies, a couple of clubs you played regularly, and if you couldn't make it because you were in Sweden or France or Germany, whatever, you would have a mate or mates who would go in with their band and cover for you for that one Tuesday night you couldn't make. We were in a club for about a year and a half, the 100 Club, every Tuesday night. The Stones had the Station Hotel and also the Richmond Athletic Ground. The Yardbirds had the Boat House down on the Thames, which was a rhythm and blues club. That was your base, from which you went out and worked other places, but you were guaranteed your regular spots.

CHAPTER SIX

Inventing the Rolling Stones

From the outside, it seemed like the Beatles were the fresh-faced fab mop tops and we were totally the other end of the spectrum. But they were just as filthy as we were, really.

KEITH RICHARDS

T he Stones' success at their Sunday appearances at the Crawdaddy induced Giorgio Gomelsky to try to get some publicity for his fledgling club by getting in touch with Peter Jones, then an editor at the *Record Mirror,* a widely circulated music publication, and now on staff at *Billboard.*

Peter Jones

I GOT A call one day from Giorgio Gomelsky, extolling a new group that was playing at the Crawdaddy; he wanted me to go to Richmond to hear them and maybe write about them if I liked what I heard. I had gotten used to agents and managers telling me how good such and such a group was. I'd met Giorgio a couple of times, knew his opinion was to be respected, but it seemed a terrible drag to have to give up a Sunday to go to Richmond, which is ten miles from the center of London.

Anyway, I turned up—across the road from the railway station, into the saloon bar of the Station Hotel. There were the usual Sunday drinkers buried in pints of bitter. Occasionally a teenager wandered through to the sort of clubroom at the back, where this new group, the Rolling Stones, was playing.

The first number I heard the Stones play was "Pretty Thing"

and it exploded, literally, like a bomb. It was an everything-happening sort of performance and it didn't need a lot of savvy to know that these boys were one of the most potent little outfits on the scene.

Later on I talked to Brian Jones who seemed to be the leader. Brian said he was sorry that the music wasn't up to their best standards. He felt they needed to warm up a little more, and said how much they depended on audience reaction to get things really swinging. I told him that I thought the group was excellent, authentic and well worth encouraging. I said I'd try to get a real disc-hardened rhythm and blues writer to see them and to see if we could get a bit of publicity going for the boys.

They looked pleased enough, but it was apparent that they'd been promised all sorts of things before and they looked as if they were going to hold back any enthusiasm until something really did happen. I went back to the *Record Mirror* office and talked to a fellow writer, Norman Jopling, who agreed to go to Richmond as soon as possible to see if he could confirm my early impression. Norman wrote more about rock than I did. He returned with an enthusiastic thumbs-up sign, and he turned in an article about them that ran in the April 1963 issue. It was the first trade-type appraisal of the Stones' actual status in the music business. The headline stretched across five columns.

The Rolling Stones—Genuine R and B

At the Station Hotel, Kew Road, the hip kids throw themselves about to the new jungle music like they never did in the more restrained days of trad.

And the combo they writhe and twist to is called the Rolling Stones. Maybe you've never heard of them—if you live far from London, the odds are you haven't.

But by gad you will! The Stones are destined to be the biggest group in the R and B scene—if that scene continues to flourish. Three months ago only fifty people turned up to see the group. Now promoter Gomelsky has to close the doors at an early hour— with over four hundred fans crowding the hall.

Those fans quickly lose their inhibitions and contort themselves to truly exciting music. Fact is that, unlike all the other R and B groups worthy of the name, the Rolling Stones have a definite visual appeal. They aren't like the jazzmen who were doing trad a few months ago and who had converted their act to keep up with the times. They are genuine R and B fanatics themselves and they sing and play in a way that one would have expected more from a coloured U.S. group than a bunch of wild, exciting white boys who have the fans screaming and listening to them.

Peter Jones

AFTER THAT ARTICLE appeared, I felt that the Stones could only cash in on it if they had a manager and, with that in mind, I contacted a live-wire publicist I knew named Andrew Oldham. I had known Andrew since he first emerged on the pop scene, trying desperately to get himself mentioned in the papers as a singer-compere under the name of Sandy Beach. Later, he actually tried the name Chancery Lane.

I told Andrew that the Stones were a wild outfit. Really wild. I said, "It looks as if rhythm and blues will make it big soon, so why not have a look at them? They're pretty brought down right now because they feel that things aren't happening fast enough for them. It'll only cost you a couple of bob to get on the train to Richmond and see them."

Andrew gave the impression he wasn't sure he could raise a couple of shillings, but he promised to talk to someone about the group.

☐ ☐ ☐

I arranged for Andrew Oldham to come see me in my apartment in New York. He is still making a desperate attempt to preserve his sixties quirkiness, but now in his mid-forties, scrambling about for pick-up jobs, strapped for money, no matter how he puts himself together, he can't bring it off. He still wears billowing silk blouses, an outsized hat that rests on his eyebrows, a kicky jacket, and carries a brocaded bag slung over one shoulder, but the circus for which he is dressed has long since moved on. He persists. He ceremoniously opens the brocade bag, takes out a candle and fits it into its holder, then withdraws a large knife, which he presses, releasing a lethal switchblade. Next he takes out cigarette papers and a square brown lump. He lights the candle, stabs the lump with his switchblade, and cooks it over the candle flame. When it is *au point* he places the melted brown substance in the paper, rolls it and starts to smoke his hash. Oldham's conversation consists of fragments, of spurts of sentences without end, of free-associated non sequiturs, but with patience it is possible to rein him in somewhat, especially in the interval when he has finished one hash cigarette and has not yet lit up another.

Andrew Oldham

PETER JONES'S CALL about this new group he found, the Rolling Stones, came at just the right time. I was only nineteen, but I had already worked for Mary Quant in her shop pushing clothes, dressing windows, making tea, and all that. After that job, I got onto Brian Epstein, who hired me to do publicity for the Beatles, when they were first starting and were completely unknown. Unfortunately, as soon as they started to hit big, I got sacked in favor of Tony Barrow, who was much more experienced. I was currently handling publicity for a young singer named Mark Wynter, but that was hardly enough to keep me going. I had just made a deal with an old-time show business agent, Eric Easton, to let me use a little spare room he had in his offices on Regent Street, a very good location. Now all I needed were a couple of clients.

I got on the train to Richmond, a scruffy place where the Crawdaddy was located, the very next Sunday after Peter Jones's phone call. Luckily, this was just before the article about the Stones appeared in the *Record Mirror*. As I approached the Station Hotel, I heard loud voices coming from the alleyway beside the hotel. I had to walk down this alley of a railway track, and there's barbed wire on one side and brick wall on the other. It was 8:30 and getting dark. There was this silhouette of a very attractive couple fighting at the end of the alley that I was walking down. I found out later it was Mick Jagger and Chrissie Shrimpton.

What knocked me out about the Stones' performance was their enthusiasm. I really dug that kind of music and they were going at it so hard, you'd have to be some kind of idiot not to get the message. They literally hurled their music from the edge of the small stand and got everybody going like crazy. There wasn't room to swing a cat. It was unbearably hot, but the fans didn't seem to give a damn. When the Stones were really laying it down, the audience danced to the music in the best way they could— using only the top part of their bodies, with their feet in place. I'd say that the one word to describe the Stones at that session was "communication." They were really getting *through* to the kids. It took me a couple of days after that evening to stop talking about them, to stop hearing their sound in my head. I went up to the bandstand at the intermission, and I asked who was the leader. Brian Jones stepped forward and said he was, but I saw that Jagger gave him a hard look. At any rate, I explained that I was a manager, that I was associated with another well-established manager of talent, and that on the basis of what I'd heard, I wanted to sign them up. I gave them my card and asked them to come up to our office as soon as they could.

To my surprise, Brian and Mick showed up at Eric's office the following day. Since Eric had no rock groups, he was all for taking them on, although after hearing them, he said, "The singer will have to go, the BBC won't like him." Nevertheless, we signed them up, and I said that the first order of business was to arrange for them to cut their first record. I knew that a fellow named Dick Rowe at Decca would be a logical person to approach because he was still dodging a lot of flak for turning down the Beatles when they came to him at the beginning of their careers. I guessed rightly, because Dick Rowe, after hearing them once at Crawdaddy, signed them up to make their first single. But I had decided that, if I was going to succeed in this business, I would have to do more than just play the usual games. I had decided that I was going to be a nasty little upstart tycoon shit. I had learned from talking to people in the business that if you let your group be recorded at Decca's studios, Decca would then have control of the copyright and the recordings. Whereas if you recorded it independently somewhere else and simply leased the recording back to Decca, who would put out the records, then your group would retain its copyrights and keep control of the record itself. So I found a studio where I could use the recording facilities by paying five pounds an hour. This was in May of 1963. The studios were called Olympic Sound and they were pretty primitive. The only personnel that came with the studio was one engineer.

The Stones had chosen a Chuck Berry song, "Come On," and when I walked in the studio, I decided I'd better be frank with the engineer, whose name was Roger Savage. So I told him, "Look, the difficulty here is that this is the first recording session I've ever been in on. I don't know anything at all about music but I'm sure

I know the right sort of sound that might prove commercial. Let's just play it by ear and try not to get too panicky about it all. Let's also remember that we've got the studio for three hours and that it's costing money and I'd like to get this song recorded within that time."

Unfortunately, the Stones didn't sound nearly as good in that studio as they had on the little stage at the Crawdaddy. They complained that without an audience they didn't have any feedback, and it was obvious that playing in a recording studio was certainly different than being able to perform in the freewheeling atmosphere of a room full of fans reacting to the music. Charlie Watts said he felt that without the right atmosphere there was nothing to force them to play the kind of music they wanted to get on the record. I had to admit that the result really wasn't very good. The engineer just slapped the tracks together and there was an imbalance of harmonica on the tape.

The people at Decca were disappointed in the tape that I sent them, and they scheduled another recording session for "Come On." The Stones complained about having to do it all over; it was somewhat of an improvement, but still a far cry from the kind of music they were producing in front of a live audience. And that's the way the critics reacted. Norman Jopling, the writer at the Record Mirror who had given them such a glowing notice about their stage performance, wrote: "The disc doesn't sound like the Rolling Stones. It's good, punchy and commercial, but it's not the fanatical R and B that audiences wait hours to hear. Instead, it's a bluesy, commercial group that should make the charts in a small-ish way."

Jopling's prediction came true in the sense that by the end of June, on the chart of the top fifty records, the Stones' "Come On" was number fifty.

□ □ □

The first booking that Eric Easton was able to line up for the Stones was a tour of Britain on a bill with the Everly Brothers in September of that year. A few interviews began to appear in the press, and in one of them Mick Jagger said, "On stage, we'll just go mad, go completely wild. We know it's useless going out to play the more advanced Jimmy Reed and Muddy Waters stuff, but we'll go through the Chuck Berry and Bo Diddley catalogue. If people don't like us, well that's too bad. We're not thinking of changing, thanks very much. We've been the way we are for much too long to think of kowtowing to fanciful folk who think we should start tarting ourselves up with mohair suits and short haircuts."

The big surprise of that tour was that on the bill with the Everly Brothers was the patron saint of the Rolling Stones, Bo Diddley. They viewed him with considerable awe, but over the course of the tour, they became more and more prominent on the bill.

Andrew Oldham

I REALIZED THAT it was imperative that they cut another disc just as soon as they could, but no matter how many titles were suggested, the Stones couldn't seem to agree on any one of them. It was becoming urgent that we find something that they would consent to do.

It was at this point that fate intervened in the person of the Beatles. One afternoon, I had left the Stones, arguing about which song they should lay down, when, as I was walking along Jermyn Street in London's West End, a taxi pulled up, and I heard two familiar voices yelling my name. They were the Beatles, John Lennon and Paul McCartney, whom I knew very well, of course, from having handled their early publicity. I got in the taxi with them and rode for a bit and told them about my new affiliation with the Stones and the problem I was having finding a song for them. They both knew about the Stones' work and actually had been to the Crawdaddy to listen to them and were very favorably impressed with their sound and their delivery. When they heard about my predicament, McCartney said, "Well, John and I are working on a couple of songs and we've got one here that's not quite finished, but maybe it's something for the Stones to do. It's called 'I Wanna Be Your Man.'" They went back to the rehearsal room with me, where the Stones were still assembled. What was missing was the middle-eight passage. Brian said that the song was fine but wondered how long they'd have to wait for it to be finished because of the pressure on them to cut another record. John and Paul talked it over for a moment, and then John said, "Listen, if you guys really like the main part of the song, we'll finish it for you right now."

So they went off to another room, and a few minutes later they came back with the completed song. And that's how it came about that the Beatles came to the rescue of the Stones and provided them with the song that was going to establish them as a popular recording group. It wasn't only the quality of the song that made the record a success, but it was also the fact that the Stones, in their brief fling at recording, when they had recorded "Come On," had become quite savvy about being able to project their music in a bare studio. Where they had been on edge and uptight in that first session, now they seemed to relax, to get themselves in the same kind of mood that produced that good music in the clubs.

I knew from my fling with the Beatles that, no matter that we had a good disc now, it was necessary for me to get the Stones and their single a publicity show. At that time there was a very popular Saturday night show called "Thank Your Lucky Stars." It so happened that the host of the program was one of Eric Easton's clients, so I was able to arrange for the Stones to get a spot on one of the programs. But the price of getting onto the "Lucky Stars" lineup was the requirement that all groups conform to the pattern the Beatles had established—uniform stage costumes, which is something that the Stones had rejected in their previous appearances. But they were anxious to get this TV coverage, so they submitted to an outfitter, who fashioned some matching houndstooth jackets with velvet half-collars and some ridiculous-looking shirts and skinny ties and boots to go with it.

With their booking on this program, I decided that a group of six was unwieldy on a stage, and I had already been considering the fact that Ian Stewart certainly didn't look like a pop musician. He was the only one of the group with a regular short haircut, he had a heavy appearance, a face that belonged more to a prize-fighter than a pop musician. I felt the time had come to make the move that I'd been contemplating for some time, so I only ordered five of these houndstooth costumes. I talked it over with Brian and Mick, and Brian was the one who took it upon himself to inform Stew when he showed up for the rehearsal for "Thank Your Lucky Stars" that he would no longer perform onstage with the group. He explained, however, that he would still get a full share as a Rolling Stone, that he would perform on the piano or keyboard, when needed, but offstage, that he would still be a part

101

of the recording sessions, and that he would perform the additional function of being the roadie for the Stones, driving the van and setting them up for their appearances in clubs and ballrooms. I guess Stew was pretty hurt by this, but I was sure I was right. Five Stones were better than six.

We had about a minute and a half to do our song, which was more than enough time for the Stones to make quite a spectacle of themselves in those houndstooth costumes, with their long hair and generally scruffy look.

☐ ☐ ☐

Despite the increased attention, there continued to be hard times for the Stones, because all this activity didn't translate into any significant income. Richard Hattrell recalls that at one point during their darkest days at the Edith Grove flat, his father relented a bit and invited him and Brian to Sunday lunch.

Richard Hattrell

TO MY SURPRISE, Brian got on extremely well with my father. Brian was very well educated, and they would talk about Shakespeare or Dickens or cricket, all sorts of things which, quite honestly, were a bit over my head. My father became fond of Brian and invited us to Sunday lunch quite often. So when the Stones made their first TV appearance on "Thank Your Lucky Stars," I managed to persuade my father to watch it. I said, "There's a pop program on." He said, "Bloody pop?! I won't have it on in my house!" I had never told him that Brian was a rock musician.

Somehow I managed to get him to sit in front of the television to watch it. Although he had very strong views on certain things in life, my father was certainly not an eccentric, but when the Stones came on . . . they came on in these incredible jackets that somebody had advised them to wear. Matching stage gear. It was a houndstooth pattern—awful, awful. High collars, it was terrible. But they were told they would have to wear it to get on this show, so they wore it. They came on and started playing, and I said, "Do you recognize anybody there, Father?" And he said, "Good God, yes! Brian! What the bloody hell is he doing there?" My father was so incensed that he went into the next room, and came back with his old army pistol from the First World War, and shot the television. Boom! Splattered the television screen, right in the middle of the Stones' number. I guess he was aiming it at Brian. "Don't you ever let that moron in my house again," he said.

□ □ □

Andrew Oldham

WHEN THEY CAME off the stage, they took one look at each other, and Brian said, "Christ, Mick, you look fucking awful." So they all took off their jackets and threw them away. From that moment on, the Stones were liberated. All groups, including the Beatles, wore matching jackets then, but the Stones said, "We don't want to look like everyone else." So when the young people saw that these Stones had thrown away their uniforms, they said, "Wait a minute, why should we, at school, why should we all wear the same goddamned jackets with our little crests on them? From now on, we are going to wear what we damn well please. And another thing—if the Stones can wear their hair long, so will we." But the headmasters said no, and that was the beginning of confrontation with a capital C.

□ □ □

"Andrew Oldham just turned up at the end of a gig one night at the Crawdaddy," Keith Richards recalled, "and said that he was in partnership with another guy and they were looking particularly for a new act to sign up for records and personal appearances. When you've been working backwater clubs for a year, and a recording session suddenly gets dangled in front of you—well, in those days, a recording contract was almost as remote as God talking to you.

"Andrew was even younger than we were; he had nobody on his books, but he was an incredible bullshitter, fantastic hustler, and he'd also worked on the early Beatles publicity. He got together those very moody pictures that sold them in the first place, so although he didn't actually have much to offer, he did get people interested in what he was doing. He came along with this other cat he was in partnership with, Eric Easton, who was much older, used to be an organ player in that dying era of vaudeville in the fifties after the war, when the music hall ground to a halt as

103

a means of popular entertainment. Eric had one or two clients, he wasn't making a lot of bread, but people in real show biz sort of respected him. He had contracts, one chick singer who'd had a couple of top twenty records, he wasn't completely out of it, and he knew a lot about the rest of England, which we knew nothing about, he knew every hall.

"Oldham and Easton got us a Decca recording contract, but first we had to get out of a contract we had signed with IBC, who had done nothing with the early tapes we had once made for them. They had no outlet. They didn't even know how to cut them onto discs, and they couldn't get any record company interested in them. This recording contract, although it was worthless, was still a binding contract, and that's when Brian pulled another one of his fantastic get-out schemes. Before this cat George Clouston at IBC can hear that we're signing with Decca, Brian goes to see him with a hundred quid that Andrew and Eric had given him, and he says, 'Look, we're not interested, we're breaking up as a band, we're not going to play anymore, we've given up, but in case we get something together in the future, we don't want to be tied down by this contract, so can we buy ourselves out of it for a hundred pounds?' And after hearing this story, which he obviously believes, this old Scrooge takes the hundred quid. The next day he hears that we've got a contract with Decca, we're going to be making our first single.

"Andrew took us out of the clubs. He got us our first record and put us on tour, a major tour of England with the Everly Brothers, Little Richard, Bo Diddley, and we'd never played a place much bigger than our flat before then. Suddenly we're in these big theaters. When those curtains opened the first time, we thought we were in the Superdome or something. It just seemed to stretch forever. We were used to tripping over each other on our stages. Suddenly we had all this room. The Everly Brothers were very good, but by the end of the tour they had a real hard job holding down that spot at the top of the bill because there was a new wind blowing, and it was blowing us in.

"I knew we had arrived when we played a certain theater in the north of England where we'd never been and we're on the bill with those big names—the Everly Brothers, Little Richard, Bo Diddley—and all the kids outside are screaming for the Rolling Stones. But that kind of popularity wasn't the reason we originally organized the Stones. We were real serious; we were evangelists at that time. It was a very pure sort of idealistic, adolescent drive that kept us going. The money, we didn't give a damn about the money—at that age, who cares? That wasn't the point. The point was to spread the music."

Andrew Oldham

MY EARLY TRAINING in hustling stood me in good stead as manager of the Stones. There was a time when I was very young, with no money in my pocket, that I subsisted nicely on various scams. For instance, when I was in the South of France, I'd go up to people on the Croisette and say, "Excuse me, I'm sorry, sir, my allowance hasn't arrived from my mother, and if you could lend me ten francs and tell me what hotel you're staying at, I'll get it back to you." I used to get about eighty francs a day, which was enough to get along on.

While in France, I met this guy who was a wandering American from Korea. He had just come from Morocco, and he invited me to share his room with him because he wanted company. He had a bag of Moroccan hash with him and that was the first time I smoked dope. A few months went by, and then I moved on to the next town without paying my share of the rent. I got a job in a restaurant, but to my surprise he came into the restaurant one day, looking for me. He was well over six feet, a huge guy, and he picked me up and hung me on the wall on a coat hook. He says, "I'm not going to hit you, because I like you, and I think I know you well enough to know that you're never going to do this again." With that, he dropped me to the floor and left.

That was a great lesson for me: If you're going to split without paying the bill, cover your tracks.

You've got to understand about the hustle. Right from the beginning, you've got to use it as your ace tool. All those early gigs, in the dance halls, the pub rooms, wherever, I'd stand in the back and when the Stones got rolling I'd start squealing in a high pitch, and that would set off all the little girls. Nothing is as contagious as a good squeal. That's what the media picked up on as "spontaneous enthusiasm." And at the early concerts, I'd organize a little group of guys to muscle their way past the girls to be up front, which, of course, paved the way for all the guys in the audience to push forward. Sometimes, if I was lucky, there'd be punches back and forth between the guys and the chicks, a wonderful image all induced by fakery.

And I helped foment riots whenever I could. I was doing publicity for Little Richard's tour in 1962, when I got kicked off the job because I sent out a press release saying, "Come and watch the teddy boys rip the seats up." That had been happening in the previous places where he had performed. But the theater owners said, "Either Oldham goes or the tour goes." So, naturally, I was the one to go. But hype and deception go with the music, man, they go with the music.

I was responsible for rock and roll being banned from the Royal Albert Hall for ten years. That wasn't when I was with the Stones, it was before that when I handled a group called the Nice. That's when I induced a guy in the group to burn an American flag onstage. It was at a charity concert for Biafra. The guy who burned the flag was later with Emerson, Lake and Palmer. Afterwards, the twit tried to say in the papers that he didn't do it, he was forced into it. What was I doing? Standing in the middle of the fucking stage holding the match for him? I owned the rights to the record that song was on, and burning the flag moved the record from number thirty-eight to number fifteen on the charts.

The overall hustle I invented for the Stones was to establish them as a raunchy, gamy, unpredictable bunch of undesirables. I had decided that since the Beatles had already usurped the cleancut choirboy image with synchronized jackets, I should take the Stones down the opposite road. Rejecting matching clothes was step one, emphasizing their long hair and unclean appearance was another, and inciting the press to write about them, using catchy phrases that I had coined, was yet another. For example, I fed some copy to a reporter for the *Daily Express* who used it in the article they printed: "They look like boys whom any self-respecting mum would lock in the bathroom. But the Rolling Stones—five tough young London-based music-makers with doorstep mouths, pallid cheeks and unkempt hair—are not worried what mums think. For now that the Beatles have registered with all age groups, the Rolling Stones have taken over as the voice of the teens."

I wanted to establish that the Stones were threatening, uncouth and animalistic. I got reporters to refer to them as "the ugliest group in Britain," and I was proud of a headline in *Melody Maker* that picked up a phrase I gave them: "Would You Let Your Daughter Go with a Rolling Stone?"—a phrase that also appeared in other publications, slightly changed to, "Would You Let Your Daughter Marry One?" By the time I got through planting all that negative publicity, there wasn't a parent in Britain that wasn't repulsed by the very sound of their name. An article in the *Melody Maker* said: "The Stones' role in music is a powerful one. They have the anger of parents on their side. Young fans now realize that their elders groan with horror at the Rolling Stones. So their loyalty to the Stones is unswerving."

□ □ □

Phil May

WHAT ANDREW OLDHAM said about himself when he first took over the Stones was accurate: "I just want to be a young, rich, tycoon shit." He had a kind of natural arrogance. His goal was to make himself very exclusive and put everybody else in the whole world outside of this little elite setup. And I think that's the attitude he infused in the Stones, and this arrogant, obnoxious attitude was what everybody perceived about them. It's an old trick. Because in the business of entertainment, you want to get kudos by behaving like a real bastard. Frank Sinatra's done it all his life. And people almost have this sort of awe about him, God, you know, he was really rude to me. They actually take it as a compliment. And I think Andrew quite shrewdly realized that wasn't a bad ploy. People would be invited down and then not be able to get in, having been told they could get in. Just a bunch of wankers, tell them they can't get in, tell them they should fuck off. That'll teach 'em. Bunch of wankers anyway. That was the aura that Oldham tried to draw around them.

I saw the Stones' first performances, and from the beginning, Mick was amazing. He was an original. He had a different way of portraying a song. Everybody before him sang with a kind of hackneyed choreography or just stood there and sang. Whereas Jagger was giving something else to the song while he was singing it.

When I first saw them down at the Station Hotel, the stage was so small and so cramped, they had to sit on stools jammed together, with the equipment and everything crowded around

107

them. But as they got out onto bigger stages and Jagger had more room, he seemed to revel in it. He naturally blossomed. And all the unique Jagger things, the seeds of them were already there. It wasn't something that he just grabbed on later in his career. I think what was so nice about it was it seemed an honest integration of the music. Apoplectic outbursts sprung from him. And he sounded like he was aware, bodily aware. And also very conscious of the power that certain of his actions had over his audience. All singers do this. You do certain things that people respond to, and you eliminate the things that don't work so well. So you are building up exposure, but not in the old-fashioned way of being schooled to it.

Mick's performance, somewhat heightened by Brian Jones's counter-performance, forever changed the sexual nature of rock and roll audiences. Prior to the advent of the Stones and the R and B music they played, audiences were very much segregated. If you went to a concert, the girls were all in the front and the guys in the back drinking beer, making derisive noises about the whole thing. The groups were supported by the chicks—they were the fans. They had pictures of Gerry and the Pacemakers on their walls, Paul McCartney, but the guys didn't do that. However, the Stones turned that around. Guys started sticking posters of Mick and Brian up on their walls, and what happened was the audience became much more integrated. Then, it was boys fighting their way to the front as much as the chicks. And there even came a point where I've seen guys knock chicks down to get closer to the stage. I mean whack 'em one. The chicks were pushed further and further back because they were physically overwhelmed—as a result the first twenty-five rows would be guys. It was simply a matter of who was physically strongest to fight their way through five thousand people and get closest to the stage. The Stones ignited that, and Jagger in particular. The way he performed, he had sexual appeal for the girls and homosexual attraction for the boys. And I'm not just talking about homosexual boys—Mick aroused heterosexual guys as well. The fact is that everybody has some homosexuality in his makeup, and it was probably the first time in their lives that it had been aroused. I'm sure if you had asked any of them that question, they'd have denied it. But there was a duality, especially in the Stones, no denying it.

By the end of the sixties, Jagger had developed a vulgar, raunchy reputation, due to media hype, but I don't think he was vulgar, not at all—I think it was his dual sexuality that upset a lot of people. But what he did on stage did not come across as vulgar. It was a very sophisticated sexual performance. When a performer can actually turn on both men and women, that's quite sophisticated. That's not just wiggling your ass.

□ □ □

By the end of 1963, the Stones had achieved a unique identity, a loyal, raucous following, and a musical style that was all their own. Nineteen sixty-three was a year filled with a succession of events that seemed to climax movements that had started in the preceding years. But then there came a fateful climax to the year itself, and the shock of it momentarily derailed the momentum of the sixties—the November 22nd assassination of President Kennedy in Dallas.

In his book, *The Neophiliacs*, Christopher Booker states that for days after the assassination, "the shock lay over Britain, blanketing everything. Then, into the ensuing void, the noise which had been rising all the year, suddenly flooded in a deafening torrent. In the last month of 1963, it became apparent that the Beatles were a phenomenon like nothing that pop music had known before. Already in their wake there were an estimated three hundred and fifty further pop groups in Liverpool alone. But it was not only in Liverpool that this phenomenon had come to the surface. A similar underground surge was also surfacing in America, particularly among the Negro teenagers of Detroit. It spread like wildfire through other cities in Britain, such as London itself, where in such teenage centers as 'The Scene,' a Soho club for 'mods,' the rhythm 'n blues of the Rolling Stones (from South and West London) was beginning to arouse enthusiasm every bit as hysterical as anything on Merseyside. 'The Scene,' run by a young man in his early twenties from Dublin, named Ronan O'Rahilly, was in one of the same cellars which, back in the early fifties, had been a center of the traditional jazz cult. It was a comment on the ever younger age level at which teenage crazes were centered that, at the time when that earlier craze had been at its height, many of the Rolling Stones' most ardent fans (the average age of their fan club being estimated in 1964 at ten) were only just being born."

By 1963 the first James Bond 007 films had appeared, as had

Albert Finney in *Tom Jones,* and pop art had produced a cluster of new artists—Richard Smith, David Hockney, Peter Blake, Peter Phillips and Allen Jones, all of whom studied at the Royal College of Art and all of whom were acclaimed at that year's Paris Biennale. Later that year, when Hockney's paintings were exhibited in New York, they were all sold on the first day of the show.

"In America," Christopher Booker writes, "the state of shock which followed the death of Kennedy lasted longer than in Britain. As the hysteria died down, a deep gloom fell over America, which was to last over two months. And then, in the first week in February, the trance was broken. The Beatles had just concluded a visit to Paris, which had turned from polite curiosity to wild enthusiasm; in England the officials at the London airport had been familiar since the previous October with the sight of up to twenty thousand teenage girls clustered like huge flocks of squealing starlings whenever the Beatles appeared there. But no one, least of all the vice-president of Capitol Records, who was actually thinking of hiring girls to scream a welcome to the Beatles at Kennedy Airport, was in any way prepared for what happened from the moment they touched down in New York on 7 February. For days the city seemed to go mad. Vast crowds of girls waited all night outside the Plaza Hotel, hoping for a glimpse or even a touch. Big stores sprouted Beatles window displays, containing everything from Beatle wigs to pictures of London policemen. The Beatles gave a concert at Carnegie Hall, something which ever since the days of Benny Goodman had been regarded as the final accolade for jazz musicians—but which, until now, had been refused to any other pop singers, even Elvis Presley. In Washington a party given for the quartet by the British Ambassador turned almost into a riot—leading to a question in the House of Commons about 'the disgraceful behavior at the Embassy.'

"These events in America were nothing to what was happening back in England itself. The fever which only six months before had run riot in tracking down every new rumor about Profumo or Keeler was now given over to the frenzied pursuit of pop singers. Almost every week some new 'group'—the Kinks, the Moody Blues, the Ivy League—emerged into the collective fantasy, and particularly as the rhythm 'n blues groups swam into ken, the Rolling Stones, the Animals, the Pretty Things, each weirder in appearance and manner than the last."

CHAPTER SEVEN

Flopping in the U.S.A.

*I must say I don't really like singing very much.
I'm not really a good enough singer to really
enjoy it, but I am getting into it a little bit. I
enjoy playing the guitar more than I enjoy singing, and I can't play the guitar either. But I
know that if I keep on playing the guitar, I can
get better, where I can't improve much as a
singer.*

MICK JAGGER

Of course the Stones' sudden catapult into the limelight
had a profound effect on both their physical and their
psychological existence. The glum, hungry troupe that
had been mired in the degradation of Edith Grove was
suddenly sprung into a strange world filled with adulation and
temptation; it proved to be not an easy adjustment to make.

With the first glimmer of success came the first serious glimmer
of dissension. During their grim struggle for recognition, they
had sustained their camaraderie. But when they started to get
bookings, Brian asserted that he was the leader of the band, and
that's when Mick and Keith discovered that unbeknownst to them,
Brian had made a secret deal with Oldham whereby, since he was
the leader, he'd get an extra five pounds out of each booking fee.
Naturally, this did not go down well with the other members of
the band; in fact, their resentment continued even when, later on,
they were all earning huge sums for their albums and tour appearances.

"It was ridiculous for Brian to tout himself as the band leader,"
Keith Richards said. "The Stones were formed with nothing like
that in mind. There was no competition because everybody's drive

was directed totally outward. There was no point in having a leader, it didn't mean anything—leader of what? Five pounds a week has got to go toward fixing an amplifier. There's no percentage in being a leader when we hadn't got any gigs to lead us to. When we started, it was just Brian, Mick and me running the band together. We lived together for two years perfectly harmoniously during very difficult times. If there was to be any tension or incompatibility, it would surely have come out when we were starving. And no gigs for months on end. It would have been easy to say, What's the point of rehearsing, we're never going to get to play anywhere."

Although these problems were beginning to develop, the reality was that their performing lives had become so frenzied there really wasn't time for personality conflicts to cause trouble. Andrew Oldham had done his job so well that the perception of the Stones as a raunchy, hell-raising group completely overshadowed their merit as a band. In fact, the screaming decibels of their fans made it virtually impossible to hear what they were playing, and only in their recordings did they reveal the rhythm and blues style that was to become their hallmark.

"At first we were always hustling to get our picture on the cover of *Fab* or *Rave* or *Teen,*" Jagger has said. "But as soon as the teenyboppers caught on, we were in for the big scream. In the beginning it was frightening. We never played to a screaming crowd before. After a while the ballroom didn't want us to do long gigs. It was dangerous, you know, so we'd only do half an hour and they'd scream for half an hour and some of them would faint it was so hot."

Andrew Oldham

THE STONES' HYPE caught on with a sudden fury that carried them beyond my wildest dreams. Whatever I hadn't invented about them, the media did, with the result that when they set out on their second British tour early in 1964, they were in constant jeopardy of being trampled, cannibalized and emasculated.

When they played the Empire Pool at Wembley, where the Mod Ball was being held, the Stones were mobbed as they left the stage and more than thirty teenagers were arrested as commissionaires fought to protect us. Four thousand fans tried to invade the Chantinghall Hotel at Hamilton, near Glasgow, when the Stones appeared there, and dozens of police and bouncers were swept aside and fights broke out inside the hotel.

There were five thousand people in the Empress Ballroom in Blackpool who went berserk when Keith aimed a kick at a kid who had run on the stage and tried to attack him. The audience overran the stage, smashing amplifiers, drums and everything else. A grand piano was hurled off the stage and shattered. Thirty fans were later treated at Blackpool's Victoria Hospital for injuries. And in Belfast ambulance men had to carry out hysterical teenage girls in straitjackets and the concert had to be called off after only twelve minutes.

If you think that was bad, it was child's play as compared to what happened on the following tour of Europe. A performance at The Hague was stopped by police after ten minutes because of teenagers' rioting, during which bottles and chairs were thrown. And at the end of a Stones' show in Paris, hundreds of stampeding teenagers smashed seats and broke the windows of the Olympia Theatre. About a hundred fifty were arrested. In Oslo, police armed with batons had to knock down rioting fans.

The newspapers in West Germany described the riot after the Stones' performance in Münster as "hell broken loose" and a "witches' cauldron." And the Geneva City Council decreed that the Stones were "undesirables" and banned them from giving a scheduled concert at a civic ice rink.

I had various scams for setting off riots at Stones concerts. For example, I'd be sitting on the stage apron, off to one side, and I'd snatch off the helmet of a policeman who was standing in front of the stage, thereby demonstrating to the audience how much they could get away with. Right away, the kids in the audience started to pluck the helmets off other policemen and that was the beginning of a nice riot.

On a European tour, I told Jagger, "Hey, why don't you give out a little 'Sieg Heil!' while you're doing 'Satisfaction'? Or maybe a couple of goose steps?" Now, Mick being the performer that he is, really took my suggestions to heart, doing 'Heil Hitlers!' and goose stepping all over the stage. And this was in Holland and Germany. Talk about riots! Every train leaving Munich was wrecked. They just tore them apart. They tore the town apart. I got a bang out of that because for me the Nazis were still fucking villains, and I had duped the lot of them.

□ □ □

Although Oldham takes full credit for the Stones' impact, his contribution was, in reality, largely limited to enticing the crowds into the theaters and stadiums. What aroused them after they got there, what set off the squeals and the riots, was Jagger's prancing, preening, posturing performance. Although accused of having contrived his moves to arouse the audience, Mick stoutly maintained that his performance was spontaneous. "I move on stage the way I do because I enjoy it," he said at the time. "Nothing I do on stage is rehearsed. I don't pose in front of a mirror for hours trying to get it right. I like it on the road, I don't know what I'd do if I couldn't go out there. I think I'd go mad. It's great to hang around, smash up a few hotel rooms, get drunk.

"I like entertaining. I suppose performing is an aid. It helps me as a person, an individual, to get rid of my ego. It's a better process than others. If I get rid of the ego on stage, then the problem ceases to exist when I have left there. I no longer have a need to prove myself continually to myself.

"When I go on the road, I just go *crazy!* I become a total monster. I don't recognize anybody. I don't even see them. 'Who are you? Forget it. Go away. Who are you? From the MM? Forget it. Get out, I don't want to see you. I'll give you two minutes! I'm doing my makeup—get out!' What a terrible monster I am. I feel guilty about it afterwards, then I laugh, because the whole thing is a joke. But Keith is worse than I am. Is he a prima donna? Oh, yeah!"

Bill Wyman, who, by now, had firmly settled into his role as bass guitarist, was very conscious of the look the Stones were assiduously trying to project. "Our hair was much longer hair than the Beatles'. The Beatles' style was to comb it forward over the eyebrows. But you could always see their ears quite clearly. Brian and Keith, you couldn't see their ears; their hair was way down on their collars. And when Charlie and I left our jobs, we let our hair grow, too. That put us all in the same boat—not wearing uniforms, having the long hair, looking unkempt. Our music was referred to as bizarre at that time; people didn't know what we were playing or how to dance to it, and they didn't know any of the songs. That is how things were when Andrew Oldham took over. He did an excellent job of publicizing us—it's a pity he wasn't as good at being a producer of music as he was being a publicist.

"The things people wrote about us in those days, and I've got press cuttings to prove it, like, 'Well, I saw them at this place, this cafe on the motorway,' someone would write to a newspaper, 'and I could see the fleas jumping off their heads.' And there was always the rumors that because we had long hair, we never bathed, we smelled, and we had filthy clothes. Those clothes used to cost three times more than the average suit because they were very difficult to find, an unusual jacket or a very groovy pair of Spanish boots, which we all used to wear. We really were bizarre, I guess, especially when we were stopped from entering a pub for a drink. They also turned us away at restaurants, and at certain shops. We'd even go in a shop to buy a pack of cigarettes and they would refuse to sell us any. 'We don't serve the likes of you in this establishment. Kindly leave.' Add to that the insults we used to have shouted at us in cinemas, in cafes, on the motorway, on the street, everywhere."

The turning point in the Stones' fortunes at that time, according to Ian Stewart, was "when Brian, Mick and Keith moved out of Edith Grove. I'll bet it was permanently condemned. Or maybe it was burned down. At any rate, Brian split away from the others because he had a hot new love affair going with a pretty model named Linda Lawrence, and he wanted to be rid of Pat Andrews and baby Julian once and for all. Brian went to live with Linda's parents, and Mick and Keith joined up with Oldham in a flat they found in North London. It was no world-beater, only two rooms and one bathroom to share, but after Edith Grove it looked as good as the Dorchester."

Jagger was the member of the band who was most affected by their lift-off from scrounging obscurity to a fame and power probably unrivaled in the experience of show business. There was no time for decompression, and since Mick was the up-front Stone, the voice, the antic rhythm-maker, the liaison with the audience, the flashy showman with his bizarre costumes and makeup, most of the media attention was heaped on him. But of all the Stones, Mick had been the most unprepared for their

115

success as performers; the other band members all had the security of knowing that they were good at playing their instruments and could always catch on with some other group— Charlie, an accomplished drummer, was constantly propositioned by other bands; so, too, were Keith, acclaimed for his virtuoso slide guitar, and Brian, for his rhythm guitar, harmonica, and his mastery of a variety of other instruments; Stew's accomplished keyboard and Bill Wyman's solid bass guitar had also established them as desirable musicians.

Jagger's talent, however, was nebulous. He could only go through the motion of playing a guitar, having learned a few rudimentary chords from Keith. Brian had shown Mick how to handle the harmonica but his ability to play it was limited. Mick could whack a rhythmic tambourine, rattle a couple of maracas, but his singing voice was unexceptional. All he really had, realistically, was style, a style that was all his own, of struts, wiggles, bumps, grinds, bobs, weaves, leaps, dips, jumps, spins, perpetual motion, completely unlaced, ominous, guileless, crafty, seductive; but unlike the other Stones, no other bands had sought him out, no impresarios, no recording companies—not until the sizzle of his performances had ignited his audiences and overnight made him a superstar, did he get full credit for his talent.

Ahmet Ertegun

JAGGER WAS AND is an incredible presence on stage. He has a bisexual look and appeal, and his style of dancing, makeup, the whole aspect of his being is directed toward arousing both sexes. I think all those rock stars were aware that suddenly something volcanic was happening— after all, they'd been up in front of audiences for a long time and nothing much happened, but now suddenly they're playing the same stuff but millions of people are screaming—they sure as hell knew something was happening, although they didn't know what, but they knew they were at the center of it. They also began to think, Man, I'm writing great music and playing great music, and the people love it, and we're selling millions of records, and we're going to be touring all over the world, and we fill the stadiums, and we're recognized in the street wherever we go, and the money's pouring in, so we're going to continue to put down the establishment, and we're going to carry this thing further and further.

I don't think the music caused things to happen as much as it was a reflection of what was happening. The songs Jagger and Lennon and McCartney were singing all made reference to sexual things, to drugs, to all things that the establishment frowned on. The Who were a violent act on stage, they broke all the instruments; Mick Jagger was an open revolutionary who did anything to shock, obscene gestures, undressing, singing songs with unprintable titles, having shows where a giant phallic symbol occupied center stage—shock for the sake of shock.

With the Stones' frantic schedule of concerts all over England, recording sessions, publicity engagements, media interviews and rehearsals, Mick had little time to assess what had happened to him and react to it. Also, that first rush of popularity did not produce a commensurate amount of income, so Mick did not have as much economic freedom as one would imagine. And then there was the reality that most rock and roll groups flashed on the scene, burned brightly for a spurt and then fell like spent rockets into oblivion. Mick knew that the preponderant odds were that the Stones would wind up in the rock and roll graveyard along with all the other burned-out groups.

With that in mind, Mick tried to continue his studies at the London School of Economics despite the rigorous schedule of the Stones, ducking back to classes whenever he could, trying to cover his absentee tracks. Being a pragmatist, Mick never lost sight of the fact that his one and only object in life was to make money. He didn't much care how. It wasn't until he was dead certain that he would make more money out of performing with the Stones than he would in a bank or as a stockbroker that he finally renounced school for rock and roll.

In the meantime, he lived in the two-room flat in North London with Keith and Oldham, sleeping in the same bed with Andrew. Mick was dating Chrissie Shrimpton and continued to dine with her at her parents' house whenever he could wangle an invitation. He avoided his own parents, giving as an excuse that he felt they disapproved of his switch from economist to rock and roller, but actually he confided to close friends that he thought his parents were "a drag." His relationship with Chrissie, whose older sister, Jean, was a star model of the sixties, was tempestuous, replete with bitter quarrels, pitched objects and threats of separation. But Mick cultivated Jean because through her he was able to meet glamorous people and get into the right places.

Mick explained himself this way: "I'm real competitive. Unlike most English people, I was brought up to be super-competitive, and winning was important. I had to be a good loser, but the point was not to lose. I was brought up in a slightly American way, as far as that attitude to winning goes. Success, winning. It stays with you."

Brian, on the other hand, not interested in winning nor success, withdrew completely from the ambitious triumvirate in the North London flat and went to live outside London with the parents of his new girl friend, Linda Lawrence, who run a guest house near Windsor Castle.

Violet and Alex Lawrence,
LINDA'S PARENTS

WHEN BRIAN JONES and Linda came to live with us, it was our belief that they would marry soon. Brian liked living in a small town. He was very likable, Brian, but very insecure. He brought us a couple of little presents occasionally, but he wasn't generous in nature. He watched his money. What we really didn't like about Brian was his quick, bad temper.

But there was a sweet side to Brian, too. He loved animals, which he constantly brought to the house. A French poodle, a goat, a cat he brought back from somewhere. He used to walk the goat down Main Street on a leash. He was rather proud of his goat. Brian never had any liquor or dope in the house, and when he first came we were sure he wasn't using any. But when he returned from the Stones' first American tour, he was very changed. Not that he started to drink or smoke in the house, but his personality was different, probably because he was drinking and whatnot outside the house.

Linda once returned from a party she had gone to with Brian, and she had a horrendous black eye. Pa confronted Brian: "You do that to Linda? If so, I'll blast you into the street." Pa was much bigger than Brian. Both Brian and Linda denied he had hit her, but later, after Brian had left her, we found out different—that he had beat her quite often.

Brian was consumed with fear. That was his most prominent trait—fearfulness. On more than one occasion, Pa had to carry him in his arms into the backstage area, so fearful Brian was of having to perform. The sight of Pa driving Brian to a performance, then picking him up, and cradling him in his arms, carrying Brian like a baby all the way backstage to his dressing chamber, was really a sight to see. Brian couldn't have forced himself to go backstage any other way. Brian was mortally afraid of his fame. He was obsessed about anyone touching his hair or his clothes, especially his hair. If a fan touched his hair, or tried to tousle it, Brian went crazy, lashed out, then ran away. Sometimes he was so upset, he began to sob, stood in front of a mirror, recombing his hair, sobbing away. He only let Linda cut his hair. He refused to let a barber touch his hair. Linda also made blouses for him, often copied from women's blouses that Brian liked. Ma also helped sew these blouses. Brian loved pretty clothes, constantly tried them on, preening for us like it was a fashion show or something.

Brian complained a lot about Mick and Keith ganging up on him. Brian wrote a lot of music, always playing it on his guitar for us, but he was bitter that none of it was ever performed by the Stones. Mick seemed jealous of him. Mick used to come to our house, that's how we know about his jealousy. Also, we used to go up to the Stones' office in London. Andrew Oldham was there. We never liked him. He was very snotty and was very obviously in cahoots with Mick and Keith against Brian.

When Linda had their baby, Brian came to the hospital and asked her to marry him. We opposed that because Brian was into drugs by then, and we feared for her. She probably would have married him if we hadn't opposed it so vehemently. Brian was concerned about Julian and wanted to provide for him.

Brian had no friends because friendship wasn't in him. He was completely introverted. Never gave anything of himself, so no one ever responded to him as a friend. Except Linda. Brian needed nothing, at least that was the impression he gave.

119

Contrary to what the Lawrences say, Brian did have at least one close friend, Ronni Money, a petite ex-dancer who is now married to Zoot Money, an established rock musician.

Ronni Money

I FIRST MET Brian Jones in 1963, before the Stones were even known, when they were just playing in Richmond at the Crawdaddy, playing the odd pub gigs and things. I met him and Linda Lawrence. They used to stay with me every weekend. There came a time Brian wanted me to live with him, not for sex—I didn't fancy Brian that way—but for me to look after him, mother him. There were times we were in bed together, but I just held him, like a child; he was insecure and fearful and he needed mothering.

Brian never spoke very much, he was very shy. And then when the Stones started making some headway, he started popping a lot of pills, and it was the worst thing he could've done because he was very paranoid anyway. Sensitive people usually are a bit. And I became a sort of nanny figure, nurse figure toward him, even though I was not that much older than Brian. I had two sons, so it was very easy for me to treat Brian like a son. I was the sole support of my sons because their father had died of chronic drug addiction. So I knew how easy it was to get sucked into drugs. My husband had gotten into drugs with Charlie Parker and his bunch. So I recognized the same weakness in Brian, knowing how easy it was to be sucked in, if you were the nervous type like Brian, needing to take a drink before he went on or pop a pill. So I worked on him to not take amphetamines. I said, "You need something to calm you down." And I knew that one didn't get addicted to marijuana because I smoked for a long time myself, and when I wanted to, I stopped just like that. But if you start to drink, nobody's got a guarantee you're not going to become an alcoholic. And if you pop amphetamines regularly, you're bound to become an addict. So I made him smoke. I said, "If you need to take something, take something that isn't going to take you." So I turned him on. In fact, he told Bob Dylan, when he introduced me, he said, "This is the woman who straightened me out."

□ □ □

But not for long. When the first crisis came along, Brian went back to his craziness, popping pills, taking acid and coke, drinking brandy—but he had a real fear of heroin, which he never touched.

The other members of the band—Charlie Watts, Bill Wyman and Ian Stewart—all had tranquil domestic lives in London, although Bill, in his quiet way, managed to have a lot of colorful bedroom activity on tour.

By the summer of 1964, the Stones were performing six or seven dates a week, but only clearing about twenty-five pounds apiece. It was a brutal schedule, since recording sessions (they had produced three singles), rehearsals and publicity opportunities also demanded time, but Oldham was not concerned about any of that, knowing that the money would soon be flowing in and the pace less hectic; what he was concerned about was that the Stones were running out of material available for recording. There were just so many Bo Diddley and Muddy Waters songs available, and Oldham realized that if the Stones were ever going to be able to put an album together they'd have to find fresh and original material. In his desperation, Oldham came up with a solution that would drastically alter the Stones' fortunes: convince Keith and Mick that they could write the songs that were needed.

Andrew Oldham | I REALLY DON'T know how I got the idea, other than having watched Mick and Keith so many times in the recording studios when they'd make interpretive adjustments of a song they were rehearsing. I got a gut feeling that there was an outside chance that they could write songs of their own.

"It had never crossed my mind to be a songwriter," Keith said, "until Andrew Oldham came to me and Mick and said, 'Look, how many good records are you going to keep on making if you can't get new material? You can only cover as many songs as there are. And I think you're capable of more.' We had never thought of that. He locked us up in a room about the size of a kitchen and said, 'You've got a day off, I want to hear a song when you come out.'

'Who does he think he is? He's got to be joking,' Mick and I said. But in his own way, he was right. We walked out of there with a couple of songs. But it was a mind-bending experience for me.

"I was a guitar player. A songwriter, as far as I was concerned, was as far removed from me as somebody who was a blacksmith or an engineer, a totally different job. I had the mentality of a guy who could only play guitar; other guys wrote songs."

Andrew Oldham

THE FIRST SONGS that Keith and Mick wrote were pretty shitty, but I had to keep pushing them because what was the alternative? We had to have material if we were going to cut more records. I had been through all the catalogues a hundred times and it was obvious that the band had already used all the best stuff. Besides, I was convinced they couldn't make it as a top group by just playing old rhythm and blues tunes. We had all witnessed with our own eyes and ears how easy Lennon and McCartney had knocked off "I Wanna Be Your Man," and I felt that Mick and Keith could do the same for us once they got the hang of it.

It didn't bother me that the first few songs were kind of drippy, although one of the songs, "Tell Me," was on the first album we cut for Decca. I had a battle with Decca over the sleeve for that album. I insisted on having nothing on the sleeve except a picture of the five Stones. No copy whatsoever, not even THE ROLLING STONES. It worked. The album sold well over a hundred thousand copies one week after its release. And the Jagger-Richards songs were getting better.

□ □ □

Despite Oldham's scheming with Jagger and Richards, Brian was still vital to the Stones' effectiveness. His instrumental dexterity, especially with his slide guitar and blues harmonica; his seductive, provocative moves in performance (Jagger picked up on these as a foundation for his own freewheeling performance); his electrifying appearance—his hairstyle and particularly his colorful and imaginative clothes, a mix of women's clothes and bizarre cullings from flea markets and antique shops; and his magnetism for both males and females when he was on stage. Although Mick began to dominate as the Stones endlessly toured Britain to increasingly packed houses, he was by no means the overwhelming presence he became later on when Brian began to be wasted by his excesses.

But in the spring of 1964, although there was intrigue and jockeying for position, the Stones' quickly escalating popularity, and the meteoric success of their first album, which shot to the top of the charts in no time, overshadowed everything else. Jagger and Richards had growing confidence in their collaboration, and when Oldham arranged for the Stones' first American tour, hard on the heels of the Beatles' great success, the Stones expected that they would find the same overwhelming response that they were experiencing in Britain.

But that proved not to be the case.

"Our first gig was San Bernardino, and they went crazy there," Keith Richards has said, "so we thought, Oh, this is going to be easy; this ain't going to be like it was in the beginning in England where we had to slog around for a year or so to make an impression. But then from San Bernardino, boom, we went to San Antonio, Texas—an arena with nineteen thousand seats and only two hundred of them filled. After that, Omaha—they looked at us like we were Martians. The only people to meet us off the plane were twelve motorcycle cops who insisted on doing this motorcade right through town. We thought, Wow, we've made it. We must be heavy. But we get to the auditorium and there's six hundred people there in a fifteen-thousand-seat hall.

"The only thing that really went down heavy there was the cop scene. It was then I realized what Lenny Bruce was talking about. We were sitting in the dressing room, drinking whiskey and Coke out of paper cups, just waiting to go on. Cops walked in. 'What's that?' 'Whiskey.' 'You can't drink whiskey in a public place.' I happened to be drinking just Coke actually. 'Tip it down the bog.' 'No man, I've just got Coca-Cola.'"

"I look up and I got a .44 looking at me, right between the eyes. Here's a cop, telling me to tip Coca-Cola down the bog. That's when I realized what it could get into.

"Nobody came to any of the shows. Nobody. New York and L.A. were hip to us, and that was it. Meanwhile we had to do a month around the Midwest, where we were the lowest of the low. All we heard was, 'What are you—a boy or a girl?' You couldn't go into a bar. Suddenly to be for a month stuck in this environment where you're a nobody, even worse than a nobody, you're a weirdo, you're a foreigner. Nineteen sixty-four in Omaha was no joke. Complete strangers, and they all hated us and wanted to beat the shit out of us."

Ian Stewart

WE WERE SANDBAGGED by that opening gig in San Bernardino. The whole place jam-packed with kids, we thought we had it made. But then, city after city we bombed—places like Pittsburgh, where there were three hundred kids in this eight-thousand-seat stadium, only three hundred of them in this big, empty place! Most places there was nobody there because they'd never heard of the Rolling Stones. In Hershey, Pennsylvania, the whole town was chocolate, for chrissakes—an empty auditorium that smelled of chocolate! Pittsburgh, Cleveland, Harrisburg, and on and on, these huge auditoriums with nothing but empty seats, and the local newspaper didn't even bother to send a reporter.

But in Chicago the gloom was lifted momentarily when we visited the Chess Studios to make a recording—that made up for a lot, because Chess was where, as kids, we used to send for all the great R and B records. Chess. It was like going to a shrine.

□ □ □

Marshall Chess, a short, tattooed, handsome man, is the son of Chess Records' founder, Leonard Chess, now deceased. Marshall was in the studio with the Stones when they recorded "It's All Over Now" and other of their early successes, became friendly with them, and later was employed by Mick to manage the band. Marshall traveled with the Stones on their tours, and subsequently produced the films *Ladies and Gentlemen, the Rolling Stones* and *Cocksucker Blues.*

Marshall Chess

MY FATHER WAS an immigrant from Poland, and he got along very well with black people, probably because he was insecure about how white people in this

124

country felt about him as a foreigner with an accent. He was a brilliant man, and he and my uncle ran Chess Records. They had a very good feel for black music and for what black people wanted in music and what they'd spend their money for. My father and my uncle couldn't read music, but they really knew how to produce records. I was brought up in their style, doing it by feeling. I was born into the record business, and by the time I was thirteen I was a full-time employee, doing everything. My primary reason for starting so early was to be around my dad, who was always on the go. I had a father hang-up—I adored being around my father. So I worked hard and got good at the job to earn his approval. We had our own studios, our own pressing plant, a totally integrated operation in Chicago, and I was around it my whole life. I had my first record label when I was sixteen. I handled performers; I had thousands of hours' experience in the studio prior to the Stones' arrival in 1964. I produced Bo Diddley. I was Chuck Berry's road manager when he first got out of prison. I made albums with Muddy Waters and all of the great ones who actually were the role models of the Stones. It was a terrific bridge to them.

When the Stones came to Chicago to record in 1964, it had been their dream for Chess to record them. Everyone wanted to get the "Chess sound." The Chess sound had a lot to do with the studio, our engineers, but mostly the input of my father and uncle. The Stones looked up to my uncle and father like gods from outer space. I always felt the Chess sound had to do with a certain sexy quality that our records had. That's what was so effective about the Stones—like Bo and Muddy, they had a natural sexiness to their music.

The Stones were one of the first white groups that my father recorded. I think my father's affinity for black musicians was rooted in the fact that he felt they were both from the ghetto—he from the Polish ghetto, the blacks from Southern ghettos—and they both had the same goal—to make money to bring materialistic things into their lives. We lived very nouveau riche Jewish. We had black DJ's around our pool every weekend, with an eye to getting our records promoted. We lived our business—lived it and loved it.

□ □ □

125

"It was frightening when we first went to Chicago and Chess Studios," Bill Wyman has said. "We walked in, and there was Buddy Guy and Chuck Berry, Willie Dixon and a lot of others. Meeting these people who inspired me to start playing guitar was more than a thrill—it was like God had arrived. The clouds open and 'Boom!' here comes Buddy Guy.

"We were unloading our van and taking the equipment in, amps, guitars, mike stands, et cetera, when this big black guy comes up and says, 'Want some help there?' And we look around and it's Muddy Waters. He starts helping us carry the guitars in and all that. It was unbelievable. The awe we all had for somebody like that, as kids we would have given our right arm just to say hello to them—and here's the great Muddy Waters helping to carry my guitar into a studio. I mean, it was unreal."

The worst incident on the American tour occurred in Los Angeles when the Stones appeared with guest host Dean Martin on "The Hollywood Palace." "We were booked to do three songs on the show," Bill Wyman recalled, "which was a mixture of performing baby elephants and the Kay Sisters. Dean Martin was the compere, falling over almost, drunk, with a glass in his hand, which we found completely bizarre that someone could actually go on camera and be drunk. And be applauded. And introducing us with insults. The whole show, totally insulting us, like: 'Their hair isn't that long—they've just got smaller foreheads and higher eyebrows.' 'Ha, ha, ha,' big roars of laughter and applause. It was like we were a comedy act. One of the acts on the show was a guy doing tricks on a trampoline. 'That is the father of the Rolling Stones,' Dean Martin said. 'He's been trying to kill himself ever since.'

"A couple of times, we damn near stopped the tour and went back to England. We almost went back after that TV show. In New York, though, the reception at Carnegie Hall was different. Keith almost got strangled by two fans when he ran into the theater with a scarf tied around his neck, and a fan each side of him grabbed one end of his scarf and pulled till he was blue in the face and just about unconscious."

Assessing their appearance, journalist Pete Hamill wrote: "There is something elegantly sinister about the Rolling Stones. They sit before you at a press conference like five unfolding switchblades, their faces set in rehearsed snarls, their hair studiously unkempt and matted, their clothes part of some private conceit, and the way they walk and they talk and the songs they sing all become part of some long mean reach for the jugular."

Andrew Oldham

IT DIDN'T TAKE much to set off the Carnegie Hall audience and get them out of control. Of course, I had some plants in the audience to stir them up. In fact, they got so stirred up, they broke nineteen seats. There had never been an act like the Stones in Carnegie Hall, and the audience went crazy. After the Stones appearance, Carnegie Hall canceled all the rock shows they had on their schedule, and I don't think they ever had another.

On that tour, Bill Wyman was the one who lined up the ladies, the one who gave out his room number from the bandstand. There were always several girls waiting at Bill's door, and he'd parcel them out. There was one girl, I recall, whose mother was patiently waiting for her downstairs in the lobby while she spent some time in Bill's room.

During that first tour, the band got a lot of clap, the price they paid for their indiscriminate fucking.

☐ ☐ ☐

There was another price that had to be charged to the tour, and that was the advent of drugs into their lives. In England, at that time, coke, heroin, hash and acid were virtually unobtainable, but everywhere the Stones went in the United States drugs were being offered to them. Ian Stewart, a straight arrow, turned them aside. Charlie Watts and Bill Wyman may have experimented a bit. Jagger went through the motions of indulging, but in fact had a fear of drugs that inhibited his extended use of them. But Keith Richards, Brian Jones and Andrew Oldham were kids in a candy shop.

For Richards it was the beginning of a lifetime of taking things—heroin, LSD, coke, hashish and morphine. Luckily for him he has an ironclad constitution that is able to absorb whatever he puts into his body and still allows him to function, as a band member, as a lover, as a composer.

Oldham and Brian Jones were not so fortunate. For them, this first exposure to drugs was the beginning of a toboggan ride that would wreck them eventually. Brian's ability to play suffered, and there were some performances that had to go on without him. Oldham was particularly susceptible to the drugs' effects, and while the Stones dragged through their miserable tour, he avoided most of it, spending his time in various parts of the country in the company of the drug set. Dressed in flowing silks and wearing makeup, Oldham reveled in the lifestyle of the affluent, organizing his days around a succession of drug-enhanced parties.

When Oldham returned to London with the Stones, he took special pains to dry out from his drug binge, but Brian did not. From that day forward, Brian combined brandy and drugs, primarily acid; as his dependency deepened he became less selective and would take virtually anything to alleviate his demons.

PART THREE

The Crest

CHAPTER EIGHT

Marianne Faithfull: The Baroness's Daughter

*If you are going to kick authority in the teeth,
you might as well use two feet.*

KEITH RICHARDS

As soon as the Stones returned to Britain in the summer of 1964, after their disastrous American tour, Oldham booked them all over Europe to restore their confidence. As placid and unattended as the U.S. tour had been, the European concerts were riotous and overrun. Everywhere the Stones went they created pandemonium—riots, police dogs, arrests, tear gas, brawls—the uglier the concerts became, the more the Stones won the esteem of the hordes of teenagers to whom they had become a symbol of what the sixties stood for.

During a performance at Helsingborg, in Sweden, out-of-control fans were attacked by the police—beaten with nightsticks and bitten by dogs. During the riot that resulted, chairs, shoes, bottles, fireworks and anything not bolted down were thrown all around the theater. In Vienna there were brawls as police were pelted with smoke bombs and rocks; and they in turn clobbered teenagers and arrested them by the hundreds.

The nastiest scene took place in Warsaw. Two thousand kids tried to force their way into the hall where the Stones were performing, and had to be repulsed with tear gas grenades, water cannons and flailing nightsticks.

The weirdest incident took place in East Berlin. In response to a rumor that the Stones were in West Berlin, over ten thousand East Berlin kids banded together and moved in a mass toward the

131

Berlin Wall, where they were savagely beaten back by border guards who inflicted a great number of injuries on the teenagers. Armored cars were used in the operation and over two hundred of the young people wound up in jail. The sad thing was that the Stones were not in West Berlin at that time.

"Car doors got torn off as we were escaping from places," Bill Wyman has recalled. "We had to go to police stations and be transferred to ambulances or newspaper trucks or whatever to get in and out of where we had to perform. Getting out of hotels through the laundry chutes, and getting in that way as well. Getting into another club in South London through the house next door to the club. We had to walk through this old lady's semi-detached house out into her backyard, jump over the fence into the back of this place and through a secret passageway.

"And when we played West Berlin, we played in the place where Hitler used to give his speeches to the Nazi youth. A twenty-three-thousand-seat stadium, with our dressing rooms in the war bunkers, and then police with dogs escorted us through a hundred yards of underground bunkers before we came up on the stage. The moment we went on stage, the whole place rioted and we had to be rushed all the way back to the dressing rooms until they quelled them—took about half an hour. We were on stage in Birkenhead, near Liverpool, where we managed to play just one note before the whole place erupted, the kids poured onto the stage and we just vaulted the drums and ran. And that was the end of the concert. I mean, it was just fervor; they weren't antagonistic, it was just total excitement and all they wanted was to touch you or grab a piece of your hair. We lost a lot of hair, in those days.

"At a concert in Sheffield, with four thousand kids there, we were told, the moment it ends, as soon as you play that last note, get off the stage immediately. They used to play 'God Save the Queen' at the end, and the audience had to stand there until 'God Save the Queen' ended, which is like a minute and a half or a minute. And usually in that time you had to be off the stage, through all the corridors, out into the street, into the car and away. But this time, we were staying right opposite the arena, so it was out into the street and then across the main road and into the side entrance of the hotel. When we came to the last number and it ended, they said, 'Go!' We all ran, and I was the last one, first making sure that my guitar was passed to the right person, because I had a very fragile guitar at that time. We all tore down the corridor, and the guy manning the swinging doors—the glass swinging doors that led to the street—had them open, and he counted, one-two-three-four, slammed shut the door, and I went BAM! On the floor, knocked out, blood all over my face. The guy had us mixed up with the Beatles. These guys always thought four in a group. Gerry and the Pacemakers, the Searchers, the Hollies, they were all fours. We were five. And I was knocked silly, so two guys lifted me and physically carried me through this door into the street where there were a couple hundred kids. I was carried out with blood running off me, and instead of all the girls screaming and pushing, when they saw I was hurt, they said, 'Oh, dear, is he all right? Oh, take care, no, don't push, no, he's hurt.' And they really took care of me, and carefully half-carried me across the road and into the hotel."

Despite the chaotic nature of the tour, Oldham continued to prod Mick and Keith to pursue their songwriting, even though their early songs were not very promising.

Ian Stewart

MICK AND KEITH have a peculiar way of working together on their songs. They work apart before they work together, that way when they come together they have something to start with. Sometimes it's not much and most times what they have doesn't turn into a song. But they often fiddle around with something when we're in the studio and it gives them a spark, so when they go off and work on it, it turns into a cut on one of our albums.

Keith Richards has said that getting ideas for songs is a totally unconscious process. "I'd go in the studio, and I'd let the rest of the band think that I know what I'm doing. I'll just start playing. And I'll rely on my intuition and instinct and all those ideas I've had during the months before we started the sessions, I'd rely on them to start coming back to me and start coming out of my guitar. Now I'll know that Charlie is sitting behind the drums. I don't have to say, 'Where's Charlie?' He's sitting here. So the minute I start playing, he starts playing. And always the rest of the band comes in, and these songs are gradually built up from the rest of the band as well as from Mick and me. The actual basic idea of the song is ours, but the way the record sounds as opposed to the original song may be quite different. What I actually do is try not to think of the songs, but I try to write records. It's sound I'm after, not so much a piece of music."

The first song that Mick and Keith wrote that made the charts was a ballad called "As Tears Go By," and it was written, at Andrew Oldham's suggestion, not for the Stones but for a virginal-looking, shy seventeen-year-old girl, whom Andrew met at a party, also attended by Mick and Keith. The girl, Marianne Faithfull, had been brought to the party by John Dunbar. John had met Marianne when he was at Cambridge and she in St. Joseph's convent in Reading, Berkshire, a dreary backwater town with persistent Victorian mores.

The town's only glamorous denizen was Marianne's mother, the Baroness Eva Sacher-Masoch, who lived as grandly in her cottage as her penurious circumstances would permit. The exotic baroness had come from Austria to Britain when she married an Englishman named Glyn Faithfull, but the marriage ended when Marianne was six years old. Since then, the baroness had concentrated all her time and energy on schooling her only child in music, painting, literature, and even took her back to Vienna one summer to acquaint her with the beauty and culture of the city where her forebears had been born, a royal lineage dating back to Charlemagne.

At seventeen, Marianne had the soft, blonde, luminous beauty of a Renoir woman, and when she walked into the room where that party was going on the night Oldham spotted her, he lost no time in introducing himself.

Andrew Oldham

THE MINUTE I saw her, I knew she was something special. She had this fantastic *virginal* look. I mean, at a time when most chicks were shaking ass and coming on strong, here was this pale, blonde, retiring, *chaste* teenager looking like the Mona Lisa, except with a great body. I didn't care whether she could sing or not—I could sell that look—and I'd learned what miracles can be achieved by clever engineers in a recording studio. And what a name—Marianne Faithfull! You can't make up a better name than that. So since I was trying to broaden my base of clients, I asked her if she'd ever thought of singing. I told her I could make her a big star if she went with me. She didn't say no, so next day I sent her a contract for me to be her exclusive manager and I set up an appointment with Decca to test her voice. Since she was underage, the contract had to be signed by her mother. I'd never dealt with a baroness before, but she was no trouble, only making me add a clause that when Marianne went on tour she had to have a chaperone.

So now I've got this convent girl with the sexy body and the virginal smile, daughter of a countess, name of Marianne Faithfull, a potential hot property, but I haven't got a fucking thing for her to sing. So I go to my resident songwriters, Mr. Jagger and Mr. Richards, and I ask them to write a nice ballad for a convent girl to sing, stained glass on the windows and positively no sex. I had observed that Mick had shown more than a little interest in Marianne at the party and that he might be motivated to come up with something better than the mediocre stuff they'd been turning out. Well, what do these two fuckers come up with? An absolute knockout, "As Tears Go By"—sentimental, lyrical, melodic—for the first time they had *composed* something original out of themselves and not tried to echo stuff they had heard. It turned out that Marianne sang effortlessly in a pleasant sort of contralto voice, with a lot more confidence than I had anticipated. The record came out in July and by September 1964, "As Tears Go By" had climbed into the top ten on the chart and Marianne Faithfull was hailed in the pop press as a shining new star.

In the years to come, her sultry voice, her graceful mien, the fact that she came from a convent and was the daughter of a baroness, her translucent beauty, her hit records, her long affair with Mick Jagger, her addiction to drugs, all contrived to make her the personification of the sixties superstar. Today, in her early forties but looking ten years older, she is forlorn and wasted, her skin blotchy, her once golden hair tarnished. But she has extraordinary recall of those days in the sixties when she was the princess and Mick was the prince and London was their kingdom.

We met in my New York apartment from time to time over the course of several weeks, talking about her glory days that ended so ingloriously. As she sits and chain-smokes and talks, she is lining up thin strands of cocaine and constantly sipping from her glass of vodka and grapefruit juice to moisten her dry throat. She is proud of the fact that she has kicked her insidious heroin addiction, but is apologetic about Sister Coke.

Undaunted, however, she still dreams of new albums she will make, new songs she will write, of her dissipated fortune that she will restore, and the misspent glory that will once again be hers.

Marianne Faithfull

AS A GIRL, I was taught absolutely everything. I was taught dancing and music and singing and piano, all those things, for some unspecified career, probably movies, I think that's what my mother really would have liked me to do, because that had been her ambition when she was a young beauty. One of the things I used to do when I was at school at the convent was fill pages and pages of my workbook with ideas for pen names or stage names. This was before I realized that my own name was actually the best possible name. But I thought one had to have another identity. I would never have gone into rock and roll, or into pop art, if I'd been entirely left to myself. I had hundreds of plans. I was going to try and get into Cambridge, or if I didn't get into Cambridge, because in those days you had to have Latin or Greek, then I would either go to drama school or I might have gone to the Royal Academy of Music and carried on with my singing. Classical singing.

I had a fantastically good music teacher at the convent, and I had a very beautiful mezzo-soprano voice. I was also interested in acting. I joined an amateur theater group when I was fifteen and I worked with them. And I remember one of the biggest things that ever happened was when Vanessa Redgrave came up to talk to my theater group. She must have been eighteen or so. And I went to the theater a lot in London. My mother made sure I got exposed to all sorts of things. I saw Callas in *Tosca* in Covent Garden when I was fourteen.

At the time I went with my boyfriend, John Dunbar, to the Stones party, I was very pretentious about pop music, and looking at Mick and Keith and the rest of them, I thought, my God, what truly awful people. Awful, mind you, but a bit fascinating, especially Andrew Oldham, who was wearing feminine silks and had makeup on. They took notice of me, particularly Andrew—even though I was only a shy girl of seventeen from a convent in a little town. I was pretty in that very strange way of a very young girl who doesn't really know about it yet, which is incredibly captivating. And I looked very different from everyone else, I think, because I wasn't dressed up and I wasn't made-up, either. And, also, I was very, very still. I picked that up from the nuns, I think. That business of not really showing your hands, keeping very still and moving sort of all in one piece.

Andrew came over to me and said, "I'm interested in you—you have a contemporary face. You are today." He didn't ask if I could sing—he didn't really care. He just said he'd like to record me. And to my surprise, a couple of days later Andrew showed up with a personal management contract, and a recording session at Decca. The first thing I was meant to sing was a Lionel Bart song, which was really much too show-bizzy for me. I couldn't sing it at all. And then, "As Tears Go By" was going to be the B side. And that turned out really well. Mick and Keith were just starting to write songs and had written "As Tears Go By" for me, tailor-made for a convent girl, and I sang it right off and that was that—thirty minutes and done. When it was all over, they were very excited about it, but nobody paid any attention to me. It was like I didn't exist, they were so excited. I finally left the studio by myself, got a cab and went to the station to catch my train. It was a weird feeling, it was a letdown. I wasn't a person to them, I was a commodity that they had created. That's what Andrew liked doing. And he was very good at it. I was a hunk of matter to be used and discarded.

So I just went back to the convent to study for the tests to get into Cambridge. But soon afterwards, Andrew sent me more contracts to sign, which I did because I was so anxious to get out of that convent. I wanted very much to be free and to have my own place and to make my own money in the world.

"As Tears Go By" came out that summer. At first it didn't sell at all, but it was a sleeper, and that autumn it suddenly took off. Right up the charts, and I became the focus of a lot of attention. I had gone from the obscurity of a convent, right smack into the limelight. It was fabulous when I first started singing in front of an audience. I loved it. I always have and still do. That was amazing. Learning, getting a sense of my power, was very interesting. But I didn't get any help from any of the Stones. Nor did I want any. They looked very common to me. I liked more intellectual sorts of people in those days. I liked John, doing his fine arts at Cambridge and all that. The Stones didn't have that kind of superficial undergraduate education that I liked, to be able to talk about paintings, reading Camus, and going to see foreign movies and all that, that's what I liked doing. They weren't into that.

So I left the convent and went on a package tour arranged by Andrew with several beat groups. And that was very good for me in a way and interesting. And it opened my eyes to what I must've thought of then as the lower classes. I realized that they were really nice, that they were real people and that they were interesting and attractive. I was already beginning to change. But not in any way connected to the Stones. Andrew just didn't relate to me—I think with Andrew, he was interested in doing a thing, and then he lost interest in it.

So I went with someone else, who was actually a partner of Andrew's, who was my manager for the next two songs I did, which were also big hits. I got married to John Dunbar in this period, when I found out I was pregnant, and we had a son, Nicholas. And that's when I began to hate singing because I felt that I was just working all the time. I wasn't really going out and doing the sort of things that someone of my age did. It was a real grind. And I didn't really like the music at all—I couldn't see where it was going to go. I was still interested in things artistically, but I didn't see any real value in what I was doing. However, I couldn't stop by then, because I'd got used to a life-style that I wanted to keep.

I wouldn't have married John Dunbar if I hadn't been pregnant. I don't think John wanted to get married, either. It was a shock. John wasn't a very conventional person at all. He really didn't want to particularly lead that kind of life. But he did love me, so he didn't mind marrying me, and in a way I think he thought it was the only way to pin me down. Because I was very much on the verge of realizing my power, and I think I was frightened of it too. I thought that getting married would tie me to the ground a bit. I needed to touch the hand of reality, yes, I really did. And I did want the baby. I was trying to become respectable, I think. I was looking for myself, who I really was. And getting married meant I was also fulfilling what I was expected to do. I really wanted to *please* too much. I wanted to be what people wanted me to be.

The trouble was people saw me as something much more than I was. The whole thing about my mother being a baroness and all that, they made much too much of it. It was awful. To have people thinking of me as an aristocrat, being deferential, but of what real importance was it that my mother was a baroness? It also made people think I was born to riches, which was a real drag. Because that meant that people didn't really think I was a serious artist. For years. I wonder if even now they don't think I get a regular allowance from my family.

I always wanted to be a serious artist. I couldn't imagine how I was going to do it, but I very much *wanted* to do it. And that's why I started acting. That's why I did Chekhov and *Hamlet*, because I thought, Well, perhaps this is the way I can be a serious artist. And I was. I could have gone far, but I didn't. I always was doing that. I was always going so far and then getting frightened by my own power and running away. It's something I've done for years.

One of the people who early on came into contact with Marianne was the young photographer Gered Mankowitz, who is the son of the British playwright Wolf Mankowitz. Gered was one of the brilliant young photographers of the sixties who brought a new kind of vibrant, impressionistic photography to the London scene. Gered was eighteen when he first photographed the Stones.

Gered Mankowitz

I WAS PHOTOGRAPHING Marianne Faithfull when Andrew Oldham, who was Marianne Faithfull's co-manager, asked me if I'd like to work with the Stones. They were already the biggest alternative British band to the Beatles. The Beatles represented everything that was straight and normal, and the Stones represented everything that was rebellious and abnormal. But I do think that the Stones' shock effect was very innocent; by that I mean, one would look at the Stones and hope that they would be wearing something that didn't conform. That they would wiggle their bums or stick their tongues out. That was it. I mean to do that on a popular TV show at the time was enough. It was actually very innocent and naive, but it was enough to go, "Wow, the Stones have rocked the boat again." And so to be asked at eighteen to photograph the Stones at that early stage of my career was fantastic, very exciting. This was 1965. Our first session, I produced photography that was used on album sleeves and tour covers and PR things and posters—all out of that first session. So the Stones and I hit it off and clicked very quickly, and I think the main reason was because I was a contemporary of theirs. I was quite self-assured and cocky and arrogant, which comes with being eighteen and having a Hasselblad camera and believing I was a photographer. I had confidence that I could handle it. And they related to me. I wasn't an older-generation person; they didn't have to conform; I wasn't asking them to smile. In fact, I was eager that they didn't smile. I was keen to promote a sullen and moody and dark and mysterious and hard image, which they wanted. So it clicked. We got on very well.

The atmosphere around the Stones in the beginning was pretty fun, although Andrew Oldham did create a certain tension. He was a very influential catalyst. He brought two elements together and somehow pointed you in the right direction and then let you spark, and something would happen. That was a great talent. He had a clear concept of what the Stones should be, and conceptually the Stones were Andrew's. Mick and Keith and Brian caught on to the conceptual idea of the Rolling Stones very quickly but at first didn't take it over from Andrew, but were extensions of his ideas. Then they began to come up with their own ideas that fit in the Andrew Oldham concept. I think that Andrew was very crucial to them. But not for long. I think that they went very different ways quite quickly, and Jagger assumed increasingly more and more responsibility for the band. Jagger, as it developed, had a brilliant conceptual mind of his own. Career-wise, he knew, and always has known, where he was going. And Andrew channeled him in the right direction and forced him to start writing with Keith. He certainly introduced them to the business concept of publishing their own songs and having B sides, which is the root of their fortune. They probably don't really think of it quite as clearly as that.

By the end of 1964, there was no doubt that the Stones were firmly established as big stars in the rock firmament, and that they had learned how to exploit Andrew Oldham's dictum that bad publicity was much better for them than good publicity. The Stratford pissing incident was a case in point—the following item appeared in the London *Evening News*:

> Summonses have been issued against three members of the Rolling Stones following an alleged incident at a garage at Romford Road, Stratford.
>
> The three are Bill Wyman, 23-year-old bass guitarist [sic; he was twenty-seven]; Mick Jagger, 20-year-old lead vocalist; and Brian Jones, aged 21, who plays the harmonica and guitar.
>
> The summonses which allege insulting behaviour were taken out privately and are returnable at West Ham Magistrates Court on July 22.
>
> The alleged incident took place at the all-night filling station as the group returned in their chauffeur-driven Daimler from a show.
>
> The three stopped at the service station late at night. Wyman used disgusting language in asking an attendant if he could use the toilet. After being told the public toilets were being reconditioned and being refused permission to use the private toilet, Mick Jagger emerged from the car, saying, "We piss anywhere, man," whereupon the three of them urinated against the boundary wall of the service station.

At the trial, the station attendant testified that a black Daimler had pulled into his station near midnight and that a "shaggy-haired monster wearing dark glasses" (Bill Wyman) had emerged from the automobile and demanded, "Where can we have a piss here?" The attendant told him the toilets were out of order and testified that Wyman's reaction was not "natural or normal, running up and down, yelling and dancing about," and that eight people got out of the Daimler and approached him, led by Jagger, who said, "We'll piss anywhere, man." The rest of the group, according to the attendant, began to chant Mick's phrase while Wyman, Mick and Brian peed on the garage wall. The attendant said that there were several people at the station who observed all this, but he admitted that not only didn't most of them seem offended but some of them actually asked for autographs (presumably after the urination).

At the hearing, Wyman testified that he never used foul language and had simply asked if he could please use the toilet because he suffered from a weak bladder, and had returned to the car when rebuffed. Mick testified that he couldn't have used an objectionable word like "piss" because even during his school days he had an aversion to foul language. Brian said it was impossible for him to be abusive toward anyone because "I am easily embarrassed."

The chairman of the magistrates who sentenced them, A. C. Morey, didn't believe any of them. "Because you have reached an exalted height in your profession," he lectured, "it does not mean you can behave in this manner." He fined the Stones five pounds each, plus fifteen guineas to cover costs.

Oldham was absolutely delighted to hear what had happened. "Pissin' on walls is made to order" was his observation as he prepared a release for the press that gave the incident worldwide coverage, thereby further enhancing the Stones' raunchy-boys image.

In the process of photographing Marianne and the Stones, Mankowitz worked closely with Oldham and got to know him very well. "Andrew presented himself to the media as a sort of stoned-out wastrel, a loony entrepreneur. But that was a contrived disguise. He was a very difficult man to gain confidence with, a very suspicious, paranoid person in many ways. Rather unreachable. You could converse with Andrew for a couple of hours and not understand a word of what he'd been saying. It's a shame. The bloke was his own worst enemy."

Oldham's assistant of several years later married Ian Stewart. Cynthia Stewart, who has remarried since Stew's death, is now a magistrate.

Cynthia Stewart

ANDREW WAS AN *enfant terrible* in the avant-garde of the sixties. He worked hard at inventing himself as a fascinating, romantic figure—long leather coats to the ankles, silk cossack blouses, hexagonal eyeglasses, stretch limos at his beck and call, arrogance studded with rudeness, inaccessibility (how often I had to cover for Andrew who, in one of his moods, would refuse for days to answer urgent telephone calls at the office), profligate shopping binges and preferred tables at the best restaurants.

You see, basically Andrew wanted to be the star of the Stones and that's what got him into trouble. He swallowed quantities of things, not heavy stuff, but Quaaludes and Demerol and acid—in fact, most of the sleeve copy he wrote for the Stones' albums was conceived while he was under the influence. For example, the legend he wrote for the 1965 album, *The Rolling Stones Now*, was Andrew's attempt at mind-bent autobiography.

The copy appeared on the album sleeve, but London Records initially refused to release it to the public unless Andrew deleted a certain passage which had suggested that the buyer should mug a blind man in order to get money to buy the album. At first Andrew refused, and there was a stand-off that delayed production of the album, but eventually Andrew lost interest in the controversy and the deletion was made. Not unexpectedly, as Andrew got more and more spacey with the drugs he was taking, the album copy became progressively more opaque and eventually made no sense whatsoever.

Oldham tried to keep separate identities for his only two clients, but Marianne was slowly being seduced by the Stones' magnetism as she grew weary of the long tour dates in miserable backwater places that Andrew was providing for her. Keith and Brian invited her to parties whenever she was in London; Jagger, too, was in contact with her, not pressing, always cool, but making contact. He was still going with Chrissie Shrimpton but that relationship was thinning, and Mick was intrigued with the baroness's daughter. He yearned for someone with class and good breeding who, by her association with him, could elevate him from the level of being a pop singer from a lower-middle-class family. Once he laid eyes on Marianne Faithfull, well-educated daughter of a baroness, with her angelic features, aristocratic carriage and upper-class accent, he set his sights on luring her from her marriage and into his bed.

Marianne Faithfull

THE FIRST TIME I met the Stones, I remember saying to a friend of mine, Barry Miles, "God, those Rolling Stones are horrible. They're all greasy and spotty." I was very critical of people in those days. That was probably one of the things that Mick liked about me, that I wasn't easily impressed, that I was very snotty. But what was good about the groups of people in the early sixties was that they really liked each other and liked being together. There was a great exchange of ideas and aspirations and feelings. They were all young and friendly and growing up together. And everybody was good-looking. And I think that was a real flaw in the whole thing. To be attracted to people because they were good-looking—that was a kind of shallowness typical of the situation. The catchword was "elegance." It seemed to me that the phrase "beautiful people" was a put-down somehow. It implied that you couldn't like someone who was clever and ugly, you could only like people who conformed to a certain type, and that's a very limiting situation. I think that one of the things that eventually attracted me to Mick was that he was clever and ugly.

At any rate, there came a time when I got fed up with singing with mediocre traveling rock bands, and I decided I had to think of something else, something new. That's when I went down to see the Stones in Bristol, to discuss it with them. By now, I'm an established name, an artist in my own right. I had made friends with Brian and Keith, and they were the ones who invited me down. Brian was more like the sort of young men I knew. He had more education than the others; more cultured, a little more sophistication. I didn't know much about music then, and Brian, who was very knowledgeable, got me interested in it. He could talk about almost anything, Brian. He was a very eclectic person. I got less interested in the superficial snobs and pseudo-intellectuals I had known—John Dunbar's friends—and I was losing interest in the life I was leading. Also, I had lost a lot of my prejudices about lower-class people. I found Brian and Keith quite intriguing. And the people they were hanging out with also intrigued me.

Besides, I wasn't getting on with John any more, at all. So we started having separate friends. John was friendly with Lennon and all those Beatle people, and I became more friendly with Brian and Keith. But not with Mick. I just slipped into their crowd and was there, always very quiet and not saying anything, and after a while, they must've liked me more than I realized. Or they got used to me. And for them I became someone who was nice to hang out with. I didn't want anything from them and they liked that. I'm not talking just about the Stones—there was a whole group that included people like Christopher Gibbs and Robert Fraser. Brian had a lot of friends in the aristocracy. I don't know why they liked him so much, but they did.

The Stone I really liked was Keith Richards, because he was quiet, laid-back, didn't come on. People like that are always more interesting because you can make them anything you like. You can fantasize them into all sorts of situations and give them feelings that they probably don't even have. I was too scared to go up and talk to Keith, of course. And he was much too shy to talk to me. But I liked him. Very much.

I had gone to Positano to get away from John and think about my disintegrating marriage and my singing career, which didn't seem to have any direction. I took Nicholas and spent a couple of weeks in the Italian sun, but when I returned to London I felt more depressed than when I had left.

Brian and Keith came around to pick me up and take me out. Not Mick. They just laughed at Mick in those days. He was considered unhip. Certainly not part of their inner group. We went out to dinner, and then we went back to Brian's apartment and took acid. Brian was the ringleader. He was the first one into acid, and that was one of the reasons they laughed at Mick—because he was so straight and so conventional and terrified of hash or acid or whatever. He drank—not often—but when he got drunk he was truly awful. Obnoxious and awful. Belligerent. A cliché drunk. I had met him a few times when he'd been drunk and usually that was when he would try to get me in bed. He was awful. He just wasn't part of what was going on, you see—not part of the sixties. Really out of step, not part of the scene. Mick was very frightened of drugs—always was. And that's been great, in a way, because he's kept his health together. And that's very important to him. But he's always pretended that he's been into dope like everyone else. It's all a sham. Anyway, getting back to that time we went to Brian's place, that's the first time I had taken acid. There were to be many more such encounters with Brian and Keith, but this was my first trip. The way it turned out, I spent the night with Keith.

In the morning, he told me that Mick was in love with me, and all that. And I was very sad because Keith was the one I liked, and I would have liked to have had an affair with him. I wished it was Keith who said he was in love with me, but then again, Keith wouldn't say that. Keith wasn't the sort of guy who said, "I love you."

But I would have liked to have had an affair with him. I would have liked that, yes. But there he was in the sheets explaining to me that nobody had to know about this night because Mick was so in love with me and all, blah, blah, blah. And I just sort of thought, Oh I see, oh dear, well, it's a shame, but I knew of Mick's interest—he had been calling me in Ischia and Positano, and when I got to Ischia, where Nicholas was with my friends, there were three letters from him. I remember thinking that I liked the thought that somebody who was somebody in the world was being romantic about me. It made me feel safe.

When I was in Positano, that was the first time that I had listened to his records. And it was only then, while I was there, that I actually got an inkling of his persona. How in everyday life he was rather bland and not very interesting. Only when he performed did he exhibit the Mick Jagger that the public knew. His persona in real life was never as intense as Brian's or Keith's. The way they came across on records or on stage, they were like that in real life. But not Mick. There was Mick, the great performer and artist, and then there was Mick in real life. And they were totally different.

When I returned to London, I took a realistic look at the life I was leading, married to John, who was taking acid all the time and putting Methedrine in his coffee in the morning. And we had a house guest who was the first junkie I ever knew. He used to come and stay for months and months and leave his hypodermics on the draining board in the morning. Our home life wasn't exactly what people thought at all. But every time I appeared in public I had to be sweet and smile, be a lady, all that shit. And that really began to drive me nuts. I think if I hadn't fucked off and gone over to Mick, John would have done very well. But I didn't give him the chance. I fucked off before he could. John's art gallery was very successful—I think he could have been somebody. But I wrecked him. I just got fed up with it. If Mick hadn't been hanging around and courting me, I suppose I would have stayed with John. But Mick's life was a bit too tempting, this very powerful man with lots of money promising me the moon with my name on it. I fell for it.

My immediate concern was that I wanted to stop and get off the routine, boring train that I felt I was on at the time. The routine I'm speaking about was singing in all those cabarets, which I hated, but had to do it for the money. Either John had to make lots of money fast, or I had to find someone else. Makes it sound very cold, doesn't it? Well, I think I was very cold. Living with Mick, canceling all the cabaret dates, lots of money and glamour, I had a great time at first. I loved it. But then I started to feel useless. And to be like what I was, I suppose—a kept woman. And I didn't like that either. I was too moral, much too moral for that role. And I was bothered, too, that things were not working out for my son, Nicholas. John hated Mick, obviously. Nicholas loved John, but it was difficult for Nicholas. That made me feel a bit bad, too. Tearing up Nicholas's family.

Another thing I felt—and this is terrible, but I think that a lot of very young mothers do feel like that—that I'd really had Nicholas too young, and I think I always resented him. Resented him for stopping my youth. Giving me this responsibility, before I wanted it. I wanted to live the life of a young carefree woman.

So for a while, I had a great time with Mick, and everything was all right. When we were together, we had a lot of power. And that's probably where it all started to go wrong. Mick and I started to get more and more press coverage all the time. Whatever we did was reported in detail. We were the beautiful couple of the sixties, and for me it was very, very exciting. To be very young, very free, very rich and very careless. But then, it went too far, and when it got too much, they had to slap us down. That's when it really became a nightmare. The drug busts, the persecution. It was really a reaction of society against what society itself had done—they had built us up too high and now they would tear us down. But that was unfair. I mean Mick and I existed, whether the cameras were there or not. We were real, we weren't the sort of people who were only real if they're in the newspaper.

□ □ □

John Dunbar

MARIANNE WAS JUST too young to make a go of our marriage. So was I. It was such a manic time. Not only was she having a music career and all that, but she was also trying to be good about the kid and cooking and housekeeping, but I was totally into the gallery and a lot of lunacy. Up all night, and all the time commotion, commotion. The two of us not home much, doing our separate things. So after a year or two of that, it wasn't really surprising that we just couldn't make it together. It was a choice that I had to make—either to devote my life to keeping Marianne together or to my own career. Before she got into smack and all the other drugs, her big kind of "out" was to spend money. She'd go into clothes shops and just buy mountains of stuff she'd never wear, thousands of pounds. Lunatic jags. She was making loads of loot but was always in debt, so unnecessary. It was just clothes, clothes, clothes, which I think she even started hiding somewhere outside the house. That was hard to take when we were struggling to get along. That pissed me off. Of course, I could have devoted my life to looking after Marianne, getting her off the clothes kick, keeping a sharp eye on her, but I was as selfish and young as she was and I wanted her to pay attention to me. If I'd been ten years older than her, then maybe—who knows? After we broke up, she cared for the child more than I did because she had loot and she could afford a nanny. I'd see him weekends. Then when she broke up with Mick, Nicholas went to live with Marianne's mother for a year or so. But when he was about five or six, I decided he'd better come live with me. He lived with me from then on.

But I remained friends with Marianne and Mick—in fact, I went to work for the Stones when they went on tour. I worked with this loony Greek guy, setting up the lights and amps and all that. It was really something to witness the reception the Stones got in Germany, Sweden, all over Europe. And Jagger really learned how to turn them on. Whether it was phony or not, it became more and more a sex act, stripping down, grabbing his joint, driving them crazy. He really went wild on the German tour. I mean, Jesus, he did everything but drop his pants and masturbate. It was wild. This performance freaked out the music—they could have been playing anything.

☐ ☐ ☐

The critic Fred Newman thinks that Jagger is wanted and demanded because he satisfies a compelling need felt by his millions of fans. "Whether he cares to acknowledge it or not," Newman says, "he is the catalyst by which an unmanageable flood of excitement is released. His expertise at pelvic gyration and rhythmic movement—he has been referred to as the Rhythm and Blues Nureyev—provides the visually suggestive symbolism that sparks the mass orgy.

"Psychiatrists have long known that the source of mass hysteria springs from repressed sexual urges, composed of both sadistic and aggressive elements. The number of occasions on which pop singers are physically assaulted by their fans—Jagger himself was recently pulled off a twenty-foot platform in a Zurich stadium and almost torn to pieces—confirms the nature of the emotions involved. Essentially therefore the concert-hall hysteria represents a sudden escape of the kind of emotions which the forces of puritanism, morality and authority—both social and parental—normally seek to contain. When a pop audience blows its top, it is, in fact, indulging in a communal act of defiance against a set of values which it feels to be unnecessarily and intolerably restrictive. It is a group protest against a society which it regards as impersonal, mechanistic and money-bound. Undoubtedly Mick Jagger, purveying as he does his own brand of untamed rebelliousness, is at once a symbol and focal point of this seething insurrection.

"The role becomes him. There exists, between him and his screaming fans, a wavelength of mutual understanding. Jagger both receives and transmits their feelings, defending them and himself from the common enemies of established order and convention. Like them, he wants out. Normal codes of behavior are derided and publicly flouted in a bleak philosophy where compromise and concession are regarded as weakness."

CHAPTER NINE

Success Is the Best Revenge

> *One thing I will say about the American press this time is that, in spite of the rubbish written by the usual idiots who come back to the dressing room and say, "Which one of you is Ringo?" we are getting great reviews.*
>
> MICK JAGGER

Buoyed by their successes in Britain and the Continent, four months after their first dismal tour of the United States, Oldham and the Stones decided to try the States again, in October 1964. But even though they had been playing to overflow European audiences for four months, that was no guarantee they would find a comparable reception on the other side of the water.

Gered Mankowitz

I ACCOMPANIED THE Stones on their second tour of the United States as their photographer. It was a big tour—forty-eight cities in about sixty days, with great lumps of time in the Midwest.

We'd fly into a place at three or four in the morning, because they had this strange routine where you'd go straight from the gig into the airplane, fly to the next town, arrive at four in the morning, go to the hotel, crash out, wake at four in the afternoon, go to the concert. So it was a very disorienting routine. There were evenings when Mick and I just sat down and talked about our girl friends. Didn't have a drink, didn't have a smoke—there were no roadies rolling up joints. There was only Stew, no one else. There was a very entertaining fellow from the William Morris Agency who was well into dope and was a sort of minder for the band. One of those handholders in this business, knows where to get anything. Whatever you want, he can get it. But he was always one day ahead of the tour because he was an advance man. So there were great periods on this tour when there just wasn't any dope present. Just those young English blokes working hard, missing home, missing girl friends, Mick missing Marianne, Charlie desolate at being away from Shirley—really, really sad. In tears on the long-distance telephone.

Of course, in places like New York, Los Angeles, Chicago, main centers, there were social events where drugs were present. You'd go out to a club, you'd get stoned, you'd get a bit pissed—nothing too out of order. Brian got very tripped out in Florida—we had two or three days off, and he and Anita Pallenberg, his girl friend, who joined him at this point, locked themselves away in their little suite, and I think basically tripped for two days and appeared on the third day very stoned.

During that tour, when Jagger and I used to converse, I didn't think he had any idea that they'd become the great band they were destined to be. At that point, he was enjoying and delighting in the enormous success they were experiencing, which at that time was unbelievable. There was still the sense of "Hey, let's enjoy it now because it might not happen next year."

□ □ □

Ian Stewart

THERE SURE AS hell weren't any empty seats this time. Wherever we went, it was bedlam. Long Beach, California, eight thousand packed in there and you could feel them throbbing to the music. A couple of teenyboppers jumped from the balcony, twenty-odd feet up, and landed on the stage. After our fifth song, we knew we'd have to make a quick getaway or there would be major trouble. As we finished that number, we ditched our instruments and ran to a waiting limousine, but even so, the crowd of kids got to the car before we could move. The entire car was covered with bodies. The roof started to collapse and we all stood up in the limo and put our shoulders to the roof to keep it from crushing in on us.

Finally cops came armed with clubs and beat the kids off the car, I mean whacked them mercilessly when the kids wouldn't move. A lot of them got hurt. We finally managed to drive a short distance to a helicopter that was waiting, and as we got off the ground we watched the kids attack the car like it was some enemy from outer space and tear it to pieces. I mean, they tore off fenders, the hood, the doors, the trunk, the wheels—it looked like giant beetles devouring a corpse from where we were in the air.

There was madness like that most everywhere we went. It wasn't pleasant to see what our music did to people.

Gered Mankowitz

RIGHT FROM THE beginning of the tour, Mick manipulated the audiences like an old trouper. I've worked with a lot of actors, and I've seen the great ones manipulate audiences, but I don't think I've seen anybody manipulate an audience better than Mick. He knew how to bring them up and knew how to tease them and taunt them. I think he sometimes brought them up too early, but he had all the movements, a lot of which I caught with my pictures. A sense of that. He was great. He took off his jacket, pretended to throw it. And the kids were throwing things onto the stage. Underpants with messages on them and toys and extraordinary things.

Robert Hughes, reviewing Mick's performance in *Time*, said, "An essential part of Jagger's act is his vulnerability. He is a butterfly for sexual lepidopterists, strutting and jackknifing across the stage in a cloud of scarf and glitter, pinned by the spotlights. Nonresponsibility is written into his whole relationship with the audience, over which he has less control than any comparable idol in rock history. Jagger's act is to put himself out like bait and flick away just as the jaws are about to close and the audience comes breaking ravenously over the stage. No other singer alive has transformed arrogance into such a sexual turn-on: it is the essence of performance, of mask wearing and play, and the spectacle has a curiously private appearance, as though the secret history of a polymorphic, unrepressed child were being enacted by an adult. What still confounds the audience is Jagger's ripe compound of menace and energy; he seems an ultraviolent wraith from Fetish Alley."

It was a newfound sense of power for Jagger, and he made the most of it. "Big outdoor concerts, if they go well," he said, "are the best. The one I remember that I really enjoyed was the Anaheim concert when they threw the shoes—it was one of the funniest things that's ever happened to me on the stage, actually, in my whole life. The way it started, a few people threw their sandals on stage—like their Jesus sandals. I don't know why, but anyway they did. Not maliciously, just throwing them up. I dodged all of them, and then, I said as a joke, I said, 'Why don't you all throw all your bloody shoes at once and get it over with.' There was a minute of total silence while the people were taking them off, and then it was 'Whoosh!' a tidal wave of shoes! The band got really mad at me because I was the only one that had previously got hit with the shoes, but now everyone was getting pelted with these shoes. None of us got hurt, but it was funny. The whole audience went home barefoot, it was so crazy.

"I get a strange feeling on stage. I feel all this energy coming from an audience. They need something from life and are trying to get it from us. I often want to smash the microphone up because I don't feel the same person on stage as I am normally. I entice the audience, of course I do. I do it every way I can think of. What I'm doing is a sexual thing. I dance, and all dancing is a replacement for sex. What really upsets people is that I'm a man and not a woman. I don't do anything more than a lot of girl dancers, but they're accepted because it's a man's world. What I do is very much the same as a girl's striptease dance. I take my jacket off, and sometimes I loosen my shirt, but I don't stand in front of a mirror practicing how to be sexy. Those screaming girls at our shows—their emotions are affection with violence and sex on top. I can feel the adrenalin going through my body. It's sort of sexual. When an audience is really going, like some of those New York or Chicago ones, the energy is just pouring off them.

When the audience isn't responding, I go at it all the harder."

Mick, however, feels that he is always in control even when it appears he is not. "When we play a really hot gig I just feel like takin' all my clothes off, but I'm inhibited on stage to a certain extent. Besides, I'd probably get arrested. Also I have inhibitions because I have to play within a musical reference. If you wander too far away from it, then the band gets lost. Sometimes I do get lost. And I mean you can't warn the band and say, 'Well, I'm going to lose control here,' because you don't know if you will. I lose control, and then come back, and that's exciting. For me it's the best part of the show.

"Of course, I do occasionally arouse primeval instincts, but I mean, most men can do that. They can't do it to so many. I just happen to be able to do it to several thousand people. It's fun to do that. It's really just a game, isn't it? I mean these girls do it to themselves. They're all charged up. It's a dialogue of energy. They give you a lot of energy and take a lot away. Maybe they want something from life, from me. Maybe they think I can give it to them. I don't know. I get a strange feeling on stage. I feel all the energy coming from the audience. I feel quite violent sometimes."

Marianne Faithfull

WHEN WE FIRST got involved, I went once to meet Mick when he was on tour, a European tour. He came straight off stage to the hotel where I was waiting, and he was absolutely terrifying. I was really, really scared. He was like some other person. And he was very violent. He was like somebody possessed. I don't think he even knew who I was. He still had his makeup on, and there was a froth of spittle around his lips. His eyes were violent. He was making sounds, guttural sounds, and he was completely unintelligible. He was a berserk stranger. He didn't say a word, just those god-awful guttural grunts. He picked me up and slammed me against the wall. Several times. He was like a mad creature from some hostile planet. Not the human race. I don't think he realized who I was. I think he just took something out on me that he hadn't been aware of. Afterwards, I don't think he even remembered it. We never mentioned it. But after that I never went to any of his performances if I could help it. I never went on tours with him or anything like that, never again.

□ □ □

Jagger, himself, was also subjected to violence. "I got strangled twice. That's why I never wear anything around my neck any more. Going out of theaters was the dodgiest. One chick grabs one side of the chain and another chick grabs the other side . . . Another time I found myself lying in the gutter with my shirt off and half a pair of pants and the car roaring away down the street. Oh, shit, man. They leap on you. 'What do you want? What?'

"There was a period of six months in England we couldn't play ballrooms any more because we never got through more than three or four songs every night. Chaos. Police and too many people in the places fainting. Pop concerts are just gatherings of people who want to have a good time, and I don't think they really have a higher meaning. People say that audiences are listening, but to what? Like the Rolling Stones on stage just isn't the Boston Pops Symphony Orchestra. It's a load of noise. On record it can be quite musical, but when you get to the stage it's no virtuoso performance. It's a rock and roll act, a very good one, nothing more.

"Rock and roll is to me . . . just sort of funny entertainment. Mass funny entertainment. There is a certain basic element in the form which is agreeable, especially performing it in sports arenas. It's like an art un-event. I prefer that to the Metropolitan Opera House."

Marianne Faithfull

WHEN THE STONES went on tour with Tina and Ike Turner on the bill with them, Mick was fascinated with the way Tina Turner moved on the stage. He studied her every gesture, her every move, all the nuances of her performance. And then when he got back to his room, he would practice what he had seen in front of the mirror, endlessly dancing, gesturing, watching himself, moving his body rhythmically, the way Tina did. What seemed spontaneous on stage was really carefully rehearsed and plotted in front of the mirror during those endless hours that Mick perfected his interpretation of Tina's motions.

Before Tina Turner was on that tour with Mick, Mick didn't really move that way on stage. It was only Brian. It was only after the tour with Tina Turner was completed Mick started to move and to do the outrageous things that eventually became the hallmark of his act. Although Mick also had picked up some motions and choreography from Brian, it was not very noticeable because Brian was more restrained. Actually, Brian was too introverted and shy to really let it all hang out.

Tina Turner says, "While we were out on tour, Mick wanted to learn a dance I did with my backup group, the pony. I knew he had been watching us every night from the wings. He tried, and I said, 'Look at the rhythm on this guy! God, Mick, come on!' I mean, we laughed because Mick was serious—he wanted to get it. He didn't care about us laughing at him. And finally he got it, in his own kind of way."

This U.S. tour not only afforded Jagger an opportunity to develop his performance but it infused all the Stones with confidence that their music now had universal appeal.

Gered Mankowitz

IT WAS A triumph from start to finish—not only their performances, but there was a sense of fun and enjoyment, especially with the American groupies. In those days there wasn't any anxiety about any sort of disease. Which is important if you think about it, because herpes wasn't thought of, VD wasn't very prevalent, and the pill had just come into wide usage. There were a lot of strange, weird groupies. I recall one girl who wouldn't actually fuck any of us, but she was just wonderful at jerking people off. That's all she did, but she was great. She had a little kit with Vaseline and oils and things. And she was wonderful. There was an innocence about her.

Whatever the sex, there was never any heavy orgiastic sort of sexual event. More like in those movies, *Porky's* or *Animal House.*

There was another girl who showed up after a concert, a lovely young blonde who had a pound of butter in her handbag that she wanted to smear over Mick's body and lick it off. I don't know if that rather unappetizing proposition was ever relayed to Mick, but in the usual backstage confusion after that concert, the blonde got shunted off to one side. She persisted, however, and tried to ascertain the availability of Keith or Brian or Charlie Watts. Finally someone said that Bill might be interested. "All right, fine," the blonde said testily. "I just want one of them and it better be soon because I'm already late in getting across town to pick up my little son."

I heard about two groupies named Mary and Kathy who had bedded one band after another—the Beatles, and many others on their long list—but for more than two years they had been pursuing Mick Jagger without success.

Finally they managed to get the Stones' attention and wangled an invitation to their flat. Mick invited Kathy to join him in bed, but she said that Mary had to be included since they had made a pact.

Mick consented, and afterwards Kathy said, "We were really disappointed. He was only so-so. He tried to come on like Mick Jagger, but he's no Mick Jagger."

What amazed me was that the Stone I thought was the least sexy was the one who had the most active sex life. Ian Stewart was the last person in the world who looked like a rock musician. He had heavy hands, heavy face, lantern jaw, and a grim sense of humor. He always had masses of stuff in his back pockets, so his ass looked huge, with great wads of keys. A very bizarre bloke in many ways. But he had a nice dry sense of humor, which was redeeming. And he'd been through it all and he was completely straight. Didn't touch anything—drugs, booze—anything.

Stew married and then divorced a girl named Cynthia, who was Andrew's assistant for years. He was a strange guy, actually, quite strange. He was the only Stone on that tour who was regularly getting fucked because he pulled one of the stewardesses on the plane. She was a red-haired, cute, racist girl from the south, who was very screwed up because she had to serve these black guys who were on the bill with the Stones, and she found that difficult. And Stew pulled her. He was the only one who was getting his oats regularly on that tour. It always struck me as pretty funny.

□ □ □

Richard Hattrell

RIGHT FROM THE beginning, there were always plenty of girls—girls screaming for attention from Mick. And the ones who couldn't get Mick, they'd try Keith, and those that couldn't get Keith, they'd get Brian, and those who couldn't get Brian, they'd go to Charlie, and when they couldn't get Charlie, they'd try Bill and Stew, and if any were left over they were passed on to me. Now the surprising thing was that many of those groupies were aristocratic girls from very good backgrounds—more than likely had been to finishing school in Switzerland. Titled backgrounds. Father was a lord or Sir Somebody or Baron Somebody or whatever. Or mother was a lady or marchioness, like that. Very aristocratic backgrounds, and I think they were kicking up against their traditional shackles, and they were looking about for excitement by larking into bed with a Mick Jagger.

Of course, their parents must have been very thick in the head or wearing blinders if they didn't suspect what their daughters were up to coming home in the wee hours of the morning, if then. Promiscuity was the buzzword of the sixties. I honestly don't think I'm a terribly moral type of person, but I think that those kids who had been so protected and been made to be so *terrified* of sex, that when sex shook itself loose, they went bonkers and were having sex just for the sake of having sex. There was no genuine love or feeling for the sex partner. They were really a bit like animals. In fact, some animals have higher sex standards and don't behave like those kids were behaving. It was sex for the sake of sex, pure and simple. The groupie was a phenomenon of the sixties, quite different from the girls who used to hang around the old-time bands.

□ □ □

Although celebrity camp followers were nothing new, the groupies of the sixties were unique in that they were not rabidly devoted to any one sex target, as were the screaming teenyboppers of Sinatra and Elvis, for example, but they were in competition with each other to see how many of the rock stars they could seduce. The most notorious of these groupies, the definitive groupie, you might say, was Jenny Fabian, whose autobiographical novel, *Groupie*, was a sensation when it was published in London in 1969. She lives in Tunbridge Wells with her husband, Michael D'Abo, a rock performer of the sixties, and their two small children. They live in a small, chokingly cluttered cottage that dates from 1537. Running alongside the cottage is a chain-link enclosure that contains a population of greyhounds, which Jenny and Michael raise and train for their owners, who are principally potentates from Saudi Arabia and other Gulf states. The greyhounds are being trained to run in dog races, which are very popular in Britain. Jenny fits unobtrusively into the corps of middle-aged Tunbridge Wells housewives, and she now looks like anything but a *groupie fatale*. She is a successful free-lancer, however, and writes for *Queen* and other periodicals.

Jenny Fabian

MY FATHER WAS a schoolmaster in a boys' boarding school on the outskirts of London. My background was upper middle class. I was an only child, attended a respected girls' private school, all that sort of thing. My father was very strict, a severe disciplinarian, terrified me; he was a schoolmaster in the home. In his eyes, I couldn't do anything right and I came to resent his bullying authority very much. My dream was not to live at home, but after I left school I had to live at home while I started work for a newspaper.

Nights, I was hanging out with a group in Soho—a very bad crowd according to my parents, because they were foreign people. It was rather chic then to hang out with French and Italians. I didn't like mods, I didn't like rockers, I liked French and Italian boys and hung out with them in the coffee bars in Soho. My parents thought they still had the say-so over me since they had paid for my education, and they had sent me to secretarial school and cooking school afterwards, thereby rendering me fully equipped to face the world, get a job, find a husband, and stand on my own two feet—they'd done their bit, and now it was up to me and if I could behave myself in the bargain, it would help.

I said I wanted to go to America, so they said, "Well you have to work to save money for that," so I got a job in a sort of beef-burgery place, about a fifteen-minute bus journey from home, and I saved fifty quid. But I decided to forgo America and move away from my parents instead. I found this bed-sitter and continued my liaisons with foreign boys but finally got pregnant by one of them, much to my mother's great distress, and had to marry him. I was underage and had to have my parents' permission. My husband was an Italian gambler. We had our first child in Soho, which was pretty gruesome, and our second one outside London in Surrey. I was stuck there in that suburban flat with the babies and nappies, when I heard Bob Dylan sing "The Times, They Are a-Changin'," and that made a deep impression on me. I thought, You're right, Bob, times are going to change. And in no time I left my husband and ran off with all my possessions plus the children to live in one of the seediest areas of London, Notting Hill, Powis Square, a famous square for poor hippies. I wasn't quite a hippie, this would be '65, '66, but I was obviously headed that way.

I'd been initiated into smoking pot by a mad poet who was very talented and amusing, but totally self-destructive, as a lot of us were. I was having an affair with this poet, who not only turned me on to dope but also on to a whole new way of looking at things. He was married with children; I was, too, but it didn't matter—we were free spirits. I smoked dope and nothing really much happened at first and took a lot of pills, but I wasn't sure what the pills were. I finally left him to go live in Powis Square with my children. Initially I couldn't go to work, they were really too young, but my husband, who was heartbroken, continued to support me. The flat I was in was very decrepit.

Next I started having an affair with a disreputable fellow who was a registered junkie. I felt a great aura of distaste and evil around him, didn't like him at all. But poets and arty types were sort of the thing before pop stars. I know Bob Dylan was a poet, but we didn't have a Bob Dylan, so poets were sort of pre-pop stars. Anyway, this junkie made me never want to take smack because there were needles all over the place and blood all over the walls, and I sort of lived what it was like being a junkie through him, and it revolted me. He was a good guy in one respect—he never tried to turn me on—he said, "*Don't!*," wouldn't let me touch it. I thank him for that. I took a lot of dope later, but never touched smack. I was carrying on with him and had family allowance and bits from my husband, but I finally broke up with him because he really was too awful.

I moved and got myself a rather nice flat, just behind Lancaster Gate, big rooms and enough of them for me to rent out rooms to support myself virtually for nothing. As my children got older, I got them into a nursery school and got this job on the *Daily Telegraph* magazine when it was called the *Weekend Telegrapher*. In this big flat I'm smoking grass from time to time, and there's a nice couple in another flat who do a little baby-sitting for me, which is handy, and in other flats there's a couple of macrobiotics groups and dope dealers. I'm only smoking maybe a quarter ounce of grass a month, but right away I got busted. That made me a fully qualified hippie now that I'd been busted—it was around the time of Mick Jagger's first bust in London.

I still had lots of contacts I'd made through the poet and the junkie. One of these contacts was a dope smuggler, quite a straightish individual—short hair—that's how you get past customs—looked like the kind of guy who would fix cars, not messy, but quite tidy. He gave me my first acid trip and took me to UFO, an underground nightclub; it was the first time I ever went to UFO, I'd heard about it, and I really wanted to go. But, he said, "You must go on acid," so I said, "Give me some," and it hit me just as we pulled up in front of the UFO in Tottenham Court Road. Acid, I discovered, was much more physical than grass. I felt like my whole insides were falling out between my legs, a really weird feeling; it hit me in the stomach, and although I've never been sick, I have seen a lot of people very sick on it. Although my stomach was falling out from between my legs, Tottenham Court looked fantastic. The entrance to the UFO had a long flight of stairs with lights that made lots of spots, so it was very difficult to see the stairs. I remember thinking, This looks like stairs here, how do I get down these? And then, finally when I got inside, it was a wonderland, all these people and mind-blowing music; Pink Floyd was playing there, and I really had eyes for their guitarist, Syd Barrett—he was the guy who wrote the initial songs for Pink Floyd. He is beautiful with his blue eyes and black hair, and I decided I wanted him, him and his mournful songs. It just happened that the managers of Pink Floyd used to go to the school where my father taught, and by being my father's daughter

I got to meet these managers of Pink Floyd, and through them, Syd Barrett. He was fantastic. But last I heard, he went off to some Spanish monastery to find himself.

Going to the UFO on acid that night opened a whole other kind of world to me. I started wearing bells on my neck and those sort of caftany things. I had an affair with a rock star I won't mention, but that was dreadful: I was only sleeping with him because he was famous; that was the second time I slept with someone I didn't find attractive. Of course, that's the whole basis of the interest groupies have in rock stars all over the world; the fact that they were famous made them attractive. Of course, they're often physically attractive as well. Syd was beautiful, exquisite, a perfect-looking individual; I can say as a young person I fell deeply in love with Syd and didn't want to be with anyone else, but you're not allowed to get what you want all the time.

I had a couple of others in between, then I met Andy Summers, who later became a member of the Police. Andy was a bass player and I thought, He's so small and pretty, I want him. (I'd look at a rock star and suddenly want him, like a kid seeing a toy in the window.) How can I get him? You've got to be inventive, because you know a lot of other groupies are also trying to get him—you've got to beat them out. I rang Andy up (very difficult to get his number) and said, "There's a boutique opening, sensational clothes, will you come with me?" He did. I was very bold in those days and really went after what I wanted. We had quite a long affair, Andy and I. I really liked him, but he left to go on tour. After him, I went through a lot of rock stars but nothing special, but I began to keep notes and that's the material I used when I wrote *Groupie*.

I got fired from the *Daily Telegraph* magazine for taking dope, but I got the union to reinstate me. But then I flew to a pot festival in Rome with some hippies, and we almost got killed in a near crash. I was very late getting back and the *Telegraph* fired me again.

Next, I got a job working for Middle Earth, because I was sleeping with one of the organizers, who was rather horrible, although I quite liked him at the time. But by then I would do just anything, not because I was stoned, particularly; I was just doing it because I was having a good time. It didn't matter to me if I slept with someone or not; I was quite enjoying sleeping with people, but I'm not saying that it was entirely sexual gratification.

I wasn't taking much acid at that stage, a lot of pills, and I may have started taking Mandrax, but I don't think so. I was mostly on uppers and downers. Basically, I smoked—the grass didn't turn me off and it didn't particularly turn me on. My attitude was, "There he is, here I am, I'm a bit stoned, why not?" In all this, I was thumbing my nose at all that strictness of my parents. Many times I used to think, if only my parents could see me now. Especially my father. I was finally having my own way instead of being told, "You can do this, you can't do that." In a way, what genuinely turned me on was the music—there's a great relationship between the music and the body, and the musician who makes you feel so good, you quite often sleep with him out of gratitude. It's all part of the chain of events. When you get a group of young women and they watch a particular group perform, and afterwards they're just dying to meet them and go to bed with them, it really is that they've transferred something of themselves to those females.

Very little of the modern synthesized music will have that effect, but the real music of the sixties affected you. I want to sleep with you for making me feel this good—I suppose in a way it's a kind of thank-you, what can I do for you? I don't know if music does the same thing for men. Of course, not every performer reaches you that way. For instance, Mick Jagger never appealed to me at all. Not my type. He is a great strutting little cock, isn't he, all plumed, definitely bisexual in appearance, whether he is or not I don't know, but that's how he grabs me.

At one point, I became saturated with my acid-groupie existence, so I went off and joined Mark Palmer with his wagons and horses. Mark's a fine horseman and he had livery horses and pointers and racehorses. I was happy to join his caravan and enjoy my dope and gypsy around the countryside with Mark's people. Brian Jones of the Rolling Stones joined us for a while but he was with some chick. Actually, I wasn't in a mood for anyone, just to enjoy the hash and sit in the wagon watching the countryside pass by.

But after a season of that I grew restless and I drifted back to pulling rock stars, going to concerts and getting turned on by the performance and putting my sights on the guy in the group whom

I fancied. It was a challenge because of the keen competition from other groupies, all trying to get the attention of the same guy I was after. To succeed, you had to have an attention-getter, like the Plaster Casters, who were a couple of middle-class girls from the Chicago area: "Excuse me, we're making this collection of erect penises, we've already got Jefferson Airplane, the Animals and Led Zeppelin—we would like to add yours to the collection. What? You'd like to see some of the others—why, of course, we'll bring them up to your room—they're all autographed."

I first heard about the Plaster Casters from Andy Summers, who was then in the Animals. He said the scene in America is more violent than in England. He said he never got mobbed in England, but in America the chicks over there come up to you after you've played and say, "Can I kiss you, sir, could I touch you, sir, would you like to ball me, sir?" He said it's funny the way they call you sir. And the groupies, they're something else. It's far more of an occupation with them than it is with the English groupies, he said. In America they really devote all their time and energy to pulling musicians, especially English ones. They go through incredible hustles to get backstage or to find out the hotels the group will be staying in, and if they score, they sometimes call their friends up to tell them who they've pulled. At first Andy thought it was rather funny, but now he said he thought it was sick, even though some of them are incredibly beautiful chicks. That's when he told me about the Plaster Casters who, he said, were two chicks who traveled all over the country making molds of group members' rigs. They plate you until you're hard and then thrust it into a container of soft plaster and wait until it sets. Andy said it was a bastard getting your hairs unstuck. I said I thought those chicks were pretty perverted, and Andy said he supposed they were, in a way.

There were all kinds of groupie scenes, like that of Paula Yates, who wrote a book on pop stars' underwear. "Excuse me, but can I come around to see your knickers? Here are some of the photos I've taken." Those kinds of imaginative groupies had success, but the ordinary fan—"Hi, I'm Susan Smith, can I come up to your room later?"—that doesn't work. You have to have something special. After I wrote my book, *Groupie*, I can't tell you the number of pop stars who came to me and said, "Hey, Jenny, can I sleep with you and be in your next book?"

BLOWN AWAY

There was a lot of sexual freedom in the sixties, of course, but
I was one of those women who did not give credit to the pill. I, for
one, didn't like it. I used the pill for a bit but then I rejected it.
Later I had a coil in, but that didn't work either. Very few women
I knew could take the pill without a problem. Everything I tried
had a side effect. I didn't want fat hips or swollen tits or stomach
cramps or things like that, all those side effects. To me, the pill was
just another con, making me more available to men for sex. It
certainly wasn't an equalizer as some say, no, it just made you
more available, and also relieved men of some of their responsibilities.

When you think about the whole rock world and the relation of
women to it, we were really sort of reduced to being chattels—
you'd be quite pleased to wash a famous pop star's socks because
they were *his* socks. And when you were with other groupies, you
could boast, "See him, I washed his socks," and your groupie
friends would be impressed.

You see, from a groupie's point of view, she was getting what
she wanted, not giving him what he wanted. All the groupies
wanted this or that pop star—"Let's see who can get him"—it was
like winning a race, that was the preoccupation of the sixties. It
was a severe competition, spiced with jealousy. "Look at that
bitch—she is having drinks with the drummer." It was a status
thing, so it wasn't demeaning, because it elevated you in the eyes
of other women, who all wanted to get in the bed that you had
gotten into, and be sitting there with that drummer. So if you can
get in the bed of your choice, you don't feel demeaned—you may
have got there by demeaning methods, but the end justifies the
means, or the means justifies the end; we'd do anything to get the
pop guy we wanted, or I would, just about, and when you'd done
it, you had achieved something—it was hard enough to get them
to notice you, much less get in bed with you. The pop guys could
afford to be very, very choosy.

When I scored with one of the members of an important group,
some of the group's image and importance rubbed off onto me,
and my friends and people like that were always asking me questions, for example, about Pink Floyd, when I was pulling Syd
Barrett. I had a sort of status, because now they could say they
knew someone who knew Pink Floyd. And when Syd Barrett took
me on gigs I could feel the stage-door groupies' envy, and I found
I liked to be envied. I was different to them, because I was with the

166

group and they weren't and they wanted to be. Though I was well aware that without Syd I would be back in the audience again, for, on my own, what was I—a nineteen-year-old groover who had just happened to pull a face.

□ □ □

Despite the surfeit of groupies who besieged him, Mick does not look upon that period nostalgically, because those young girls were subjected to a great deal of unnecessary brutality, and not by the rock stars. "In the early sixties," Mick has said, "peace and flower power and all that didn't exist. That didn't happen till later, like '66 or '67. That was a product of the Vietnam War. Before that it was very violent for a while, because people didn't know how to control kids. When we came, say, to Memphis, there was just little girls who would run to the front with their Instamatics and snap-off bulbs and they would throw things on the stage, gifts. And they'd scream all the way through—we wouldn't have to play, hardly, because you couldn't hear anything but the screams. But what happened was that the authorities didn't know how to control them, so the police used to hit them over the head with their nightsticks, these little children, like their own children. It was quite horrible because these communities didn't realize they could control these little girls just by being nice to them. But later, when the peace thing took hold, the little girls stopped screaming and they got more into the music, and they got politically or socially a bit more aware.

"Toward the end of the sixties, rock and roll became industrialized. By industrialized, I mean it became organized, routinized and big businessized. Before that, it was kind of amateur night and idealistic, hopeful and all that. Then it changed when people saw there was big money in it. I suppose you could say that was a good thing, because it meant that you didn't get those cops knocking down little girls in Memphis any more."

The suddenly surging bigness of rock and roll came on Mick quite differently than he had imagined when he was a poor Dartford boy dreaming of unattainable riches. To go from obscurity and poverty to big money and overwhelming fame in less than a year was an enormous challenge, much harder to deal with than the hopelessness of those months in the cold and filthy Edith Grove flat. Of the principal Stones, only Jagger hooked onto his celebrity, wealth and power without breaking stride. Keith developed an acute drug dependency, as did Oldham, and Brian Jones not only became immersed in drugs but he also developed a paranoia toward the band that interfered with his participation in their recording sessions and their tours.

The vulnerability of this fellow Stones was not lost on Mick. He had given up the London School of Economics because he had gambled that a rock band, if successful, could bring him more money more quickly than any business job that might have come his way. And now that his gamble was paying off in such a big way, Mick began to calculate how he could gain complete control of this group that was such a gold mine. He knew that Richards was no threat to him because drugs had neutralized him—besides, Mick needed Keith to help compose the music. Oldham also figured not to be a problem because unlike Keith, who could handle his drug intake, Andrew was being destroyed by the quantities of acid, hash and amphetamines he was consuming. It was especially important to eliminate Oldham, Mick knew, because he insisted on being the producer of the Stones' albums, but Oldham had had no experience as a producer and he simply got in the way of the capable people who were producing their albums. Also Mick himself had become very skilled at studio technique, mixing and sound production, and he wanted to eliminate all interference with his absolute control.

Ian Stewart, Charlie Watts and Bill Wyman posed no problem for Mick, for all three were backseat players who were content to perform their tasks, pocket their take, and avoid the politics of the band. With Brian, however, Mick had his only difficulty. Even though Brian was constantly on something, and even though his musical skills were often impaired, he was still in control of himself and continued to look upon the Stones as his band, the band he had recruited and organized, whose basic sound owed its origins to him. Brian was aware of Mick's conniving, wary of being stripped of his power and tossed aside, and it was this wariness, plus Brian's dope-accented hostility toward Mick, that thwarted Jagger's ambition to make the Stones his band.

It was destined to be a long, drawn-out struggle that would end tragically, for although Mick would eventually succeed in driving Brian out of the band, in the process the Stones would lose that spark, that touch of soul, that made them what they were in the sixties.

CHAPTER TEN

Ominous Rumblings of Discontent

There are things about Brian that are like Cocteau.

ANITA PALLENBERG

After the success of the American tour, Jagger, filled with new confidence, came back to an England that was also feeling a euphoria resulting from a consummation of the social and political revolution that had been underway for almost a decade. "Here at last," the author Christopher Booker says, "at the beginning of 1965, was the shining, youthful, vigorous new England which had thrust its way irresistibly up through the decaying, class-ridden atrophy of the old; an England whose destiny was in the hands of a young, vigorous, Kennedy-style government; an England bathed in the dazzling release of an unprecedented new talent and energy; the England of brilliant young playwrights, of irreverent film directors and television men, of a glittering new classless culture that was the cynosure of the world. Alongside these more prominent standard-bearers of the revolution were the host of outriders who had equally helped to transform the flavor of English life—the fashion designers, the hairstylists, the cookery experts, the antique shops, the discotheques, the little restaurants, the casinos, the color supplements, the spy novelists, the interior decorators, the television conversationalists—all interwoven, feeding off each other and providing a unique color and excitement in everyday living."

After his success in the States, Jagger felt that now, for the first time, he truly belonged among those celebrity standard-bearers of

169

the revolution. He was secure in the knowledge that the band had universal appeal; the success of "As Tears Go By" proved that he and Keith were bona fide songwriters, and that gave them the impetus to embark on writing a string of hit songs; the American gate receipts provided him with the first substantial money that he had ever received; the attention he was receiving in the media and on the street made him realize he was well on his way to attaining the celebrity status he so coveted; and he was excited over the prospect of possibly acquiring Marianne Faithfull as his live-in girl friend. Money and aristocracy were his twin goals in life, and although a rich British aristocrat would have been more desirable, he was happy to settle for the well-schooled, ladylike daughter of an impecunious Viennese baroness.

But, ironically, although everything was on the rise for Mick and the Stones, the man who helped engineer the rise, Andrew Oldham, was on the skids.

Andrew Oldham

NINETEEN SIXTY-FIVE was the year it all came together for the Stones, but for me personally it started to come apart. Basically what happened was that I got heavily into drugs, and I was in no shape to contribute much to the Stones. My memory of their U.S. tour is fuzzy and full of gaps. I vaguely recall lying on the beach in Miami or somewhere warm while they were slogging around the States performing.

That's when a short, fat, New York promoter, oily hair, oily skin, oily personality, named Allen Klein began sniffing around the Stones. He had already contrived to take over the Animals and Herman's Hermits, but Brian Epstein had sent him packing when he made his move on the Beatles. Now, however, he was moving his heft in on the Stones, and in my zonked-out condition I was certainly not in very good shape to resist him.

As for the Stones, their prosperity was gung ho. Decca paid one million pounds for world rights to the Stones' recordings, the United States and Canada not included; a separate contract provided for an additional eight hundred thousand pounds for those rights. By July 1965, the Stones had sold ten million singles, five million LPs, and had earned five million in personal appearances. Chauffeured Rolls-Royces, town houses, country estates were the order of the day, and there was limitless booze, dope, clothes and sex.

Mick and Marianne Faithfull fast became London's glamour couple, Brian had become involved with a seductive German model named Anita Pallenberg, and the Stones' music, composed by Keith and Mick, was sweeping the charts: "Satisfaction," "Get Off of My Cloud," "19th Nervous Breakdown," "The Last Time," and the albums *Rolling Stones Two* and *Out of Our Heads*.

The sixties were now in high gear, dominated by music, acid, clothes and multilayered sex, each one feeding off the others. There was also an acidy epidemic of "dropping out," and for every ambitious Stone, there were twenty hippies who fucked off for the "other" life.

☐ ☐ ☐

Chris Jagger

MICK WAS ABLE to deal with success— that was the virtue that saved him. I can't tell you how many rock people cracked up when they got successful. Busted or dead. They didn't have the confidence to deal with success, not the sudden success of the rock world with all that adulation and enormous money. They were poor boys, from provincial places, and all of a sudden they're being asked to make all kinds of decisions and they don't know what the fuck is going on. So success overwhelms them. It's much harder to deal with success than to deal with failure, because with failure, you keep trying, but success is something else. In a nutshell, that's what I think happened to Andrew Oldham. He could wheel, deal and manipulate as long as he was comfortable in his familiar world of conniving to "get there," but once there, I mean, once suddenly on top of Everest, and then, "Oh, fuck, what do I do now?" Success wrecked Andrew Oldham, and it wrecked Brian Jones, and it made a wreck out of Keith Richards although somehow he kept staggering to his feet, like a punch-drunk prizefighter who refuses to get knocked out.

☐ ☐ ☐

In Brian's case, it was not only the meteoric success of the Stones as a group but also the startling success of Mick's and Keith's

171

songs that slowly wrecked Brian. The alcohol and drugs that Brian thought would embolden him and enhance his position had the opposite effect, and as he felt control of the band slipping from his hands and passing to Mick, he grew increasingly desperate.

"In the beginning," Bill Wyman has said, "Brian was the most popular member of the band as far as fans, girls, everything was concerned. He did most of the interviews in the early days. I'm talking about the first six months of the year. And then when we went to other countries, where people didn't think of us as the Rolling Stones—they always thought of someone and his band, you know? Like they did in America. It's the only place in the world, even now, that they say, 'Mick Jagger and the Rolling Stones.' In the rest of the world, it was 'the Rolling Stones.'

"When Mick and Keith started to write the songs, at Andrew's direction, Andrew became very matey with them and they became a tight three. And the other three of us were kind of secondary in Andrew's mind. He was probably right. He recognized that that was where the talent was and that the songwriting was necessary to carry us on. Brian took it personally that suddenly it was being called Mick Jagger and the Rolling Stones, and he took it personally that he wasn't the most popular member anymore as far as the fans were concerned. He was the second most popular, because Mick started to get more mail than him. And Brian was unable to stay normal in that environment of having an awful lot of money all of a sudden, as many girls as he wanted, as much food. He would go to extremes, and he got very mixed-up. When it came to about '66, '67, he started to be less good at his instrument, and he started to try to rectify that by playing bits and pieces on all kinds of instruments and was never on the second guitar, so it put more of a burden on Keith as a guitarist. And in the end, he just wouldn't turn up at the recording sessions and other events. And he also had bad health a lot, and he missed so many gigs with us in those six or seven years. I've never missed a gig, Mick's never missed a gig, and I don't think Keith ever missed a gig. Charlie's missed one. But Brian probably missed fifty in that time. He missed eight or nine days on an American tour when he was sick. And he missed all kinds of odd gigs in England where we had to play with four of us instead of five. We never brought a reserve in—that was unthinkable. We just played more to compensate.

"But, listen, Brian was okay. He was a very nice guy sometimes.

But sometimes he was a real shit, it depended on his moods. At a given moment, he could be really, really evil if he wanted to be, but for the rest of the week he could be great, fun, enjoyable. I spent a lot of time with him on tours going out. Me and him, mainly, in those early tours would be the two that were going to the clubs and trying to find girls and going to parties, while the other three usually stayed back because they all had steady girl friends. Brian was free and easy and running, and I used to run with him, basically.

"He used to pick a girl up in Birmingham or Manchester and say, 'Come home with me to London for the weekend.' So this girl of seventeen or eighteen would jump in the van with us and come home. And then we'd get to North London and drop Charlie off, and then we'd get to Hampstead and drop Mick and Keith off. And then we would come into the center of London and drop Brian off and he would leave the girl in the van. And he used to say, 'Oh, no, no, no. I'm sorry, I've got to do this or that,' and he would just desert her. And it was always Charlie and I who had to fork out some cash and make sure that she had somewhere that she could stay the night. On a couple occasions I had to take girls home to my house. And I had to ask Charlie if he could come with me because otherwise my old lady would never believe it. We'd put them up for the night and then put them on a train back to Manchester and pay for it, and I'd feel damn silly about the whole thing. That was the way Brian was. He never rested comfortably in the environment when it got big. He never relaxed into it like the rest of us did and accepted it and took it in our stride. He didn't, he couldn't handle that."

Gered Mankowitz

I NEVER REALLY cared for Brian. He was the first of the band that I met; he was the only one I met socially prior to working with them. I grant that he had the ability to be incredibly charming and polite and well-mannered. And he was very well-spoken. Charming sort of middle-class accent. Terribly full of social grace, and in the Stones' early days, able to be very pleasant. But there was another side to him, a manipulative side to him that was very difficult to cope with. He could be very hard, very cruel. Enjoyed laughing at people's mistakes. And very rapidly I realized that he would put photo sessions in peril just to make my life difficult. He would try and screw up pictures—he'd make faces, he'd cover, he'd hide from the camera. You know, he'd play games trying to be a difficult sort of elf. A little naughty boy. If somebody was going to make trouble, it seemed to be Brian. And I think the other Stones began to give him enough rope whenever they could. So I began to realize that if he wanted to make grotesque little faces, that would become a feature of my pictures of them. If he wanted to hide behind a newspaper in a portrait, he was so well-known, everybody knew that was Brian Jones behind the newspaper, we didn't have to see him, so I let him hide.

I presumed he did this to get attention, that he was beginning to feel overshadowed and neglected. I think he became paranoid about his role in the band, because he had been the leader of the band, he had initiated it.

□ □ □

Brian's drift toward self-destruction was temporarily abated somewhat by the arrival in his life of an exotic, worldly, cat-eyed German model named Anita Pallenberg. She would eventually have a profound negative influence not only on Brian but also on Keith and the rest of the Stones for the next decade, but when she first arrived on the scene in 1965 she gave no inkling of what was to come. She appeared backstage at a Stones' concert in Munich, seemingly just another of the ever-present groupies whose only goal in life was to have sex with a Stone. With her long-legged blonde-model looks, she was able to maneuver herself past security and into the dressing room area. Her purpose in going backstage was to meet Brian, whom she had seen perform in a previous concert in Hamburg.

At the moment she appeared, Brian had just come off the stage distraught and close to tears over an incident, real or imagined, that had occurred on stage during that night's performance, an incident that he interpreted as another instance of Keith and Mick's "ganging up" on him. So when this beautiful, intriguing blonde appeared alone in his dressing room, bearing a piece of

174

hash and some amyl nitrite, obviously interested in him, sympathetic, apparently not the usual groupie, Brian wasted no time on preliminary small talk.

"I don't know who you are," he told her, "but I need you. Will you come spend the night with me? I can't be alone. Stay with me tonight—*please*."

"It was a strange way to start an affair," Anita recalls. She and I are sitting in the living room of her London flat, which overlooks the Thames. I had seen photos of Anita taken in the early sixties, smilingly slim and beautiful, and other photos taken in the late seventies when heroin had ravaged her, a bloated, dulled woman looking ten years older than her age. At that time she was all over the newspapers when a seventeen-year-old boy committed suicide by shooting himself in her bed when she was living in Connecticut. But then, during the late eighties she cast off the drugs and alcohol that had wrecked her and gradually reclaimed some of her attractiveness.

"There was nothing sexual about Brian's asking that I stay with him," she is telling me. "I could see how upset he was. He needed someone to comfort him."

That was the beginning of a relationship that, good and bad, was to consume Brian for the rest of his life. Besides her good looks, Anita had other attractions for Brian. She came from a family of artists, writers and musicians, Germans who lived most of their creative lives in Italy, and Anita reflected that background. Also, Anita spoke several languages and had a worldly sophistication that intrigued Brian. In her late teens, Anita had won a scholarship to study graphic design in Italy, which eventually led her into modeling. Her bookings as a model required extensive travel, and it was when she was on an assignment in Germany that she went to the Stones' concert, where she became intrigued with Brian.

Anita Pallenberg

THAT FIRST NIGHT that Brian and I spent together, he cried the entire night. We were in bed and I held him in my arms and he couldn't stop crying, like he'd been holding back all this pain and now he was able to let it go. It was all about Mick and Keith and the others. I didn't make much sense out of it at the time since I didn't know about these band things then and what was going on, but I tried to comfort Brian and hold him and that was a crazy way for a long affair to begin.

I didn't leave Munich with Brian, because I had a modeling assignment in Paris, but I did go to hear their next concert, which was in Berlin. What madness that was! The music was very rebellious that night, very wild, and the atmosphere was really charged up. I was watching from backstage. Mick was doing his sexy number and the girls were throwing their panties on the stage, then quite suddenly it all began to turn ugly, with the audience pushing and shoving their way onto the stage, and the Stones all dropped their instruments and ran. To get back to the hotel we had to go through the underground concrete bunkers connected by tunnels where Hitler and his staff had operated during the war. That was my introduction to the Stones—escaping that mad mob of wild teenagers by running through Hitler's bunkers. The Stones were great favorites in Germany—Germans didn't respond to the Beatles, who were like goody-goodies, the way they reacted to the Stones. They were the naughty boys, long hair, scruffy, dressed in beat-up jeans, funny jackets and jump suits and not the pretty matching costumes of the Beatles.

I stayed with Brian at his hotel that night and he asked me to go back to London with him. He really liked me, I could tell, and I responded to him. Brian was very attractive, very unusual, very intriguing. I couldn't go to London with him just then, but I told my agent to get me some assignments in London, which he did a couple of months later. That's when Brian and I began to have a serious relationship.

Brian was very moody, which I like, and he was physically attractive as well—he looked kind of like a girl in a funny kind of way; sexually I like girls as well as men and Brian seemed to combine both sexes for me. At the same time, he was funny as well. He had a great sense of humor—how could I not love a man who could make me laugh? I think laughter is a very important part of loving. I could never love a man who didn't make me laugh. Also, Brian was very outspoken, blunt, said everything on his mind, outrageous things, and he had a wonderful curiosity— curious about new things, new places, wanted to know everything that was going on, wanted to meet new people, new ideas, learn

176

the new dances. And he spoke some German, which we could use when we had something private to say and other people were around. The other Stones were more like, what should I say— frightened. Brian was much more ready to go to strange places, to meet people he didn't know. Not like Keith who, in those days, sort of sneered at anybody who tried to get too close to him. Except for Brian, all the Stones at that time were really suburban squares. Mick's girl friend, Chrissie Shrimpton, was a secretary type, nine to five, Miss Proper, hairdresser's on Thursday, and so was the girl Keith had, very normal, very plain, no challenge. Charlie Watts had a kind of drab wife he kept in the background, and Bill Wyman, too—you know, background women, with personalities like elevator music.

I was aware that these other Stones didn't approve of me when Brian brought me around. Especially Mick. They looked at me like I was some kind of threat. Mick really tried to put me down, thereby putting Brian down in the process, but there was no way that this sort of crude, lippy guy was going to do a number on me. I was always able to squelch him—I found out, you stand up to Mick, he crumbles. He tried to get Brian to stop seeing me, called me poison. He ordered his girl friend, Chrissie, not to go near me. I figured he was jealous because I was the one close to Brian.

In temperament, I was closely tuned to Brian. I felt like he did about most things, so we got along very well right from the beginning, liking to investigate, experiment, get into mischief. And we got introduced to a lot of mischief by Robert Fraser, who was a London art dealer, Eton type, connected with high society and royalty. Robert's London house was the center of social activity for people like Christopher Gibbs, a very fashionable Chelsea antique dealer, Donald Cammell, an American painter who also gave great parties at his studio, the photographer Michael Cooper, Paul Getty, Tara Browne who would someday inherit the Guinness fortune—a fascinating group of people who were on the cutting edge of what was happening in high society, great cultural evenings, wonderful intellectual talk, plenty of hash and marijuana and speed and LSD. Brian and I were having a ball.

□ □ □

It was certainly a turnaround for Brian who, after the American tour, had been in deplorable condition, heavily into the deadly combination of whiskey and amphetamines. When the Stones were in the United States, at the recording session for "Satisfaction," Brian was in such bad shape he was not able to perform and even had to be hospitalized in Chicago for several days. As far back as that, Mick and Keith were plotting ways to ease Brian out of the group, and that was the situation when Anita came into Brian's life.

What Anita did for Brian was to restore a dominant trait in his personality—a feeling of superiority, a kind of swagger, an arrogance. Brian was delighted to drive Anita around London in his new Silver Cloud Rolls-Royce, and to further impress her he once again concentrated on his appearance, those innovative blouses and jackets and jewelry that were distinctly his creation. Anita tinted his hair to match the color of hers, which caused many people to believe they were brother and sister. The net effect of Anita's attention was a restoration of Brian's self-confidence.

Anita Pallenberg

BRIAN WAS VERY SHORT, especially his legs. He was a head shorter than I, and he could barely see over the steering wheel of his Rolls. He worried about the look of his teeth, which were capped, but I made him forget his defects and just think about the positive side of Brian Jones. Mick resented me, I think, because I brought this new positive force into Brian's life. It seems to me that Brian could have regained control of the Stones at this point except for one thing—much as he tried, he couldn't compose songs for them to sing. God knows he tried, and Andrew Oldham locked him in a room same way as he did with Keith and Mick, but it didn't work. Brian was a fabulous musician but he just couldn't write songs. There were times he'd spend the whole night with his tape recorder, creating music and recording it, but in the morning he'd listen to the tape and always destroy it.

□ □ □

There was one weakness that Anita and Brian shared that would eventually prove their undoing—a proclivity for drugs. At the gatherings at Fraser's house there were always inviting bowls of a variety of drugs and everyone helped themselves. It was there

178

that Anita and Brian first took acid, the fashionable drug of the sixties, and it became a part of their sex lives. The LSD gave them great sexual freedom, Anita said, and allowed them to indulge in sexual fantasies they had suppressed: Brian's latent femininity, Anita's need for sexual dominance. Back when Anita was a young student attending art school in Munich, her first sexual experience was being raped. For a long while after that, she told me, she avoided men, and went only with women.

On one occasion, at Brian's urging, Anita dressed him up to resemble Françoise Hardy, a French singer whom Brian admired, and they spent the evening in a strange kind of role reversal, with Anita pretending that she was Brian seducing Françoise as impersonated by Brian. When they were in one of these sex modes, it could last several days, during which they were totally incommunicado with the outside world.

Anita Pallenberg

BRIAN HAD A volatile temper, and he would react to frustration with physical violence. I'd leave him, against his wishes, to take on modeling jobs for a few days, and when I'd return he'd come at me with a fury, beat me mercilessly. He was short but very strong, and his assaults were terrible—for days afterwards, I'd have lumps and bruises all over me. In his tantrums he would throw things at me, whatever he could pick up—lamps, clocks, chairs, a plate of food—then when the storm inside him died down he'd feel guilty and beg me to forgive him. He also felt guilty at having kept extra money for himself back when the Stones first started to get gigs. He felt that that was why Mick and Keith were getting back at him, why they hated him. He had a guilt about that.

But Anita feels that the real reason Jagger and Richards decided to put Brian down and get rid of him was because they resented him. Anita thinks that Mick, in particular, envied Brian and, in fact, took on his persona. From the very start, Anita feels, Brian was a role model for Jagger, for when Mick and Keith were up on the stage awkwardly trying to make themselves look like sex objects, Brian already had two illegitimate children.

179

Anita Pallenberg

BRIAN WAS THE one who did the hustling, getting the band together and believing in it, unlike Mick who couldn't make up his mind whether he wanted to be an accountant. Brian was saying in the early days, "Look, it's going to happen!" At the same time he had it in his hand so he could control it, but when they found out he was right, that they did become a hit band as he predicted, instead of appreciating what he did, they resented it. And that's when Brian's doom was sealed. They had a vendetta, Mick and Keith, a real vendetta.

Anita feels that Mick's resentment was further fueled by the fact that in his association with Brian he discovered that, like Brian, he also had a strong feminine component that asserted itself on stage. Anita says she put up with Brian's craziness because she was fascinated with his talent. "But he was a tortured personality," she now says, "insecure as hell. He was totally paranoiac."

Ronni Money

I WAS AT the Scotch of St. James Club on one of those nights when everybody in London seemed to be there. I was at a table talking to Jimi Hendrix and Eric Burdon when I caught a glimpse of Brian on the other side of the room. We hadn't seen each other for a couple of months. He spotted me, shouted out my name and came dashing over—hugs, kisses, all that— then he introduced me to Anita Pallenberg, who was with him—we had never met. Anita's first words were, "So who's this one? Another one of your one-nighters? I thought I'd met all of them by now."

I didn't get too steamed over the remark—catty women don't really get to me—but Brian whirled around and smashed her in the face. "You can't talk to Ronni like that, you bitch!" he yelled at her. Her nose was pouring blood and the waiters were using napkins to try to keep the blood off her dress. That's how we met.

As time went on, I got used to these violent incidents involving Brian and Anita. She usually got the upper hand because she

180

simply overpowered Brian with her force and energy, which derived from a steady diet of amphetamines.

□ □ □

Phil May

THE PRETTY THINGS had taken over a large house on Chester Street, which is near by Buckingham Palace. It was owned by the father of a friend of ours. The son was an out-of-work gambler—good public school, but never managed to make a living in his life. But his father let him have this house. We rented five floors of it. And Brian and Anita moved in with us, but that caused some problems because there was quite a lot of friction set up in the media about the antagonism between the Stones and the Pretty Things—all media hype, of course.

The Stones were successful by then—on their fifth or sixth hit record. But Brian was very paranoid because there was obviously a lot of strain going on within the band, between Brian on the one hand, and Mick and Keith on the other. Mick and Keith were incredibly close. A tough double act to come up against if you wanted to control the band, if you wanted to override them. They were a powerful couple. And Brian was made even more nervous because he feared that living in the same house as us would even estrange him further from his situation with the band, since we were being hyped in the press as mortal enemies.

Even though we had some bizarre times with Brian, I liked him a lot. But he did do some crazy things. Once we came back from a tour and found that Brian had gotten hold of all our records and tapes and completely mutilated them—burned and twisted them. Another time he had written scurrilous things with shaving foam all across the bathroom mirrors. On top of all that, Brian had completely got it into his head that we were a sort of threat to him. Or a threat to the band. But, of course, the real threat to Brian was posed by the other Stones. Case in point: A friend of Brian's was driving him down to a gig in Bristol, and they left in Brian's car ahead of the Stones who were all going in a van. Brian's car broke down about twenty miles from Bristol, but Brian told his friend not to worry, "The lads will be coming along in a minute." But when the other Stones came along and saw him broken down on the side of the road, they leaned out the window, made faces at him, and kept going, intending to play the gig without him. That was a bold rejection because there would be an awful lot missing from that night's performance without Brian and his slide guitar. So that shows you how strained the relationship had become.

Brian and Anita Pallenberg had a crazy relationship. They fought a hell of a lot. So sometimes she stayed there, sometimes she didn't, when he'd beat her up. Brian was unpredictably violent. On one occasion, we were sitting downstairs in the basement when Brian came in. We were listening to the Stones' first album—people sitting around, smoking joints, listening—when suddenly Brian went crazy, picked up a guitar, and crashed it down over the head of our drummer, Viv Prince, smashing the guitar to smithereens. But Viv was so stoned, he kind of said, "What?" He didn't realize what had happened. Brian was so paranoid he thought because we were laughing and smoking joints that we were pissing on the album. That was his paranoid side, but then again he could be very, very gentle. He just had these outward explosions like a little kid.

☐ ☐ ☐

Marianne Faithfull

ANITA WAS CERTAINLY into black magic. And although I can't really say whether she was a witch or not, there's no denying the fact that Anita was sort of a black queen, a dark person, despite her blonde looks. Her whole sort of background tied up with all that, her family, everything about it. Of course, I was just the opposite, I mean the opposite of all the kind of Nazi rigmarole that she was into, all that stuff. My granny was Jewish, so there was certainly a clear-cut line between us. But "beautiful" and "wicked" are certainly two adjectives that could be linked together in describing Anita. It's very hard to define wickedness, but when Anita looked at you sometimes with that incredible smile on her face, it was not a smile you had ever seen before, it was a smile that seemed to be a camouflage for some great dark secret that she was hoarding. She gave off a superior aura, a very seductive quality, and when you couple that with the fact that she was incredibly beautiful with an incredible figure, great style, very bright, very tough—her toughness was a predominant trait of her personality, the way she just didn't give a damn about anything, but I really can't say how much of that could be related to her heavy involvement with drugs and how much of it may have derived from other sources, sources within her. The best way I can describe Anita is that she was like a snake to a bird and that she could transfix you and hold you in place until she wanted to make her move.

☐ ☐ ☐

I asked Anita about Marianne's allegation that she had powers as a sorceress.

Anita Pallenberg

OH, SHE'S PROBABLY referring to that spell I put on Brian. She knew about that. Brian and I had had a big fight and he threw me out of the house—literally opened the door and threw me out on the street. So, all scraped and bloody, I went to a friend's house who took me in. I was sitting there, in tears, angry, getting my wounds treated, feeling terrible, and I decided to make a wax figure of Brian and poke him with a needle. I molded some candle wax into an effigy and said whatever words I said and closed my eyes and jabbed the needle into the wax figure. It pierced the stomach.

Next morning when I went back to where I was living with Brian, I found him suffering from severe stomach pains. He'd been up all night, and he was in agony, bottles of Milk of Magnesia and other medications all around him. It took him a day or so to get over it. Yes, I did have an interest in witchcraft, Buddhism, in the black magicians that my friend, Kenneth Anger, the filmmaker, introduced me to. The world of the occult fascinated me, but after what happened to Brian, I never cast another spell.

But I do look very deep into things because of my astrology. I am very careful about my astrological charts. And I also have other charts for nutritional gastrology, what to eat, when to meditate. I have a quality that I can look very deep into things, I mean I can see through things and see what is beyond them. That is because I have a very old soul from another time that entered my body and lives in me. I feel younger now than when I was eight years old. When the soul entered my body I felt very oppressed, very heavy, that something was bearing down on me. But now I am young and released with this new soul in my body.

□ □ □

Kenneth Anger, a filmmaker whose works often deal with the occult, has an unequivocal judgment of Anita's Satanic powers: "I believe that Anita is, for want of a better word, a witch. I was going to film a version of *Lucifer Rising* with the Stones. All the roles were to be carefully cast, with Mick being Lucifer and Keith as Beelzebub. Beelzebub is really the Lord of the Flies and is like the crown prince next to the king in the complicated hierarchy of demons. Beelzebub is like a henchman for Lucifer. . . . The occult unit within the Stones was Keith and Anita and Brian. You see, Brian was a witch, too. I'm convinced. He showed me his witch's tit. He had a supernumerary tit in a very sexy place on his inner thigh. He said, "In another time they would have burned me." He was very happy about that. Mick backed away from being identified with Lucifer. He thought that it was too heavy. When he married Bianca, he was wearing a rather prominent gold cross around his neck."

CHAPTER ELEVEN

Glamour, Villainy and Degradation

*You get to the point where you have to change
everything—change your looks, change your
money, change your sex, change your women—
because of the business.*

MICK JAGGER

The exuberant mood of London was depressed somewhat in 1965 by the escalation of the Vietnam War. In February the United States Air Force bombed North Vietnam for the first time, and tens of thousands of American troops started pouring into South Vietnam. Demonstrators against the war began to appear on London streets and around the American Embassy. But when an unusual summer heat wave engulfed London, the mood of the city swung back to the discos, the mod restaurants and the music. Pirate radio stations suddenly materialized, bombarding Britain with rock music from offshore ships. London was filled with such moviemaking endeavors as Charlie Chaplin's *A Countess from Hong Kong*, Antonioni's *Blow-Up*, and *Alfie;* Hugh Hefner was unveiling his first Playboy Club; and American tourists were clogging King's Road, Carnaby Street and all the other celebrated haunts of swinging London, especially the clubs and theaters where the new rock superstars were appearing.

Despite all the pressures on Jagger—his new superstar role, his manipulation of the other Stones, the necessity of dealing intelligently with the huge amounts of money that were suddenly inundating him—he kept faith with his credo: Stay cool, never show emotion. His studied manner was one of aloofness, always keeping his distance. He avoided friendships, submerged his affection and his anger.

He allowed only one person past his personal barricade and that was Marianne Faithfull, who during those chaotic years was the only one who knew Mick intimately, who was privy to his emotional ups and downs, his disappointments, his vanity, his triumphs. In the years she lived with him, Marianne saw a side of Jagger no one else ever saw; she was very likely the only woman that he ever really loved, although now he proclaims, with uncharacteristic emotion, "Marianne, you know, she nearly killed *me,* forget it! I wasn't going to get out of there alive!"

Marianne Faithfull

ALTHOUGH IN THE end Mick became intent on replacing Brian, in the beginning Brian was in effect his role model. Everything about Brian in those early days fascinated Mick. The way he behaved on stage, the way he walked, his style of dress, and especially his attitude toward music. I think Mick learned everything about the technique of playing the blues from Brian. Brian's attitude toward Mick, his freewheeling embracement of alcohol and drugs, fascinated Mick, who after all came to London a very unsophisticated eighteen-year-old boy from the hinterlands.

Although Brian was associated with drugs all his life, he never got into heroin or any of the heavier drugs and really confined his drug taking to acid and to prescription pills, which were provided for him by various doctors. Jagger was somewhat intrigued with this side of Brian and on occasion took a little acid and a few pills, but was mostly afraid of drugs, certainly avoided any dependence on them and, for the most part, pretended to be interested in drugs rather than indulging in them.

But Mick was very clever about acquiring the elements that eventually were to form his public persona. For example, when I began to appear on the stage, Mick, who had never shown any interest in theater before, came to virtually all my performances. Not so much when I performed Ophelia in *Hamlet,* but when I was doing *Three Sisters,* which was in a theater at the bottom of King's Road, he came to every single performance of that play. Before he came to see me in the play I don't believe he took my acting very seriously, sort of regarding it as a way to keep me quiet and giving me something to do. But after he saw the way I performed the part, he did an abrupt about-face, and I think it touched off something seriously competitive in him and for the first time planted in him the notion that he might want to be an actor as well as a rock performer. Not only was he jealous of the success of my performance, but the fact that I was being acclaimed critically for my acting ability was very upsetting to him, because he had firmly cast me in the role of being his pretty girl friend who stayed in the house and didn't assert herself. The last thing he wanted was for me to become someone in my own right. So he came every night, every single performance, three months, night after night. He didn't always come from the very first act to the end. Sometimes he would come in at the intermission and just see the last act, or sometimes he would come in and see the first act and leave, but he was always there. It was amazing considering how little attention he had paid to my activities before. Mind you, it was a fantastic production, with Glenda Jackson as Masha. And I think the whole theatrical experience opened up Mick's eyes as to the possibilities it presented for him. And then, too, I think Mick took some pride in my performing. He was very much in love with me then, as I was with him, and looking back on it, I think that what I represented for Mick was some sort of wish fulfillment. He had this fantasy of having a girl friend who was an idealized fairy princess, and I was like that then. I had long blonde hair and that sort of face, I belonged to royalty since my mother was a baroness, I came from a distant country, and it's ironic that the very quality in me that Mick loved so much was something that I disliked about myself terribly, something I wanted to crush. I thought it was a sappy image, and I didn't realize, being as young as I was, that it would pass soon enough, and that if you could look like a fairy princess for a few years in your lifetime, enjoy it. Don't try to change it. But I didn't have the maturity to see it like that. I wanted to change. I wanted to be grown-up and worldly, and maybe I turned to drugs to hurry it along.

The fact of the matter was that I loved Mick very much then and I think we both realized that we had to split up as a matter of self-preservation. I was destroying myself, but he was giving me an excuse to destroy myself. And I came to realize that I had to get out if I was going to grow up because he wanted to keep me frozen as a girl of eighteen. The worst thing of all about being with Mick was that he was absolutely obsessed with the notion that you must never show emotion or else people would think you weren't cool. The result of that was that, over the long time that I was with Mick, everything that I felt used to get bottled up inside me. I could never show anything or discuss anything. I remember that on one occasion when Mick and I were in Morocco and were walking up in the mountains with our friend Christopher Gibbs, I suddenly burst out in uncontrollable tears. Christopher was very concerned and wanted to know what the matter was and I couldn't talk. There wasn't anything to tell him. It was just all those emotions exploding in the midst of that beautiful terrain.

Of course, one of the by-products of not being able to talk to anybody or express anything was that I didn't develop any understanding of what was going on in my life. Being very young, very confused, there was no way I could come to grips with the good and the bad of my everyday life. And as a result there are still some things to this day that I don't understand. Of course, the last person in the world I could discuss anything with was Mick. We never talked about anything really personal, about anything that really mattered to us. I tried on some occasions, but it didn't work. In a way he resented it, as if it were an intrusion into a private part of him that he didn't want to share with me. There was a time toward the end of our relationship when he realized that I was making a gesture at discussing our situation with him, and after he rejected my gesture, he would later on try to talk to me and I would reject him in order to get back at him. This went back and forth and, as a result, we never discussed anything.

There was another thing that we never faced and that was the fact that after the very beginning of our relationship Mick was never very interested in having sex. I always felt that whatever sexual drive Mick had, he used it up on stage and there was very little left over for his personal life. At any rate, it certainly didn't exist between us. Even when we went to exotic places like Morocco and we climbed into our draped, four-poster Moroccan bed for a siesta, Mick was only interested in reading a book and not in me. I felt that I was pinned against the wall by the whole superstar structure. I often thought that it might have been a help if Mick and I had tied on a good drunk together, maybe if we had loosened up that way, we might have stood a chance of talking and of getting ourselves on track. But that was the sixties, and we just didn't drink. I suppose the prevalent belief was that to take LSD or smoke hash was a pure sort of organic thing and that alcohol was going into the straight world of our parents, and since that was what older people did to get off, we absolutely rejected it.

The thing about drugs is that when you are taking drugs, you simply don't speak. You are. You don't talk about anything. You just are. You exist individually, you are separate entities with no connection between you. But when you drink, the alcohol gives you a feeling of comradeship, a feeling that you need each other. Mick was giving of things, especially in the beginning, like flowers or little gifts, but there was no giving of himself. I think that our problem was very similar to the problem that Yoko must have had with John Lennon: to get him to stop filling every minute of the day with nonsense business—this, that and the other thing, none of them very important. To stop running on that treadmill and actually live. Mick never learned to do that. He was always wanting to be somewhere he wasn't. Even on a small level. If he was in the country he wanted to be in the city. If he was in the city he wanted to be in the country. And this restless ambivalence made you feel rather strange if you were in a relationship with him. As for me, I would have loved to have set up a home in the country, to have furnished it, and made it something of our own. Then I could have started to be my own person. There was a house that I wanted him to buy but he wouldn't because he said it was too far from home. Of course, it was a long way, near Wales, but I fell in love with it. It had a trout stream and three mountains in the background. I would have put in gardens and made it a thing of beauty. Of course, the house that Mick did buy in Stargroves did give me an opportunity to create a lovely garden, which I made in the shape of the four of diamonds composed of red and white roses. It was sort of like Alice in Wonderland.

This aspect of their relationship was completely hidden, and London only saw a glamorous couple who with the clothes they wore, the places they went, the cars they drove, set the fashions of their day. The teenage offspring of lords and earls competed to entice Mick and Marianne into their social groups; newspapers and magazines entreated them for interviews and photo sittings;

sellers of yachts, luxury cars, stately homes, besieged them; stock-brokers and bankers lusted for their business; designers begged them to wear their clothes—a certain miniskirt on Marianne would ensure the sale of thousands of copies, as would an article of clothing worn by Mick on stage; but more important for the clothing people was what Mick and Marianne originated in the way of clothes, most likely rummaged from a thrift shop, for these costumes were often emulated by their fans if designers were quick enough to copy them and get them in the stores.

"I'll tell you how come Mick made it so big," his younger brother, Chris, says. "He instinctively knew how to deal with fame. He had thought about it so much when he was poor, how he would act, what he would do when he became famous, that he was prepared for it—you know what I mean?"

As far as Brian was concerned, the overwhelming fame that engulfed the Stones was not the fame that he was looking for. He was losing control of the band to Mick; he was having his troubles with Anita Pallenberg whom, in frustration, he had beaten se-verely on several occasions; he yearned to compose original music for the Stones but Oldham, Jagger and Richards rejected his ef-forts as incompetent; he was hopelessly enmeshed in alcohol and dope, and he was convinced that vicious intrigue and animosity were swirling around him. By 1967, he felt particularly betrayed by Jagger's insistence, over Brian's vehement objection, on pro-ducing an album called *Their Satanic Majesties Request,* which was an obvious and inferior imitation of the recent Beatles hit, *Sgt. Pepper's Lonely Hearts Club Band.* Mick maintained that Brian was out of step, that the psychedelic music of *Sgt. Pepper* was the sound of the future and that rhythm and blues, which Brian wanted to stick to, was now hopelessly dated. The fact that in this showdown Mick prevailed was bitter proof to Brian that he was no longer in command of his own band. It did not matter that *Their Satanic Majesties Request* was a failure, thus proving that Brian was correct in insisting the Stones should stick to R and B, which was the sound their followers wanted to hear. Mick was too deeply en-trenched for the one failure to affect him, and conversely Brian was in no shape to pursue the matter aggressively.

Ian Stewart was the only one in the band who tried to befriend Brian, to understand him and help him, but he found it a thank-less task.

Ian Stewart

BRIAN HAD A phenomenal musical talent. He was one of those people who could make sense out of almost any instrument he picked up, quite quickly. He could play clarinet, sax, he wasn't bad on piano, and also, later on, he got quite keen on some of those African instruments. But he was so wrecked all the time that he could never play properly. He seems never to have been able to find himself, he had a lost quality, not knowing what he wanted to do, or unable to express some part of himself. He was actually quite a nice person who didn't want people to think he was nice. He wanted to be known as an evil character, but he wasn't really, and the end result of it was he just had to be so off to everybody. He treated his parents like dirt, and his parents are very nice people. And the other thing was, as soon as he actually got the money to do it, he felt he had to get drunk all the time and take any pill that anybody offered him. He was so zonked most of the time, he just couldn't play. He was certainly intelligent enough to realize all this would lead to his own destruction. He must've known that. Maybe in the back of his head he conceived of himself as being the young rock and roll martyr.

I, personally, got along with Brian all right. But basically the thing I didn't like about him was he wasn't very honest. All the other guys in the band were very straight. But Brian would tell you one thing and you knew perfectly well he didn't mean it. What really bothered Brian was knowing that the big rock money was in the writing and the publishing, not the performing—he had a complete mental block against writing songs, he just could not do it. And because Mick and Keith wrote all the songs, which they were encouraged to do by Andrew Oldham, there was an unholy trinity of Mick and Keith and Andrew Oldham, and a very unholy trinity it was, I promise you. And Brian was just out of it. He would say at the time, "They won't play my songs," but he couldn't write songs, he just couldn't. He would come to the studio with things he had written but they were awful. Terrible. On the other hand, Mick and Keith could just begin with snatches of things and develop them into songs like "Satisfaction," reaping in enormous royalties that none of the others participated in.

This was an enormous factor in Brian's frustration that he tried to cushion with booze and dope and all the crazy things he did. Brian was Welsh, you see, and Welsh people are very devious.

They are basically dishonest. And another thing that a Welsh person'll do: If you get in a fight with a Welsh person, they're always laughing, right up till the moment they take a swing at you. You've never got any idea it's going to come. And it's not like you're going to fight an English person, a Scottish person, there's usually a row first. A Welsh person will be laughing, acting friendly, then bam! a crusher to the jaw. You never know where you are with those people. I don't like them at all.

I think Brian's sin was being so goddamned stupid about himself. There was no need for him to get in that out-of-it state that he used to get into. I really think he did it because he thought that was the way rock and roll stars should behave. But it wasn't in his nature to behave like that, really, because he was quite well-educated, he was quite intelligent, he had an awful lot going for him, and he could've been quite a superior human being. But, No, he thought, I'm a Rolling Stone, I have to take the pills, I have to take acid, I have to be rude to people, and that's the way he was. It wasn't so much narcotics as drinking brandy all the time. He got into this thing that a lot of jazz musicians got into, where they lived on brandy. Brandy's a good food substitute, and if you drink a lot of brandy you don't need to eat. The result was that he just stank of it. You couldn't go near him. So he was pissed most of the time then, steadily pissed. And he could never resist acid either, so he didn't talk a lot of sense, and everything was like dreamy and all that kind of shit.

I'm quite sure that Mick had tried almost everything, but he's very bright, so he's always managed to take it or leave it and not have it interfere with how he functioned. And Keith in those days, whatever he was into, it did not have any effect on his performance, either writing or playing. So he felt very contemptuous of Brian for getting himself in that state because Keith had to play all the guitar on all the records. And I used to get the rotten job of taking Brian home. He was a menace in the recording studio.

I remember one time I went to pick him up and drive him to the studio. He thought he was going to a recording session but when we got there the studio was empty. We had recorded the song "Little Red Rooster" the night before, and all there was was a note from Mick telling Brian where he had to play, where not to play, like that. "I can't believe this," Brian said, "you guys had a session and now I'm just to fill in?" I felt bad about it, but what the hell, when he was at a session all he wanted to do was put in Indian drums or play the Mellotron, and nobody wanted that. But Brian did have a good musical sense—I'll give him that—he could pick sounds out of the air.

□ □ □

Despite his troubles, his lost days and his setbacks, there were times when Brian suddenly shook off his oppression and became the jaunty, irrepressible person he once was. He continued to wear bizarre, stunning clothes, costumes really, an amalgam of men's and women's clothing—a broad-brimmed plumed hat that could have been worn by one of the three Musketeers, a tunic with pearl buttons, striped silk pants, a woman's satin blouse, gaily colored silk scarves tied to his wrists and knees, several beaded necklaces, and high-heeled boots. Designer Ossie Clark credits Brian with having originated unisex clothes, and Jagger with having helped popularize them. Both Brian and Mick enjoyed wearing some of the clothing of the women they were living with. It was this strong masculine-feminine force, which manifested itself when they were performing, that caused some people to regard them as bisexual.

Marianne Faithfull

WHAT AMERICANS DON'T understand is that homosexuality in English society is not the same as it is to Americans. It's quite common for Englishmen to have some sort of early homosexual experience, and it is something that is accepted in school life in England. I also think it's almost a stylistic thing, that it's the heart of narcissism. It's just the desire, a very strong desire, to have people be in love with you. Whether it's a man or a woman isn't really important.

I have read accounts that Mick came home from a tour one day and found me in bed with a girl friend and was furious and had a temper tantrum and all that. I did have girl friends and I did have affairs with them, and it is quite probable, although I don't remember it clearly, that Mick did find me with one of my girl friends one day, but it's inconceivable that he would have been angry. He knew about my girl friends. He knew and he didn't mind. His attitude was that he'd much prefer me to have a girl friend than a boyfriend. Same as I preferred him to be in bed with a man rather than a woman.

I heard that story about Frank Sinatra—and from someone who knew—finding Ava Gardner in bed with another woman and freaking out. What I was told was that he came home unexpectedly and found Ava in bed with Lana Turner. And he really went out of his mind. I just don't understand that. Of course, there's a great difference between having the odd love affair with a girl when you're very young and actually being a dyke. But what of it? It all has to do with love and affection. It's just that for most of us it's something you grow out of as you get older. At least I know I did.

I know it's been said that there was something between Anita Pallenberg and me but that simply wasn't true. I was in awe of Anita because she was very powerful, very beautiful, very clever. But that's as far as it went. There was something compelling about Anita, as if she had some great secret locked up in her. No matter how I tried to dress, Anita always made me feel dowdy and badly dressed, lacking in style, and lacking in sophistication. I guess part of my feelings could be traced back to the fact that it was Keith that I really liked and would have liked to have been with, but Anita was the one who got him when she left Brian. So emotionally that would have some effect on how I felt about her. There's no doubt I was jealous of her, primarily because she was easier in her own skin than I was in mine.

□ □ □

Brian wasn't the only problem that confronted the Stones. Their manager, Andrew Oldham, had become so addicted that no injection existed that could have picked him up. His drug dependency had robbed him of his imagination and vitality; his incompetence as a record producer had rendered him useless in the recording studio; the Stones had advanced far beyond his simple machinations to establish them as rock's bad boys; Mick had developed a pronounced antagonism toward him; and the New York promoter, Allen Klein, had succeeded in pushing him aside and establishing himself with the Stones as their new manager.

Gered Mankowitz

I REMEMBER VERY clearly the night at Olympic Studios in 1967, when Andrew Oldham knew that he and the Stones were finished. It was because of a breakdown in communication between the group and Andrew. Also I suspect that Allen Klein might have been manipulating Mick and Keith against Andrew. Whatever the cause, the band and Andrew split because they were just going different ways. I think drugs had a lot to do with it. I also think that the business was changing so rapidly, the idea of a controlling, manipulative, conceptual, entrepreneurial manager in the Andrew Oldham mold was beginning to be untenable for a band that had become world famous. The band had to take over their own career at this point.

□ □ □

Andrew Oldham

THE PRESSURE ON me got so bad, there was this convent in Highgate where I used to go every Friday night for the weekend to avoid a nervous breakdown. I had this psychiatrist who would give me electric shock treatments at the Bethan Nursing Home, and then I'd check into the convent where the nuns would take care of me until Monday morning—bring me my medicine, serve me my meals, watch TV with me. I was into shock treatments because I was in a bad depression that could no longer be lifted by booze or dope. I knew that I was losing my grip on the Stones, that Allen Klein was getting control of them, and I took to the nunnery for refuge. It was the psychiatrist who set up the convent for me.

I was depressed about a lot of things, one thing being that the bands were not in control any more—the Stones and others—the public was catching up to them. It had gone serious. The drugs had gone serious and the only message to take away was: We were wasted but had a good fucking time.

□ □ □

Ian Stewart

IN THE BEGINNING, we were impressed with Allen Klein and took him on to co-manage with Oldham because Klein had the reputation of being the first accountant who got the record companies to pay the recording artists a decent percentage. For example, the original Beatles' deal with EMI was for a ridiculous one or two percent. Klein was the first person who confronted these record companies and maintained they could quite easily afford to pay eighteen or twenty percent and still make lots of money. So he revolutionized the artist's participation—I'll give him that.

Unfortunately, he wasn't prepared to stop at that. He could've stayed with the Stones, getting them their seventeen, twenty percent record deals, and in so doing he could've made a lot of money for himself, but he was greedy. In the case of the Stones, he wound up with the copyrights to all their important songs. And there also wound up in his bank account a $1.25 million advance he had obtained from Decca on behalf of the Stones. This was 1966, so that was a sizable sum to have banked with interest.

□ □ □

This is how Klein allegedly did it: Oldham and the Stones had a company named Nanker Phelge Music that was their song publishing company in England. Oldham assumed that the $1.25 million in advance royalties from Decca had been paid into Nanker Phelge Music. However, he later discovered that the money had been sent to Nanker Phelge USA, a company Klein had formed in the United States, with himself as president and only stockholder. Oldham sued Klein, alleging that Nanker Phelge USA had been used as "a vehicle for diversion of assets and income" from Oldham and the Stones to Klein "for his own personal use and benefit." Klein denied these charges. Ultimately, the suit was settled, with Klein to take over Oldham's interests in the Rolling Stones and to pay him $1 million. In the process, Klein was able to remove Oldham as co-manager and get the Stones all to himself.

In another lawsuit, the Stones sought $29 million in damages

196

from Klein and claimed he had used his position as their manager "for his own personal profit and advantage." Klein denied these allegations and that case was eventually settled as well.

Cynthia Stewart

ANDREW WAS AN easy mark for the likes of Allen Klein. Andrew's failing was that he was not a businessman—an ideas chap, an expert on hype, yes, but he didn't know how to handle money, how to invest, how to squeeze the record companies, none of that side of being the manager of the Stones. Andrew had started a record label, Immediate Records, to provide the Stones with their own company, but it was a disaster. Andrew just didn't understand how businesses work, nor did he devote the time such a business requires.

So when Klein showed up with all his glib talk about what he had done for other rock stars and groups and what he would do for the Stones as co-manager with Andrew, why Andrew just lit up and welcomed him with open arms, thinking him some kind of savior-genius. My own opinion was that Klein was a cross between a New York gangster and an undernourished wrestler. It was as clear as the nose on his face that he meant to oust Andrew and take charge, but Andrew was too befuddled with drugs to know or care.

What appealed to the Stones was Klein's absolute assurance that he would clean up their tax messes, double or triple their royalties and make lucrative investments for them, holding himself out as the Big Daddy of business. I saw a lot of Klein in those days and I found him to be rough, brusque and rude, but when he wanted to achieve something he could turn on a certain amount of rather charming persuasion.

An amusing footnote to Klein: He was absolutely potty about Marianne Faithfull but she paid him no mind, as he was far too common and rough-edged for Marianne. But despite her indifference, Klein was always giving her gifts, even going so far as to present to her, on one occasion, a talking myna bird.

But what always seemed strange to me was that in all those years both with Andrew and after, I never saw any money being distributed. What I mean is that after tour dates there must have been large payments by the promoters but I never saw any funds either being received by Andrew or distributed by him. Of course, those concerts generated gobs of cash, and I know that the custom with rock concerts is that the promoter has to pay either before or right after the concert ends, but I wondered how these payments were made. I was almost always with Andrew during a tour when a concert ended, but not once did I see him receive a payment from a promoter. Nor later on did I ever see Klein handle receipts. And yet, knowing Mick and how he was about money, I'm sure there was some kind of system whereby the huge amounts of cash got distributed.

□ □ □

Through Mick, before Mick got wise to him, Klein was able to get an introduction to the Beatles. But not all of Klein's schemes worked. He was charged with evading federal income tax on the large amount of money he made from selling promotional records supposed to be given free to disc jockeys to promote sales. A federal jury convicted him and he was fined and sent to prison. Judge Vincent L. Broderick, who sentenced him, said, "In my judgment Klein lied during the trial."

On another occasion, Klein was involved in a Beatles' lawsuit started by Paul McCartney. McCartney's lawyer told the court that Klein "cannot be trusted—he paid himself commission to which he is not entitled and is asserting entitlement to even more. [He] cannot be trusted with the stewardship of the partnership, property and assets. He has not cooperated with the accountants, and there is ample evidence that the standard of bookkeeping has been lamentable."

The presiding judge, Edward Stamp, agreed that McCartney had solid grounds for mistrusting Klein, although there was no evidence that he had pocketed any of the Beatles' funds. Klein denied that he had taken unauthorized commissions from the Beatles' funds and he said that, in fact, his company had taken less commission than he was entitled to. Judge Stamp described Klein's assertion as "the irresponsible patter of a second-rate salesman."

Marianne Faithfull

MICK'S OBSESSION WITH business matters resulted from the problems he was having with Allen Klein, who had become involved in the Stones' financial affairs. I got to know Klein during this period, and I found him to be a very vulgar man who was manipulative and certainly not someone to be trusted, but, nevertheless, I didn't mind him for what he was. However, Mick really hated him. I had never known Mick to hate anyone like that. It all began when Mick suspected that Allen wasn't giving him a fair shake on the accounting. That is, the accounting for the Rolling Stones' recordings. I don't think Allen Klein has ever given anybody a fair shake on the accounting, to tell you the truth. The only way one can deal with Allen Klein is not to inquire too closely into what he is doing. Because if you start worrying about that, then you don't get anything out of him. Allen always tells you beforehand that what he basically does is to make a record deal for much more money than you could get without him. Therefore, he feels entitled to cream a lot off the top. But even with his creaming off the top, you will make more than if you hadn't used him. That's his sales pitch—that's the way he wheels and deals, and Mick came to resent that when he didn't get full royalties. All of Mick's best records, starting with *Beggars Banquet* and including *Sticky Fingers,* were tied up by Klein so that the royalties go to Klein first and then they go to the Rolling Stones, which meant that Allen was in a position to take his outrageous percentages before sending on the residue to Mick. And, of course, Mick mightily resented getting what was left over rather than getting the chief cut of the pie. One thing about Mick is that he has a great head on his shoulders and he learns very fast, and he realized that he could just as easily use Klein's tactics to make a record deal without using Klein.

One of the lawsuits that Klein definitely did not win involved surreptitious dealings he had had with a British music publisher, David Platz. With Klein's connivance, Platz came to control certain rights to the Stones' music. In a proceeding in the High Court of London, the presiding judge found Platz guilty of wrongdoing and dishonesty toward a company called Westminster Music Ltd., of which he was managing director. Westminster was part of a larger company controlled by an American, Howard Richmond. Klein and Platz were trying to bully Richmond into relinquishing control of publishing copyrights Westminster had to many pop songs, including those of the Rolling Stones.

The
London
Times

EVIDENCE BY BEATLES MANAGER "A LIE"

Mr. Allen Klein, a former manager of the Beatles and the Rolling Stones, lied when giving evidence in the high court in support of a senior music company executive who was paying him 1,500 sterling pounds a week for "unspecified services," a judge said.

In a reserved judgment on a dispute over the assets of Westminster Music, which controls the rights to many songs of the Rolling Stones, George Harrison, Procol Harum and other well-known artists, Mr. Justice Walton said that Mr. David Platz, managing director of Westminster, had committed the "grossest possible" breaches of contract.

The case, which lasted 77 days, involved a dispute between Mr. Platz and Mr. Howard Richmond, an American music publisher. The judge ordered Mr. Platz to pay damages and granted an injunction restraining him in his conduct as managing director.

The judge said that Mr. Platz and Mr. Klein were "thick as thieves." Mr. Klein sued Westminster over Rolling Stones' copyrights, yet Mr. Platz was paying him a 500,000 U.S. dollars fee and 1,500 sterling pounds a week during the trial. Their collaboration was aimed at "softening up" Mr. Richmond.

Mr. Justice Walton said that Mr. Klein had changed parts of his evidence quite dramatically on the second day, claiming a "mental block" on the first. "I do not accept that there was any mental block at all. His original answers were just untrue," the judge said.

□ □ □

After getting rid of Klein, Jagger attempted to recover from the carnage left by him by putting his financial affairs in the hands of Prince Rupert Loewenstein, a partner in the prestigious banking firm of Leopold Joseph. Prince Rupert is an authentic member of the House of Hapsburg whose lineage would link him to the Austrian throne if there were an Austrian throne. In an office encased with dark wood paneling, the prince scintillates elegance from his Savile Row dark-blue suit to his custom-tailored shirt with his initials discreetly on the cuff. He uses a gold-rimmed pince-nez for reading, and has the diction and polished demeanor of the actor Robert Morley, whom he resembles.

Prince Rupert Loewenstein

I HAD MET Mick Jagger at some function or other and we got to talking about finances, and he told me that the Stones had been in the grip of a character named Allen Klein who had done them in financially, and he asked whether I would take on the Stones as a client and try to put a traditional structure into their financial life. This was the first client from the music world for our firm. We had, of course, had a few clients of high standing in the acting profession, but the unsavory reputation of the Stones was something else again. I discussed taking on the Stones with my partners, but they were very much against any involvement, saying it would be bad for the image of the firm. It was very hard to win them over, but I finally prevailed.

My next problem occurred when I went to a prestigious bank in Geneva with whom we had been dealing for years on behalf of our clients, who were people of means and position in society. However, when I discussed with a high-ranking officer of the bank how I planned to invest the Stones' money with his bank, he turned us down flat, and there was no way of talking the bank out of it. "How would it look," he said, "if the Rolling Stones came in to cash a check and our other clients would see them in the lobby of our bank? Our valued clients would flee. Absolutely not."

Eventually I found a bank that accepted the Stones' accounts, and I applied the same principles to the Stones' money and income and assets that I would for any client—businessmen, people with inherited wealth, whatnot—there was no reason to treat a rock band's considerable income any different than you treated the income of a business or anyone else. Because the Stones led a wild and rather unpredictable life was no reason that their accounting had to be wild and unpredictable.

During the early sixties, when considerable earnings had come in from their early albums, that is, '64, '65, '66, the tax rate in Britain was eighty-three percent on earned income and ninety-six percent on unearned income with a threshold of fifteen thousand pounds. That meant that after fifteen thousand, you paid those rates. Now young rock stars, mostly uneducated and naive, would see a check arrive for them for one hundred thousand pounds, let's say, for a hit record, and they thought it was theirs to spend, so they rushed out and bought houses, a Rolls-Royce, three Rolls-

Royces, with no reserves for taxes. So when the tax man came around, they were in trouble. Of course, copyrights and such could be sold as assets. It would have been very easy to transfer income to capital, but the accountants who were handling their affairs simply didn't do that. It called for a different and sophisticated concept of accounting.

The big change in the record business was that more companies came into being as the groups themselves began to proliferate, and serious competition began to develop for the top groups who were having phenomenal sales of their records and albums—the Beatles, the Stones, the Who, and so forth. These new companies realized that the lower the price, the smaller the profit but the bigger the volume, and with the big volume they would make much more money than if they tried to keep the price higher. So they were willing to pay huge royalties to get the groups who were the big money earners. That was the big change in the business.

Also, as the years progressed, the attitude toward rock stars began to change. The staid people of the community no longer regarded them as freaks in relation to the conduct of their affairs, and so they were able to achieve certain respectability. For example, Mick Jagger's little girl now goes to a very good public school (what in America's called a private school), and I would say that the stigma of the rock star in general has been erased. But back in the sixties—when the police staged their drug busts and when there were arrests and trials of Jagger, Richards, Brian Jones, and members of the other bands as well—I've heard criticism that they were staged raids and that the police were just picking on them. Well, I don't agree with that. After all, these performers were singing songs that were extolling drugs. Just listen to the lyrics to some of the songs. And they were really inciting the kids to use drugs through music. After all, they were the heroes and the kids looked up to them. So I think it was only fit and proper for police to go after the ones who were promulgating this propaganda.

As far as the business goes, once the income tax rate went down to sixty percent, we had no problem any more structuring the Stones' income, so that they were left with a very reasonable amount of their income. But my primary accomplishment for the Stones was to undo the financial harm Allen Klein had inflicted on them. Some of the things Klein had schemed were irreparable, but all in all I was able to de-Klein the Stones to the point of allowing them to get back on track.

□ □ □

Tony Palmer

WHAT HAPPENED IN the sixties, financially, happened with a real vengeance, because money had started to flow, and as the music became more and more popular, spreading to greater and greater numbers of people, up popped big business when it smelled—aha!—Money! *Big* money to be made here. Money like the music business had never seen before. And so, big business took over this cultural upsurge, and then, of course, almost immediately took it away from its roots. That was the reason, I think—I discussed this very point with John Lennon—that was the real reason that Lennon and McCartney stopped. Because they could see that happening.

That is why they set up their new company, Apple, because they thought, If it's going to be big business, let's manage it ourselves. But they couldn't, of course. They were ham-fisted business people and they were easily duped by that dreadful man, Allen Klein. And so, disillusioned, they thought, Ah, this is absurd—we're not going to do this anymore.

Their withdrawal caused Jagger to think that the Beatles had copped out—he said so at the time. But Jagger lacked Lennon's and McCartney's intelligence and he didn't perceive what was happening to him. He allowed himself to be used by Klein. It was, after all, Jagger who brought Klein into the group, who encouraged Klein. And Klein was a prototype of all the predatory sharks swimming around in the rock waters, ripping off naive superstars like Jagger and the Stones. That's when big business took over Jagger.

So you have a progression of things that start off as a relatively unsophisticated attempt to make individualistic music, to make our own culture, to make our own gesture, really. The Jagger end of it propels itself forward, making bigger and bigger gestures, finds itself frustrated and empty, hollow, uses the Vietnam War *pro tem*, as it were, because that's a cause, we can keep on going, folks. But while that's happening, behind the smoke screen of the Vietnam War, big business is very surely devouring everything in sight. And having devoured it, it's all over. Because, in the devouring process, vulgar predators like Klein chew up all that which is delicate and nurturing. And the wreckage, the human wreckage, of course, is devastating. Whether you're talking about Jim Morrison or Mama Cass or Janis Joplin or Brian Jones or Jimi Hendrix. I used to live on the other side of the square from where Jimi Hendrix lived. The night Jimi died, he actually came to see me. He lived only two blocks away. He came in very drunk, maybe also drugs, I don't know, and he went down to my basement where he used to keep some stuff. After a while, it occurred to me he might have gone down there and fallen asleep. So I went down to look for him later but he'd gone. He had gone back to his house, and later that night he suffocated in his sleep—choked on his vomit.

□ □ □

With the elimination of Oldham, and then Klein, and with Prince Rupert reorganizing their finances, Jagger brought in a new manager who he knew had the experience both in the music business and in record production to help the Stones recover from their run of bad luck. It seemed a rather quixotic choice at the time, since the new man had never been a manager, but as it turned out, Jagger's selection of Marshall Chess was exactly the manager the Stones needed.

Marshall Chess

MY FATHER DIED when he was fifty, from overwork, chain-smoking, stress. Our company was sold, and that's when I phoned Mick in London and asked him for a job. To my amazement, he invited me to come over, and shortly afterwards I was hired to be their manager. It was a transition period. They had just kicked out Allen Klein, and Prince Rupert was just getting involved (he knew less than nothing about the music business and I think he was brought in for his social standing and his tony banking connections). The Stones were fairly broke, so I had to get rid of Decca, and we got them a new, lucrative deal with Atlantic.

From the very beginning, my relation with the Stones was a love affair. I fell passionately in love with them, I lived for them, I lived with them, they were my whole life. As a matter of fact, I lived for over a year on the top floor of Keith's house on Cheyne Walk, and I was on intimate terms with Keith, Anita, Mick, all of them.

As for the songwriting—Mick and Keith—that was the heart-beat of the Stones. I was in on all of it and, let me tell you, I think there was magic involved. The music is what hooked me and kept me around. There was magic there, all right. When we would be recording, we would go three days, four days, three weeks, nothing happened, not a track laid down. Then all of a sudden one night, magic would happen. Four or five basic rhythm tracks would emerge out of nowhere, utterly amazing, the whole band playing as one, the kind of thing only a magical combination of musicians can achieve. I had heard the same thing happen before at Chess, when that great creative thing happens—that's my buzz.

On one tour Mick let me play my trumpet with them on the last three numbers. I would come on stage and play some trumpet riffs—that was my bonus. They never gave me a money bonus—they were sort of cheap that way, they didn't take care of their people financially—but money or no money, that was one of the greatest periods of my life.

What I did for them was help them develop a system to create. It was very expensive, but I think it really worked. We had to leave England, because of Rupert's tax plan, so I took the Stones to different countries, so that every album we recorded was in a different environment. I would rent a studio for two months, and at midnight every night they'd come in and begin. Sometimes they'd have trouble and I'd send for a keyboard player, like Nicky Hopkins or Billy Preston, to add that little bit of spice, so that if Mick and Keith were caught in a rut they knew they could get another musician in there to pull them out and help change direction. Bobby Keys was another guy who would help—he was a horn player. Ian Stewart was in on some tracks, sometimes he wasn't, depending on the style. Once they got the basic format, they'd make cassettes and construct off them. Keith had books of lyrics from which he adapted certain phrases. A song eventually called "Tumbling Dice" was at first called "Good Time Women," with a totally different set of lyrics.

During these long sessions, which went on for weeks and weeks, I got increasingly into drugs. I spent a lot of hours taking drugs with Anita Pallenberg, sitting in the same room with her, the two of us, for days at a time. It was Anita who introduced me to heroin, which at the time was rather a rarity. Speed, acid and grass were the drugs, but I became heavily involved with smack. Anita and Keith had been into it for a long time.

In the six years I spent with the Stones, I never had one argument or problem with them. They never told me what to do, and they backed me totally even when, as a complete heroin addict, I was totally in charge of their careers. "As long as our records go to the top of the charts, and each one sells more than the last one, we don't care what you do"—that was their attitude. They gave me a big expense account, total freedom, and I gave them everything I had in return. We had a great marriage. How many guys would let a junkie run their shit? They stuck up for me. I remember several meetings with Prince Rupert when he brought up my addiction—"What about Chess, he's a complete junkie, how can we trust him?" But the Stones remained faithful. I think it's ironic that their first manager, Andrew Oldham, and I both wound up as druggies.

Anita, Keith and I did go for "cures" in Switzerland, given by a doctor, who put us on Elucidril and barbiturates. He'd put us to sleep for five, six days. The Elucidril did nothing. What we really did was sleep through the withdrawals, but he didn't cure whatever it was that made us addicted, so three days later, after we finished the cure, we were right back on smack. It was a joke.

CHAPTER TWELVE

Acid Dreams and Other Nightmares

Sometimes an orgasm is better than being on stage. Sometimes being on stage is better than an orgasm.

MICK JAGGER

By 1967, the Stones' music had swept the world. In that year alone, they sold ten million singles, five million LPs and their audiences poured more than three million dollars into box offices to attend their concerts. The songs they were playing, "Satisfaction," "Let's Spend the Night Together," "Have You Seen Your Mother, Baby, Standing in the Shadow?," were not only reflective of what was going on and how teenagers felt, but also, because they used simple rhythms and traditional chord patterns and meter, they were able to preserve the fundamental requirement of rock music—that it be solid music for dancing.

On top of that, Jagger had emerged as arguably the best-known rock star in the world. Both as a gyrating, inventive performer and as a colorful public figure, accompanied everywhere by his beautiful aristocratic girl friend, Marianne Faithfull, he had captivated the media. And Marianne also contributed to the attention they were receiving by such behavior as posing in the nude for Salvador Dali, and by getting into a flap with a fashionable, staid London restaurant because she came to lunch without wearing a bra. When a reporter asked her if she had an ambition in life, her reply got wide coverage: "Yes," she said, "it's always been my ambition to be killed by some lover in a fit of passionate jealousy."

When Mick and Marianne were asked about the possibility of marriage, they each reflected the sixties' attitude of disdain. "Marriage spoils the whole game," Marianne said. "It's just not the scene. It's disillusioning."

Jagger was more deliberate and thoughtful, but equally disdainful: "In London we don't live in that kind of society anymore. There are no pressures to get married, not even from your own family. In a small village you're under great stress if you're going out with a girl, but not here. I've been going out with women for years—very happily, a beautiful edification of the spirit, but I've never considered marriage. Not even if you want to produce children, not even then. Of course you have a responsibility to the children—but what matters to the child is not whether they're illegitimate or not, but whether they've had a happy home life. I was a happy child but I don't think it would have made any difference really if my parents hadn't been married.

"As far as I can see the marriage thing is security not so much for the children as for the woman, because she hasn't reached the stage of economic independence in our society."

When he was asked what he'd do if the woman he loved wanted to marry him, he said, rather grudgingly: "If she wanted it, yes, I'd give it to her if that's what she really needed, but I don't think that would ever arise. It wouldn't be my kind of woman who needed that kind of security. But if I did meet one who really wanted to get married and who I wanted to have children by and spend the rest of my life with and she couldn't make it unless she was married—I'd marry her."

And what about Marianne? Jagger was asked. "Well, it's very nice with Marianne at the moment," Mick replied, "but I can't speculate on whether it will last. I don't think about things like that."

Marianne Faithfull

ONE OF THE things Mick liked about me was the way we discussed his ideas for songs. It made me feel that I was doing something very creative, in a way. It's a funny thing, that. I think women can slip into that. Living through a man. Letting somebody use them and not thinking that it's at all strange. But now I think it's very odd that I put myself at his disposal like that. Because I was more educated than he was. I was very good with words. And I gave him books to read that would give him ideas. For instance, I gave him *The Master and Margarita*, an eerie book about Satan coming to Moscow to assess the damage of the revolution. That's one of the things that started the song "Sympathy for the Devil" from the LP *Beggars Banquet*. The sinister theme of that song is largely derived from that book.

And when Mick was working on the words for a song, he'd go over them with me. That was something that was really very good between us, I think. And in a way, I'm quite proud of that, my contribution to that. But after a while, I got to hate it very much. And then years later I read a book about Scott Fitzgerald and Zelda, and I really identified with her. I should think artists do that a lot. They use the life around them for their subject matter. And if you're living with somebody who writes, your life will be used. They're going to feed off of you. I eventually hated that, but at first I liked it, I enjoyed it. I did come up with all sorts of things. Lines in songs. And eventually, I wrote a whole song, which was "Sister Morphine." I wrote the lyrics, Mick wrote the tune. Sometimes I get credit, sometimes I don't. When we wrote it, we were living together, and I recorded it. After it came out, it was taken off the market very quickly because it was a drug song, and there was protest. On that first version, it credited "Jagger, Richards, Faithfull." But then Mick recorded it for the album *Sticky Fingers,* and by then we had split, so he took my name off it. But then Keith wrote a letter to Allen Klein, who was publishing it, and said that I had written the words, so then I got the money for it. But I never got the credit. Just Mick and Keith, and Keith had nothing to do with it.

I think that Mick did some of his best work, really, in the period we were together. And I think that the reason for that was because I am interested in many things, and he was still young enough and open enough to be receptive to new things. With me, he wasn't the repulsive chauvinist that he later became. About women and their place and all that stuff. In the early time, when it was still good, I really felt that we were partners, that we shared feelings and reactions. I never wanted actual credit for the lines I would give him. I thought then, and I still do, in a way, that if you live with an artist, that's part of life. All I do now is make sure I get back from people what I put in, which is fair. When I was with Mick, he would try to do that, but he wasn't really good at giving of himself. But he tried. Even though he was the more dominant person, we had a kind of interdependency. I accepted my role, although I was very jealous as well. But I tried not to show it—in the sixties it was very important to be cool. If you died in the attempt, you could at least have it on your gravestone: "She Kept Her Cool." What happened was that in the end I realized that if I didn't cut out I was going to die in the attempt. And I really couldn't live in the shadow of someone like Mick Jagger forever—however much he loved me. But I feel I was an important influence on them and their records, their best records, really—*Beggars Banquet, Let It Bleed* and *Sticky Fingers*. I was in the studios during all the recording sessions, and I learned an awful lot.

What Marianne learned was a creative process and studio technique that had evolved haphazardly as Mick and Keith struggled to learn how to write and produce a record, and, later on, an album. Their imaginative mastery of the very complicated process of taking a simple song once it was taped and enhancing it with all the electronic apparatus available in a high-tech studio has been the key to the success of their songs, although, of course, studio inventiveness is meaningless unless the song itself has strong ingredients.

The sound that the Stones were producing evolved more by accident than design. They had started by trying to imitate the music they heard on the recordings of such greats as Muddy Waters, Bo Diddley and Little Richard, but in their attempt to imitate, they were unwittingly producing a different sound, a sound rooted in the style of the original performers, but in their failure to produce an exact imitation they found a sound and a style that became an interpretation of the originals, not a replica.

Sally Arnold is a Londoner who managed several of the Stones tours, and she was privy to many late-night sessions when Mick and Keith did some of their songwriting.

| **Sally Arnold** | THE TIMES I sat in on Mick and Keith composing occurred late at night on tour after a concert. The first thing they'd do is listen to that night's concert, which had |

been taped, and they'd analyze it and discuss it, sometimes putting in one song for another, or rearranging the order. They'd smoke some dope and then begin to play a few chords and such on their guitars. Maybe throw a couple of words at each other, phrases, Keith would start a riff and they'd build on it. I remember one night we were traveling by train, and I was in a compartment with them when they were jamming together and a tune just started to come out of it and they began to fit some words to it. They had started with some old blues stuff, some blues chords, and then they'd sort of slid off on their own and they really seemed to have fun building on it. Mick doesn't play the guitar very well, but for composing it didn't matter. Mick'd be the first one to admit he's not much of a musician, Keith has all the talent there, but what Mick really cares about is his voice. There was one time Mick came down with severe tonsillitis and the doctors desperately wanted to take his tonsils out, but Mick was terrified that it would change his voice so he wouldn't let them do it. He preferred to suffer.

Bill Wyman and Charlie Watts have a very realistic attitude toward the protocol involved in cutting a Stones' song. "Mick and Keith run the show as far as choosing what tracks go on the album," Bill has said, "because they write the songs and they're the producers of the records. So that is their big thing. But as far as anything else is concerned, it's very much a group decision. If we're going on tour, who we work with and what we do, it's all voted on—it's very democratic, actually. For myself and Charlie, who provide the rhythm tracks, there's not too much variety unless they want to try a different bass style on something. If they need an overdub on percussion, they use someone else, not Charlie. What Mick and Keith do after we finish the tracks is overdub the odd guitar, horns, keyboard maybe, vocals, work on vocal ideas, write lyrics and mix. There's very little that Charlie and myself are involved in. You don't want five or six people in the studio saying, 'Turn the bass up, turn the guitar down, there's not enough piano'—it gets too many cooks into one kitchen."

When the Stones recorded at the RCA studios in Los Angeles, the studio engineers, Jack Nitzsche and David Hassinger, had never experienced anything like the method used by the Stones. "After a playback," Hassinger said, "you had to get an okay from the Stones before mixing. And an okay from the Stones was Mick and Keith. Not even Andrew. That's why I liked Andrew. He never claimed or appeared to be *the* Rolling Stones. Mick, Keith, and Andrew seemed to have that understanding. The determination and what was said musically was always Keith. If a *feel* wasn't right, Keith got it every time. You knew if it was a good take by Keith's smile. I always remember looking at Keith and if he was smiling we had a good take. Keith never said anything. He just smiled. And it would never be questioned, never a discussion."

Nitzsche not only engineered but also played piano on some of the tracks. "There was no guidance at all on those records. And very little need for it. What the fuck, this was the first time I'd seen a band get together and *play*. They changed my whole idea of recording. Before I'd just been doing sessions, three hours to get the tunes down. Working with the Stones made sense right away. Booked studio time for twenty-four hours a day for two weeks and if ya didn't get it, fuck it. The great new thing about them was they'd never record a song the way they had written it. If it didn't work nobody thought twice about making it a tango! They tried every way possible. Nobody had that big ego thing about keeping a song a certain way. That changed me. That was the first really free feeling I had in the studio."

Marianne Faithfull

I REALLY LEARNED a lot from Mick. I didn't realize how much I had learned until I started to record on my own, and then I found all those things stored away in my brain that I didn't even know were there, which I must have heard or picked up when Mick was recording. When you're young you soak up information like a sponge and you don't even realize it. Mick also formed my tastes, my musical tastes. Without Mick, I would never have been exposed to a hell of a lot of black music and soul and stuff like that which he exposed me to. I would have missed out on it. My personal music taste when I met Mick was extremely weird. The only person that I liked really, that I could relate to, was Otis Redding.

As for Mick, I taught him to open up to a whole new world—theater, dance, pictures, furniture, fabrics, architecture—a whole new world. I took him to the ballet for the first time and he loved it. It was a particularly fortunate time because he was just developing his dancing technique on stage and at that time he was not a caricature. He was amazing, truly amazing the way he moved, his natural instincts. And I thought he really must see Nureyev because what he was doing was so similar to Nureyev's style, and they even looked alike. I think we would have gone to the ballet much more often, but it was just such a jam with all the photographers and the media. That was inhibiting and it cut off a lot of things we might have done together. But there were beautiful pictures and all sorts of new things for him to learn about without us having to go public. I even got him interested in the beauty of lace.

Despite her efforts, however, Marianne found that Jagger's interest in this new world was transitory, that his shallowness kept him from emotional involvement, from any real connection with these new artistic experiences. Nothing touched him because he didn't seem to know how to reach out and embrace new sensory reactions and new emotions.

Marianne Faithfull

MICK HAD VERY little insight about himself. I often heard him say that he'd rather not know what he's like. "I am what I am," he used to say, "and everything just happens, doesn't it? So I let things happen to me and then react." That's just the way Mick was but I can't complain. I chose to live with Mick. I made that decision. And then I hated it and resented it. I hated so much being in the shadow of somebody like that. I really felt hunted and used. I felt that all my experiences were being drained out of me as if by a vampire and used by him in his work and it left nothing for me. And then I felt a rage against society, too. I felt it was incredibly unfair that we were persecuted as we were. We really weren't doing anyone any harm, and I had this incredible feeling that they really wanted to take away our power, which is the worst thing you can do to somebody because you're born with it and you need it, and if people try to remove it, it's like taking the sting from a bee—

you're finished without it. And I know how that feels because for a long time after the sixties I felt as if someone had unplugged me from the life-force and my power wasn't there. And I know that when I went on stage to act in those years, I would stand there waiting to go on, waiting for that feeling of my power, and it wouldn't come. And it was awful. And then eventually—I don't know why or how—I got it back again. It took an awfully long time. It took almost ten years.

When I performed Ophelia, I still had it and I fought bitterly to keep it. But then I think I must have decided if someone was going to fuck me right up, it was going to be me, not anyone else. That's what got me into drugs—trying to destroy myself before they beat me to it, but after I got myself into that, I decided I didn't like it. I didn't like being a junkie. Not at all. But by then I had lost my option of choice. I had discovered that drugs as an escape was a fallacy—what they are is imprisonment. Also, to be honest, there was something . . . how shall I say . . . romantic about it.

This is very dodgy stuff, isn't it? Because some sixteen-year-old, fifteen-year-old kid might pick up wrong on this. But, truthfully, from reading De Quincey, Baudelaire, Oscar Wilde and others, I had this very romantic idea of taking drugs. And the sort of journey and experience that you could get from it, if you didn't die. I'm very lucky that I didn't die, which I certainly could have. And then it would have all been absolutely pointless, because there sure was nothing romantic about it, and the journey finally led you into hell. It wasn't at all like Baudelaire or De Quincey or Oscar Wilde. It wasn't even like being Dorian Gray. I thought it would be, but it wasn't.

Drugs kept me from being a terrorist—by that I mean there came a point where I think I felt that either I was going to have to explode out into something, into actual acts of violence in some way, or I was going to have to implode and contain it. And I decided to keep it in. So I turned the violence against myself by taking drugs, which did violence to me. But that destructiveness could easily have gone the other way. If I had fallen in with Erika Meinhof, for example, I can see I could have readily joined my terrorism to hers and exploded in violence against society. I could have. I really could have.

Getting involved with Mick Jagger, that life I was leading with him, that, too, was part of the violence. There I was, trapped in an image that I couldn't stand. And since then, my life has been very much involved in trying to align my own real self with people's image of me. And I still haven't got it right. I don't really care about people's image of me, but I would like it to correspond with how I really am. I don't want to have to act out something for people. And I feel that now, when I do an interview, when I go and promote my work, I don't have to. I can be myself. I don't know how people really see me outside England. Of course, there I have a stigma and nothing I can do will make any difference. But when I go to other places, I can be myself. I can talk how I talk and be how I am and people accept it, you know? And I've got rid of the rage. I really have. Of course, I can still tap the rage when I want to, when I'm on stage and I need it, I can plug into it, as an emotion I once had. I can recall it, if I need it. I've learned to be an actress. But when I performed Ophelia, I had not learned how to be an actress, so instead of being able to plug into something, I *became* Ophelia. I had to do it in a primitive way, like a child would. Acting was one of the things I always wanted to do. And I enjoyed it as long as I had marvelous words to say, but then, after that, I was cast in terrible plays, and it was awful. And I really saw the other side of the coin. What it's like having to do a play night after night with absolute shit. I did *The Collector*, which isn't all bad, but it's not very good; it certainly is no match for *Hamlet* or Chekhov. And then I did *The Rainmaker*. I did it on tour. It really was the other side of the coin—staying in really cheap theatrical digs and having to do it every night. But I hated it. And I realized that I wasn't really an actress. And the audience resented me as much as I resented them. The producers wanted me in the part because I had a name that could possibly sell tickets. And I didn't get on with the other actors, because they felt very much that I was an interloper.

But when I did *Hamlet*, that was pure joy. Nicol Williamson was amazing. He made me see *Hamlet*. He did a very unorthodox Hamlet. He was wonderful. You had to cut through the way he looked. He didn't look like the sort of classic, romantic hero. In a way, it was like being in a contemporary drama, at least that's the way it affected me, as if I were the Ophelia of the sixties.

The key that opened the door to the dark, decadent world that Mick and Marianne inhabited was LSD, acid, the mysterious drug of the sixties. Of course, hashish, marijuana and heroin were around, but acid was inexpensive, easily available, and was perfectly suited to the psychedelic, mind-bending spirit of that time. More than any other single factor, LSD (lysergic acid diethylamide) fascinated, confused and captivated the Jagger Generation. It appeared quite suddenly, established itself as a dominating force, and then disappeared just as suddenly as it had materialized. But while it flourished, "taking a trip" did not mean a voyage by land, sea or air, but a nightmarish adventure of the mind into territory never seen before, whose aftereffects usually lasted two or three days, depending on one's metabolism.

An American named Steve Abrams, who left the University of Chicago in 1960 to matriculate at Oxford, is a recognized authority on LSD and has written and lectured extensively about it. Abrams never left London and to this day lives in cluttered digs in St. Luke's Mews, a section of the city where cabbies fear to drive and where patrolling bobbies are everywhere. Abrams is a six-foot-four-inch Ichabod Crane with a shock of graying hair, intellectually composed, an anomaly in this neighborhood of pimps, fences and hoods.

Steve Abrams

THE MYSTERY ABOUT LSD that seems baffling is why, unlike all other drugs, it made a sudden and quite overwhelming appearance toward the beginning of the sixties and then, as if on cue, just as suddenly and mysteriously disappeared as the sixties ended. The solution to that mystery lies in the fact that LSD did not emanate from Aldous Huxley, Michael Hollingshead, Humphrey Osmond or Timothy Leary, but that it was almost totally supplied by the CIA, which supervised its distribution all through the sixties and then decided to withdraw it around 1970. When the Beatles took their psychedelic trips that led to songs like "Lucy in the Sky with Diamonds" and the Stones wrote "Something Happened to Me Yesterday" and other acid-inspired songs, the lysergic acid diethylamide that inspired them was provided by the CIA, which was the only source of the drug all through those acid years.

216

□ □ □

Abrams was studying ESP at Oxford when he was contacted by a man named Robert Lashbrook, who was with a Washington, D.C., organization called the Human Ecology Fund. At first, Lashbrook professed interest in his ESP experiments, but subsequently, at a meeting that included Lashbrook's boss, Dr. Sidney Gottlieb, it was revealed that the Human Ecology Fund (HEF) was in actuality a branch of the CIA and that its chief mission was to test a new drug, LSD. The CIA was buying the drug in large quantity from a Swiss-based pharmaceutical firm, Sandoz Laboratories. In fact, the CIA, Abrams discovered, was to buy Sandoz's entire production of LSD —a mammoth ten kilos, which, over time, would have been enough to have turned on the entire Western world.

Steve Abrams

DR. GOTTLIEB WAS in charge of an operation called MX-ULTRA, whose purpose was to find out how LSD could change a person's behavior by covert means. Specifically, the CIA wanted to know if, by administering LSD to a captured enemy agent, they could break down his resistance and get him to reveal his secrets. And if that wasn't possible, they conversely wanted to know if they gave LSD tablets to our own agents to take in the event of capture, would it so scramble their minds that they couldn't reveal the secrets they knew to their captors. Gottlieb honestly believed that LSD was going to completely change the world's espionage methods.

Lashbrook and other agents in the London office had begun their experiments by using LSD on themselves and making notes of its effects. But the acid was so strong and so unpredictable that all they had succeeded in doing was making themselves loony. They lived together like karate students, unpredictably spiking each other—karate students are taught to be prepared to be attacked at any given moment, and that's what was happening with these CIA agents. They were so spaced-out by the drug that the notes they took about one another's reactions were totally unreliable, if not unreadable.

That's when they decided to enlarge their experiments outside their own circle. They began to go into bars and drop acid in people's drinks, then follow them home or take them to safe houses and perform experiments with them.

The HEF agents also released acid to rock groups in an effort to assess its effect on performance and creativity. All the big pop groups had one guy who was their delegated dealer and who kept the group supplied with the drugs it wanted, so it was relatively simple to distribute acid to particular bands by contacting these designated dealers. Paul McCartney once handed me some acid, together with a copy of *Sgt. Pepper's Lonely Hearts Club Band,* and said, "Take this acid, Steve, and then listen to the music on headphones." I did, and while colored lights were bursting and spinning spheres collided, tangerine trees and marmalade skies, newspaper taxis and looking-glass ties rode their melodies all around my trip.

By now, CIA agents were distributing acid all over the place and, of course, as a result, before long the CIA guys were losing track of where they had placed the acid and with whom.

Some of those CIA fellows were able to take acid trips and come out of them under control, but LSD was such a powerful and unpredictable drug that many of the HEF men became unhinged from it. The same thing was happening in the U.S. I knew about a group of CIA men assigned by Dr. Gottlieb who were given drinks spiked with LSD, which is tasteless and colorless and gives no hint of its presence. One of the men, who had been an outgoing and well-adjusted fellow, emerged from his acid trip in a very depressed state and acting irresponsibly. His wife and children became alarmed. He was put under the care of an uncle of mine, Dr. Harold Abramson of Mount Sinai Hospital, in New York. After a couple of weeks, Dr. Abramson advised the CIA that this man was suffering from a severe psychotic condition that had been induced by the LSD experiment and that he should be committed to a sanitarium that the CIA ran for those of its personnel who developed psychotic disorders.

The night before he was destined to enter the sanitarium, this man, who was a respected scientist, dived through a closed tenth-story window of the Statler Hilton in New York and fell to his death.

I had heard about another activity, this time in San Francisco, where whores were paid one hundred dollars a head to pick up tricks, take them to a CIA-rented pad that had a two-way mirror, behind which sat CIA observers taking notes on how the victims behaved after the prostitutes put LSD in their drinks.

By 1970 it was more than apparent that acid was of no practical value to the CIA, and it recalled all of its stockpiles and its personnel. The operation in England was shut down, and with that decision, acid, the drug that had captivated the sixties generation quickly dwindled.

□ □ □

Marianne Faithfull

WHAT PIQUED MY curiosity about LSD was a long talk I had with John Lennon one night when we were all at the Ad Lib. He said that his first time with LSD was when a London dentist laid it on George Harrison and Lennon, without telling them, at a dinner party at his house. He put it in the coffee. John didn't know what it was, and he thought that the dentist, who was a mixed-up swinger, was probably getting into it for the first time. Probably thought it was like smoking a joint. John said the dentist had warned everybody not to leave but that they thought he was trying to set up an orgy and they skipped out and went here to the Ad Lib nightclub. John said that when they got to the club they thought it was on fire, and then John thought no, it was a premiere, but actually it was just an ordinary light outside. They were jiggling in the streets and shouting, "Let's break a window"; it was just insane. They were completely out of their heads. When they finally got on the elevator, they again thought it was on fire, but actually it was just a little red light in the elevator. They were all hot and hysterical, and when they arrived at their floor—this was a discotheque that was on an upper floor— the lift stopped and the door opened and they all came out screaming.

John said he had read about the effects of opium in the old days, and he thought that's what was happening to him. He said that this seemed to go on all night but all he could remember was George driving him home in his mini, only in his condition, God knows how George managed to do it. They were going about ten miles an hour, but it seemed like a thousand to John, and Patti

Harrison was urging everyone to jump out and play football. George's house seemed to be a big submarine, John said, and he believed he was steering it. John said he stayed stoned for a month or two as a result of that trip.

I asked John if he had been on acid when the Beatles made *A Hard Day's Night* but he said no, he was on pills. He said he started taking pills when he was seventeen, which was when he took up music. The only way to survive in Hamburg, he said, was to play eight hours a night, and you had to take pills for that. You got them from the waiters. John said he'd always needed a drug to survive. The other Beatles, too, but John had more pills, more of everything. But for him, John said, LSD was just another mirror. It wasn't a solution to anything. It was more of a visual thing and a therapy, looking at yourself a bit. It did all that. But it didn't write the music.

There was another time I got to talking to Paul McCartney about acid. "God is everything," he said. "God is in the air between you and me. God is in the chair you're sitting on. God is everywhere and everyone and everything. The way I happened to find God is through taking acid."

☐ ☐ ☐

Gered Mankowitz says that the first time he became aware of acid was when he accompanied the Stones on their American tour. He discovered that Brian Jones was taking acid when he saw him go out of control during a performance.

Gered Mankowitz

ON THAT OCCASION, Stew picked Brian up by his jacket and shook him in the wings as they were coming off stage, yelling, "You are a piece of shit and if you don't play properly, I will personally break your bollocks!"

But Brian went on taking acid all through that trip. I myself never touched acid. As far as I'm concerned, acid was a real evil, the most dangerous drug around. Oldham was heavily into certain things, but he always seemed to have it under control, and when he didn't have it under control and went off the rails, he would disappear and try to do something about it. He'd clean up his act quite quickly. Whereas Brian just started going downhill.

On tour, at our hotel, I met Bob Dylan, who was a friend of Brian Jones—Brian introduced me to Dylan in Brian's room. And there was definitely some drug thing going on there. So what I'm pointing out—portents of a drug-oriented, orgiastic world—were beginning to creep in, but they weren't a way of life. They weren't crucial. They were another thing to enjoy or another thing to experiment with. I think at that point everybody had it very much under control.

The first person to go was definitely Brian, who just didn't know when to stop. As for Anita, I didn't like her. She was manipulative, wicked, evil. There was definitely a clique around those days, of manipulating people into situations. Anita was part of that clique. Spiking drinks with acid began to be prevalent. People would put acid in people's drinks to "see what would happen." There was a club in London called the Scotch of St. James—it was right next door to my studio. Very cliquey, trendy music club and several people had their drinks spiked there with dicey results. All of that was beginning to creep into the rock and roll sixties society. And I felt that Pallenberg and Brian were not beyond doing that sort of thing. I did not trust them. I wouldn't go and spend an evening with them because I feared I would have my drink spiked. I became paranoid. In my view, Pallenberg and Brian were very manipulative, dangerous people, but I never was involved enough with them to be exposed to the danger.

Many of the psychedelic acid posters of the sixties, a brand-new genre never seen before, were the work of a man named Michael English.

Michael English

I DID POSTERS for most of the rock groups, including the Who. I used to go off every weekend with Pete Townshend and others—we used to go to a house near Victoria and take acid trips. Acid was really the drug of that period. I learned so much from it. It was great for painters and musicians. It destroyed a lot of people, but for me, it opened my eyes so much. It enlarged my sensibilities; I saw the world anew, it was like a rebirth for me; I suddenly began to understand the laws of color and the laws of visions, really, the sort of visions that you could conjure up in your mind, and I'd use all that I'd learned from those trips in my work. I could never have done my sixties paintings without acid. It really had a phenomenal effect on my work, as it did for Pete Townshend. He had a bad trip the first time, somebody spiked some food, terrible time. I remember saying to him, "You can really learn something wonderful from it if you have it in the right environment and are ready for it, and have an experienced guide." So I got some acid and we all took it—Pete, myself and some other people who were very close friends of his—and he was able to have a deep experience from it. I think it made his music a lot richer, his lyrics, certainly, a lot more meaningful. Not that he could actually compose while on a trip. You can't, but it's the memory of what you've learned that's valuable.

A bad trip is when you lose control of the feelings and images that come up, and if you lose control they tend to get rather nasty—like nightmares. I've experienced them, but I was always aware that they were part of the drug. I remember sitting in a chair and looking in a mirror, thinking about something else, my mind a million miles away, and there was dust on the mirror and some finger marks in the dust, and a light was shining obliquely on the mirror so all the dust was visible because of the light. Suddenly, I got the most tremendous shock—I'll never forget this—that whole mirror came alive, all those marks became alive and became like a rotting undergrowth, and normally if I had lost control of that vision, I'd have been in a bad way and sucked into a very bad trip. I went into the mirror, but I went in knowing that I was in control—I sort of held back, and I think that was the secret of doing acid properly. The whole time, I was holding rein on it and learning from it. But, of course, enjoying the adventure of the experience as well, even though subconsciously I was learning from it. I was very lucky to have that reaction.

I think a lot of creative people learned a lot from acid trips. But granted, it's very dangerous, very dangerous. I remember taking a trip with Brian Jones in his flat that he had in Ebury, and I nearly had a bad trip because I got involved with the passing of time. Brian had a book called *The Expanding Universe*, just a picture book that began with a girl with a cat in her arms, sitting on her chair, and the next picture, you see her from about a hundred feet away, and then you expand outward into outer space, so by the end of the book you are out into outer space with all the galaxies. I was looking at that book, getting increasingly frightened at the way time was related to space, and the whole thing got too overpowering for me. I damn near let go, and I think that was the closest I ever got to losing control. If you lose control, of course, it could lead to anything—jumping out of a window or running in front of a bus or jumping into the Thames—anything.

Brian was my favorite acid partner. Very kind, very friendly, very feminine sort of person, Brian was much more appealing than Mick Jagger ever was. Brian was a very gentle person but self-destructive—he used to drink vodka and take acid at the same time. It was considered dangerous to mix alcohol and acid but Brian didn't seem to care. Mick and Brian never got on well together, in fact, they got progressively worse, and things got really bad between them. Brian was very selfish, but he was also very talented, such a gentle person, but he just didn't get on with Mick, and after a while, there was a real struggle for influencing the group; Mick turned it into hard rock, Brian wanted it a little softer, with more meaning in the music. Mick was all business, always in control, whereas Brian was surrendering himself to acid. As a result, Mick eventually took the Stones away from him as easy as you take candy from a baby.

□ □ □

Andrew Oldham

KEITH RICHARDS HAS said that the only times that I hit it off with Brian was when we were both high, and that's the truth. Other times, we had no use for one another. But on one memorable occasion when we got on acid together in New York, Brian took me to visit the offices of the notorious Dr. Max Jacobson, known as Dr. Feelgood because of his mysterious injections. This was in 1966. We had spent a good part of the night with some fabulous black hookers who cruised in a Rolls-Royce. I shouldn't call them hookers—they were a lot more than that. At any rate, at three, four in the morning, Brian takes me to Dr. Jacobson's brownstone. We are ushered right in, past several people in the waiting room. I'm amazed that a doctor would have office hours at three in the morning but there he is in a dirty white smock that's got blood spurts all over it. And on his desk are the remains of half-eaten sausages and sauerkraut, as God is my witness. There's a line of several booths that have people in them. At that time I had a case of herpes that Jacobson gave me some ointment for—the herpes was so bad, my nerves were going to my cock. Then came the injections for which he was celebrated. A hot jab that gave a tremendous lift. While I was getting jabbed, I looked in amazement at the citations that covered the walls—from the Kennedys, Lyndon Johnson, Dietrich, so on and so forth. I mean seeing those famous people was a fucking trip. And then I saw that sitting in one of those booths giving dictation, while Jacobson injected him, was Alan Jay Lerner. It blew my mind that the great songwriter was there working on a show under those weird conditions. It was no wonder he was having trouble writing new shows.

Jacobson had wrecked a lot of lives with his amphetamine injections, and I had no doubt that if Brian had lived in New York he would become yet another victim because the injections did give you a big, glowing high but they also resulted in a killing down. I guess that's why Lerner and the others were there in the night, to get injections to pick them up when they started to fall.

□ □ □

The Stones were planning a tour that included Australia and New Zealand, but they knew that Keith Richards would not have been able to get visas because of the trace of drugs that he had in his system. In order to pass the blood test, Keith had a blood transfusion, substituting new clean blood for the contaminated blood in his veins. Afterwards, he used to joke around, by going up to his close friends and saying, "How do you like my new blood?"

"Although he tries to deny it, there were a couple of occasions," Andrew Oldham says, "that I know about when Keith Richards replaced his blood to get rid of the telltale heroin that would show up on blood tests. On one occasion we were both in a clinic in Switzerland, Keith in a room on the ground floor, me up on the third floor. We used to call back and forth to each other from our balconies, bragging about whose new blood was better."

Tony Palmer

WHEN YOU TALK about drugs in the sixties, there is no resemblance to the drug scene of today. Compared to today's drugs—heroin, coke, crack and the like—the drugs of the sixties were kiddies' play. Marijuana is far less damaging than alcohol (this is a contentious statement, but I believe it to be true). The reason that Lennon and a lot of others took LSD was because they saw it as part of the liberation of their imaginations. I discussed this with Lennon, who believed that alcohol loosened the tongue, whereas LSD would loosen the imagination. It would allow him the flights of fantasy that, within a Western culture, would seem to be impossible. And he identified LSD with Eastern cultures, in which he was very interested. He had taken trips there, and he was fascinated by Eastern culture long before he ever took LSD. And it was suggested to him that LSD might be a way in which he could, as it were, leap forty years of Brahmin training. The Maharishi (both intellectually and culturally absolutely discredited now) had this course wherein after God knows how many weeks, hours, days, months, years, you could convince yourself you were flying. Literally. You were sitting in a squat position and flying. But, you know, that was after a five-year course. So John thought, Well, Timothy Leary is saying, "Here's LSD, which can give you that flying sensation," so why not? Alcohol loosens the tongue, LSD loosens the mind.

The drugs of the late sixties were predominantly pep pills and acid. After all, Jagger was arrested for having four pills on him, and they were only pep pills. A whole middle-class generation was taking Valium and atrium and dopium and God knows what else. But these were all perfectly acceptable because they were mostly being taken by bored and frustrated housewives. But poor old Jagger comes along in his funny clothes, has four pep pills on him and is arrested. So you have to understand that when you talk about drugs in the sixties, you're really talking about comparatively harmless substances. It's only later, with the advent of heroin, that the drug scene took its nasty turn.

Heroin existed, of course, but I have a book on heroin addiction that lists a total of only 163 registered heroin addicts in England in 1969. So that wasn't a problem. When you talk about drugs, therefore, I think you have to see it in this light: the kids saying, "We don't want to go down to the pub drinking beer, we'll smoke dope." A fairly harmless gesture, really, which makes one conclude that Western culture simply did not allow the mind to be liberated in the way that Eastern culture undoubtedly did.

But I don't mean to minimize the wreckage that was left behind when hard drugs like heroin came into use. Whether you're talking about particular people, such as Dave Crosby, for example, who was an absolutely blown-out hulk of a man. Or the walking dead and the ungrateful dead, like Keith Richards, Marianne Faithfull, Anita Pallenberg and the like, who are off heroin now and still function but whose creative spirits have been battered—I don't think you should ever underestimate the wreckage that was left behind. There are thousands and thousands of people around the world who live without any purpose, just empty hulls, a hollow generation of hollow men, hearing only the meaningless whispers of the past. That's the downside.

□ □ □

PART FOUR

The Fall

CHAPTER THIRTEEN

The Persecution of the Stones

Oh who is that young sinner with the
handcuffs on his wrists?
And what has he been after that they
groan and shake their fists?
And wherefore is he wearing such a
conscience-stricken air?
Oh they're taking him to prison for
the colour of his hair.

A. E. HOUSMAN

Mixed in with the high-flying success the Stones were having, along with the record concert crowds, the phenomenal album sales, the Rolls-Royces, stately homes and all the other accoutrements of their exalted status, there was some dead weight, heavy sacks of trouble destined to inhibit their flight and perhaps ground them: amphetamines, marijuana and acid, slowly dominating them, monopolizing their lives.

In the mid-sixties, at the height of the Stones' popularity, the police mounted a drive aimed at making them an example of the narcs' determination to crack down on drug users. It was ironical that the one who bore the brunt of the police action was Jagger, one of the Stones least involved with drugs. But it was a relentless and quite vicious campaign that the police waged, as this scorecard attests:

1967

February 27th: Sussex police raid Keith's house and find "various substances of a suspicious nature." Among those present are Jagger and Marianne Faithfull. Keith and Mick arrested.

May 10th: Mick and Keith in court to answer drug charges. Bail set at one hundred pounds. On the same day, Brian Jones arrested for unlawful possession of cocaine, Methedrine, cannabis resin. He posts two hundred fifty pounds bail in Magistrates Court on May 11th.

June 27th–29th: Mick and Keith tried on drug charges. Mick spends two nights in Lewes Prison, Keith out on bail. Mick found guilty of illegal possession of four pep pills found in his jacket at Keith's house party. Fined one hundred pounds and sentenced to three months in jail. Keith found guilty of permitting his house to be used for the smoking of Indian hemp, fined five hundred pounds, sentenced to one year in jail. Bail for Mick and Keith set at seven thousand pounds each.

July 31st: London Appeal Court. Keith Richards conviction quashed. Mick Jagger given conditional discharge with one year probation.

October 30th: Brian pleads guilty to smoking cannabis. Judge Seaton sentences Brian to nine months on occupation of premises on which cannabis was smoked, and three months on possession of it, sentences to run concurrently. Brian remanded to Wormwood Scrubs prison. Bail denied.

October 31st: James Comyn, QC, and Brian's psychiatrist, Dr. Leonard Henry, appear before a High Court judge to plead for bail on medical grounds. Bail granted: Seven hundred fifty pounds sureties and Brian must agree to see a court-appointed psychiatrist.

December 12th: Brian's sentence set aside. Fined one thousand pounds and three years probation.

1968

May 21st: Brian arrested and charged with possessing cannabis. Appeared at Great Marlborough Street Magistrates Court, bailed for two thousand pounds.

June 11th: Brian committed for trial at Inner Court Sessions.

September 26th: Brian fined fifty pounds with one hundred five pounds costs at Inner Court Sessions, after being found guilty of unauthorized possession of cannabis.

1969

January 13th: Brian's appeal denied.

May 28th: Mick and Marianne Faithfull arrested for possession of hashish. Released on fifty pounds bail.

July 8th: Marianne found in drug-induced coma.

July 18th: Marianne Faithfull enters Bexley Hospital for heroin treatment.

December 19th: Mick fined two hundred pounds plus costs for being found in possession of cannabis resin. Marianne acquitted.

Marianne Faithfull

I REMEMBER JOHN Lennon saying, "I can't believe that I'm so important that they would go to all this trouble to do this to me, to tap my phone, to follow me, I feel I'm going crazy, because I know that this is happening. Or I think I know." But nobody really believed him, and he nearly went insane.

There's no doubt in my mind that our group was set up for the same reason. All that persecution. The fact that every time any of us were in a car we were stopped and searched. There was one occasion Jagger was stopped and he said, "You're not going to search the car until I get my lawyer," and the cop said, "I'll get you next time." Another time, one of our many, many busts, the cops very obviously planted something during their search. Mick set the guy up—the detective, whoever he was—to pay him off, and filmed the payoff with a hidden camera. Needless to say, all charges against Mick were immediately dropped.

But all that persecution takes something vital out of an artist. I believe that's why the Rolling Stones, artistically, did not live up to their early promise. They lost it. They gave in, very much so. I think that drug persecution also did in Lennon, but I think if he had lived, he'd have got over it and would've really started to write much more important work. With Mick, it was just the reverse.

We were in bed one Sunday, reading the newspapers, when Mick exploded at a piece in that rag, *News of the World,* that was headlined, "Investigations into Pop Stars and Drugs." What followed was a description of a place where LSD orgies took place with Mick as a participant. At that point Mick had never touched LSD, but this kind of fabrication was nothing new where *News of the World* was concerned. They had made the mistake of confusing Mick with Brian and of further confusing hash with LSD. Mick was steamed, and when he appeared on a TV talk show that evening, he announced that he was going to sue the *News* for libel.

The *News* is the most combative and underhanded paper in Britain, and when Mick and I heard certain peculiar noises when we used the phone, Mick suspected that we had been bugged. We also noticed that a blue and white van was rather permanently parked near our house, so we figured we were being both watched and listened in on.

We tried to be careful about what we said and where we went, but we made one stupid mistake that was to cost us dearly. At some point Keith phoned to invite us down to his Redlands house for a weekend party. One of the guests, Keith said, would be a man named David Schneidermann, whom we had all recently met and who was a fantastic drug supplier. He was a Californian who dressed in proper suit and tie and carried a leather attaché case in which he had almost every kind of drug you could think of, including several types of LSD, one of them a brand called "Sunshine" that was very popular at that time. There were several old friends at Keith's house when we got there—the art dealer Robert Fraser, Christopher Gibbs, an antique dealer, the Beatle George Harrison and his wife, the photographer Michael Cooper—plus Schneidermann, Fraser's Moroccan servant, and a man named Nicky Cramer who was a prominent member of the King's Road jet set.

On the Saturday morning of that weekend, Schneidermann had come to our rooms and distributed Sunshine to all of us. It was Mick's first trip ever—I guess curiosity finally got the better of him. By afternoon we all began to emerge from our rooms, floating on our LSD trips. We drove around the countryside in the afternoon, returned to the house in the early evening. George Harrison and his wife went home, which reduced the group to the eight men and me. I took a bath, but since my clothes were rather wrinkled and soiled from our afternoon excursion, I took a large fur cover off our bed and wrapped myself in that. I joined the men in the living room where they were watching television.

It was around eight o'clock when I heard Keith say, "Look there at the window—some old girl peeking in—probably hunting autographs." As he said it, there was a loud banging on the door.

◻ ◻ ◻

"It just so happened," Keith Richards recounted, "that we had all taken acid and were in a completely freaked-out state when the police arrived. There was a big knock at the door. Eight o'clock. Everybody was just sort of gliding down slowly from the whole day of sort of freaking about. Everyone had managed to find their way back to the house. TV was on with the sound off and the record player was on. Strobe lights were flickering. Marianne Faithfull had just decided that she wanted a bath and had wrapped herself up in a rug and was watching the box.

"Bang, bang, bang—this big knock at the door and I went to answer it. Oh, look, there's lots of little ladies and gentlemen outside . . . He says, Read this, and I'm going whaa, whaa? All right.

"There was this other pusher there who I really didn't know. He'd come with some other people and was sitting there with a big bag of hash. They even let him go, out of the country. He wasn't what they were looking for.

"When it came down to it, they couldn't pin anything at all on us. All they could pin on me was allowing people to smoke on my premises. It wasn't my shit. All they could pin on Mick was these four amphetamine tablets that he'd bought in Italy across the counter. It really backfired on them because they didn't get enough on us. They had more on the people who were with us, who they weren't interested in. There were lots of people there they didn't even bring up on charges.

"But we were just gliding off from a twelve-hour trip. You know how that freaks people out when they walk in on you. The vibes are so funny for them. I told one of the women with them who they brought to search the ladies, 'Would you mind stepping off that Moroccan cushion, because you're ruining the tapestries.' We were playing it like that. They tried to get us to turn the record player off and we said, 'No, we won't turn it off but we'll turn it down.' As they went, as they started going out the door, somebody put on 'Rainy Day Women' really loud: 'Everybody must get stoned.' And that was it."

Marianne Faithfull

THROUGH MY ACID haze, I remember being amazed at the number of policemen who were crowding into the room. Eighteen or nineteen of them, three of them policewomen, who I guess had come to search me. Actually, if Patti

233

Harrison had stayed and Anita Pallenberg had been there—she canceled out at the last minute—there would have been three of us—so the police had been tipped off accurately.

The whole raid, we believed, was a setup triggered by *News of the World,* who later admitted that they had given information to the cops about us—where we were, how many of us, all that stuff. We suspected they had picked up the information on a phone bug and surveillance. We also believed information was supplied by that fink, Schneidermann, who, despite having an attaché case chockablock with drugs, was not searched. When a cop asked to see the contents of his case, Schneidermann said it was full of exposed film and couldn't be opened and the cop let it go at that. Also, Schneidermann mysteriously disappeared that very evening, never to be seen again.

□ □ □

"What usually happens is that someone gets busted, the papers have it the next day," Keith Richards said. "For a week the police held it back to see how much bread they could get off us. Nothing was said for a week. They wanted to see. Unfortunately none of us knew what to do, who to bum the bread to, and so it went via slightly the wrong people and it didn't get up all the way.

"Eventually after a couple of weeks the papers said the Rolling Stones have been raided for possession. The first court thing didn't come up for three months. Just a straight hearing. That was cool. The heavy trial came in June, about five months after. It was really starting to wear us out by then. The lawyers were saying, 'It seems really weird, they want to really do it to you.'

"In the States you know the cops are bent and if you want to get into it, okay, you can go to them and say, 'How much do you want?' and they'll drop it. In England you can drop fifty grand and the next week they'll still bust you and say, 'Oh, it went to the wrong hands. I'm sorry. It didn't get to the right man.' It's insane."

Ian Stewart

THREE DAYS AFTER the Redlands bust hit the papers, our new LP, *Between the Buttons,* passed the million-dollar sales mark and brought us a sixth consecutive gold disc from the Recording Industry Association of America. Considering what we were bringing into the treasury of Great Britain, you'd think they'd be toasting us instead of running our balls through the wringer.

□ □ □

To handle their defense, Mick and Keith chose Michael Havers, a barrister who was highly experienced in both the prosecution and defense of criminal cases. Since the 1960s, Havers has risen to the top of his profession; in successive Conservative administrations he was Attorney General and Lord Chancellor.

Lord Michael Havers

WHEN MICK FIRST came to see me, I was impressed with his intelligence—he was an A level at the London School of Economics—and his personal charm. He spoke in two tongues—a quite proper London accent and a Cockney put-on, which he used interchangeably. I told him to restrict himself to his London accent on the witness stand. I thought the prosecution had a very weak case against him, with just a few airsick pills at issue, and I told him that I didn't think there was a chance in hell he'd be convicted. I didn't know that Keith, Mick and the others were all on acid that day, but neither did the police, so that was an element never introduced at the trial.

I did tell Mick that once in the courtroom he would have to disregard everyone but me, never to guess at an answer but to say that he didn't know or that he forgot, because if you guess, I told him, you'll always guess wrong. It seemed to me that Mick would get off because the police had thoroughly searched the place and found no incriminating evidence at all, that the shadowy character, Schneidermann, was an obvious plant, and that, as evidence, the four amphetamine pills were just too flimsy to merit serious consideration.

One of the peculiar aspects of the case, widely reported in the press, was the infamous Mars Bar rumor. When the police entered the living room, so the rumor went, they found that the woman on the couch had a Mars Bar protruding from an intimate place in her anatomy. At no point in the trial was there any men-

235

tion of the scandalous Mars Bar but nevertheless the tabloids continued to refer to the proceedings as the Mars Bar trial, replete with rather graphic references to what occurred.

I actually went round to the house with my wife to have a look, and she pointed out several Mars Bars on top of a bookcase but that's all there was to it, some Mars Bars on top of a bookcase plus the vivid imagination of some tabloid writers.

□ □ □

On June 27, 1967, Mick and Keith were brought to trial at the West Sussex Quarter Sessions with Judge Leslie Block presiding; the prosecutor, Malcolm Morris; for the defense, Michael Havers.

POLICE SERGEANT JOHN CHALLEN: I first went into the drawing room and then went upstairs to a bedroom. There I found a green jacket in the left-hand pocket of which I found a small phial containing four tablets. I took the jacket downstairs and Jagger admitted the jacket belonged to him. He said the tablets also belonged to him and that his doctor prescribed them. I asked Jagger who his doctor was, and Jagger replied, "Dr. Dixon-Firth." I asked what the tablets were for, and Jagger replied, "To stay awake and work."

PROSECUTOR MALCOLM MORRIS: Did you ask Jagger about these drugs?

DR. DIXON-FIRTH: He said they had been given to him by a friend and that he needed something to get him through the following day.

JUDGE BLOCK: Did you gather he was in possession of these pills?

DR. DIXON-FIRTH: Yes, sir.

JUDGE BLOCK: Did you ask to look at them?

DR. DIXON-FIRTH: No.

MR. MORRIS: A doctor must know what he is prescribing. He must know the effects of what he is prescribing. You didn't know at all what you were prescribing.

DR. DIXON-FIRTH: I knew they were pep pills. I did not know the precise formula.

MR. MORRIS: Are you really saying that if a patient came to you, as Mr. Jagger did, and said, "I have some pep pills," you would say, "All right, you can take them if you need them but not too many."

DR. DIXON-FIRTH: Yes, providing I was satisfied after discussion that they were appropriate for him.

MR. MORRIS: How can you know? You were not there.

DR. DIXON-FIRTH: Because I know what pep pills contain normally.

MR. MORRIS: A hard drug may be described as a pep pill?

DR. DIXON-FIRTH: I would not describe it as a pep pill.

MR. MORRIS: Now you know the constituency of this, would you still call it a pep pill?

DR. DIXON-FIRTH: Yes.

JUDGE BLOCK (to the jury): I have ruled in law that these remarks cannot be regarded as a prescription by a duly authorized medical practitioner and it therefore follows that the defense open to Mr. Jagger is not available to him.

I therefore direct you that there is no defense to this charge.

Lord Michael Havers

THAT WAS A vicious summation, tantamount to telling the jury to convict, despite the evidence and despite the principle that a man is innocent until *proven* guilty. Of course, it only took the jury five minutes to bring in their verdict that Mick was guilty. I was totally unprepared for such a verdict, and unfortunately I had not drawn up papers for an immediate appeal. I did request bail but was refused and the judge remanded Mick to prison. He was handcuffed and put in a police van with a group of other criminals and taken to Lewes Prison, where he was fingerprinted, processed, given prison clothes and put in a cell.

Judge Block was an old retired naval officer, dead now, who shared the prejudice most adults had against the Stones, hatred really. Also, West Sussex was a posh community, a chichi place that resented the fact that one of the Stones had a house there. Would bring down property values, you know?

The following day, Keith came to the same court for his trial, to face charges that he had allowed guests to smoke cannabis resin on the premises at Redlands. Mick, in handcuffs, was brought back to the courtroom to wait for his sentencing. After what had happened to Jagger, I no longer took it for granted that, despite the preposterousness of the case against him, Richards would escape punishment. I could only hope that by attacking the flimsiness of the incriminating evidence I might deter Judge Block from again charging the jury in such a prejudicial manner as to virtually dictate a sentence of guilty.

□ □ □

PROCEEDINGS AT WEST SUSSEX QUARTER SESSIONS, JUDGE LESLIE BLOCK PRESIDING. JUNE 28, 1967

PROSECUTOR MALCOLM MORRIS (to the jury): The police went into the drawing room of Keith Richards's house where loud strains of pop music came from the radio. The television was turned on but whether anyone was watching it at that time was not clear.

In the room were eight young men and one young woman. The settee in the drawing room was the main piece of furniture and there was a stone table. On the table was a tin marked "incense" and incense was what the tin contained. Also on the table was a briar pipe bowl, which was taken away, carefully preserved, and the contents analyzed and found to contain traces of cannabis resin.

On that same table a woman detective constable noticed some ash. This she carefully scraped off and put into a small transparent bag. Analysis showed that this, too, contained cannabis resin.

In one of the bedrooms on the first floor, a Detective Sergeant found a pudding basin containing three cigarette ends and a quantity of what appeared to be cigarette ash. Analysis showed this to contain cannabis resin.

Also in the drawing room was a man who is not before the Court and indeed is not now in the country.

You are not concerned with the names or identity of anyone at that party other than Keith Richards. The case is a charge against him and not anyone else. The man referred to was named Mr. X, and in his right-hand breast pocket was found a tin containing two pieces of brown substance shown on analysis to contain sixty-six grams of cannabis resin. In an envelope in another pocket was found a quantity of herbal cannabis resin, untreated cannabis resin. In the drawing room where Richards was entertaining his guests, there was a strong sweet smell, which no one could fail to notice.

In the submission of the Crown, you cannot have any doubt at all that Keith Richards was permitting his house to be used for the purpose of smoking cannabis resin.

You will hear from Detective Inspector Lynch, of the Drug Squad of Scotland Yard, who has taken part in raids on many premises where cannabis resin was being smoked and who is familiar with its effects. He will tell you about the unusual smell it produces and of its effect of tranquility and happiness and how it tends to dispel inhibitions.

It seems, you may think, it may have had exactly that effect upon one of Richards's guests.

This was the young lady on the settee. All she was wearing was a light-colored fur-skin rug, which from time to time she allowed to fall, disclosing her nude body. She was unperturbed and apparently enjoying the situation.

How people behave in their own house is usually no concern of anyone else. The only significance of that young woman's behavior is when the police arrived she remained unperturbed and apparently enjoying the situation.

Although she was taken upstairs where her clothes were, to be searched, she returned downstairs afterwards still wearing only that fur rug—and, in the words of the woman detective constable looking after her, in "merry mood and one apparently of vague unconcern."

It is obviously important in a case like this that you should not jump to conclusions or allow unusual behavior to prejudice you against Keith Richards.

We are not in any way concerned with who that young woman was or may have been, but was she someone who had lost her inhibitions? And had she lost them because she had been smoking Indian hemp?

There were no glasses containing alcohol in the drawing room, and you may think in any event that this is something which Richards could not fail to see and appreciate.

You may conclude that the reason why he was not surprised at her behavior was that cannabis resin was being smoked then and there on his premises.

DEFENSE COUNSEL MICHAEL HAVERS (to the jury): It is one of the sad things about any case which attracts public attention— whether it is a murder, fraud, action civil or criminal, or as now a case involving a well-known pop group—one of the unhappy accidents with the nature of the crime is that interest mounts and mounts, and in the end rumor overtakes reality and there is a risk that prejudice creeps in.

On February 12, sometime before three o'clock, a well-known national newspaper gave information which led to this raid.

The house belongs to Keith Richards, who bought it a comparatively short time before. In passing, he had told some friends: "Come down and see my new house." They gathered at Redlands at about midnight on Saturday night. Included in the party was a man called Schneidermann, a man virtually unknown to Keith Richards. They had met in New York the previous year. How he got there and who brought him down was something no one may know. But Schneidermann was there, with all the trappings and kit of someone interested in drugs.

Let me tell you the background.

On February 5, a week before, the newspaper published— not in relation to Mr. Richards, but to Mick Jagger—an article, which if untrue was a grave and disgusting libel. The consequence of that was that immediately, on behalf of Mr. Jagger, a writ was issued by his solicitor and served upon the *News of the World*.

In the remaining five days this man was subjected to being followed and observed wherever he went or whatever he did. A van or car was constantly outside his flat.

And within a week, this well-known national newspaper tips off the police to go to West Wittering—not just for anything, but for drugs. We know it was for drugs because the warrant was issued for drugs.

If a newspaper publishes a story and it is found to be untrue, how many thousands of pounds would a jury like you award?

It may be coincidence because a well-known national newspaper publishes this libel on Mick Jagger and the same well-known newspaper tips off the police the following week.

In that party was a man not known to the Rolling Stones as a group, conveniently from across the seas and loaded to the gunwales with cannabis.

Schneidermann is the only man on whom was found any cannabis. He has gone out of England—with a return ticket in his pocket.

What had to be proved by the Crown is that Richards knew and permitted someone else to smoke cannabis in his house.

You have heard about a naked girl and a strong, unusual smell. A strong, sweet smell is the opposite to the smell of cannabis. If the place was drowned in this smell, and this girl was in this euphoric state, you would expect people to be rushing around getting rid of the traces. But a policewoman looked through the window and she would have seen them because she had a grandstand view. But nothing of the sort happened. Was the girl's behavior such that you could draw from the evidence that she had been smoking cannabis?

Had any of them stopped to think whether this was fair to the girl? She was not on trial or able to make a defense.

She was a girl who remained technically anonymous, but the consequence of this was that she is described as a drug-taking nymphomaniac, with no chance of saying a word in her own defense or of cross-examining anybody.

I am not going to allow this girl into the witness box. I am not going to tear that blanket of anonymity aside and let the world laugh or scorn as they will.

Keith Richards now took the stand to testify in his own defense.

PROSECUTOR MORRIS: Is it your defense that Schneidermann had been planted in your weekend party as part of a wicked conspiracy by the *News of the World*? Is that any part of your defense or not?

RICHARDS: Yes, it is, sir.

MR. MORRIS: Is your defense that Schneidermann was planted by the *News of the World* in an attempt to get Mick Jagger convicted of smoking hashish? Is that the suggestion?

RICHARDS: That is the suggestion.

MR. MORRIS: What you are saying is that because the *News of the World* did not want to pay libel damages to Mick Jagger, which they might have to do if what they had printed about him was untrue, they had planted or arranged to have planted Indian hemp in your house?

RICHARDS: Yes, sir.

MR. MORRIS: This misfired and the only result of that criminal conspiracy is that you are in the dock?

RICHARDS: Yes, sir.

MR. MORRIS: Are you quite clear of what you are saying?

RICHARDS: Yes.

MR. MORRIS: This party was mainly of your personal friends?

RICHARDS: I can only say that in my profession there are people who are hangers-on who you have to tolerate. On this occasion, there were two or three people I did not know particularly well, but did know well enough to allow them to come down.

MR. MORRIS: Can you say anything about these hangers-on?

RICHARDS: Two were hangers-on, one of them Schneidermann.

MR. MORRIS: How did Schneidermann come to be in the party?

242

RICHARDS: He knew one of the other friends. As far as I can gather, he knew a party was going on and he asked if it would be all right to go along. I had seen Schneidermann over a year ago in New York and once since in a club in London the previous week.

MR. MORRIS: From what was found on him it is clear he smoked Indian hemp?

RICHARDS: Most definitely.

MR. MORRIS: Did you know that then?

RICHARDS: Not at the time, sir. None of my friends there smoked hemp to my knowledge.

MR. MORRIS: It would have been possible for Schneidermann to plant Indian hemp if he had so wanted?

RICHARDS: Yes.

MR. MORRIS: In particular, if he had been injected into your weekend party for the purpose of incriminating Mr. Jagger, he could have put anything else into Mr. Jagger's clothing or anything else?

RICHARDS: Yes, sir.

MR. MORRIS: Nothing was found in Mr. Jagger's clothing?

RICHARDS: No, sir.

MR. MORRIS: So if you are seriously suggesting that this was part of a plot, it is a curious plot in that nothing in fact was done to associate Mr. Jagger with Indian hemp.

RICHARDS: He was associated with the whole raid, which is enough, I am sure.

MR. MORRIS: There was, as we know, a young woman sitting on a settee wearing only a rug. Would you agree, in the ordinary course of events, you would expect a young woman to be embarrassed if she had nothing on but a rug in the presence of eight men, two of whom were hangers-on and the third a Moroccan servant?

RICHARDS: Not at all.

MR. MORRIS: You regard that, do you, as quite normal?

RICHARDS: We are not old men. We are not worried about petty morals.

MR. MORRIS: After she had gone upstairs with a woman police officer, did it come as a great surprise to you that she was prepared to go downstairs again into the drawing room still wearing only a rug, where there were about a dozen police officers?

RICHARDS: No, sir. After all she had taken off her dirty clothes she had been wearing all day. The rug she was wearing was big enough to cover three women. The girl did not embarrass easily.

MR. MORRIS: You do not think it was because she had been smoking Indian hemp and had got rid of her inhibitions and embarrassment?

RICHARDS: No, sir.

MR. MORRIS: You were all just sitting around the drawing room doing nothing in particular?

RICHARDS: Yes, sir.

MR. MORRIS: Was anyone smoking hashish or hemp?

RICHARDS: Not to my knowledge.

MR. MORRIS: Would you have objected to anyone smoking Indian hemp?

RICHARDS: Yes, because I knew that if the police came I would be standing here—and I am.

JUDGE BLOCK (TO THE JURY): Put out of your minds any prejudice you might feel about the way Richards dressed or about his observations on petty morals. You are trying a man well-known in the entertainment world and inevitably in such circumstances an enormous amount of publicity has been given to the proceedings.

The issue you have to try is a comparatively simple one. You have to be satisfied that cannabis resin was being smoked in the house when the police went there, and you have to be satisfied that Richards knew of it.

You should exclude from your minds everything you have read in the newspapers about two of the house party admitting or being convicted of being in possession of certain drugs.

Finally, disregard the evidence as to the lady who was alleged by the police to be in some condition of undress, and do not let that prejudice your minds in any way.

The jury deliberated for an hour and came back with a verdict of guilty.

Mick and Keith were brought before the judge. The expectation was that Keith's sentence would be a fine and probation, but the judge gave him a year's imprisonment and a fine of five hundred pounds.

Now it was Mick's turn, and his sentence was three months in prison and one hundred pounds costs.

Marianne Faithfull

I WAS STUNNED, in fact I didn't quite grasp the impact of the judge's penalties. Mick and I looked at each other as the bailiff handcuffed him and led him away. There were tears down his face, as there were down mine. Mick was taken to Brixton Prison, and Keith, handcuffed to Robert Fraser who had been given a six months jail term, was led off to Wormwood Scrubs.

□ □ □

"Now Wormwood Scrubs is a hundred and fifty years old," Keith has said, speaking of his incarceration. "I wouldn't even want to play there, much less live there. They take me inside. They don't give you a knife and fork, they give you a spoon with very blunt edges so you can't do yourself in. They don't give you a belt, in case you hang yourself. It's that bad in there.

"They give you a little piece of paper and a pencil. Both Robert and I, the first thing we did is sit down and write. 'Dear Mum, don't worry, I'm in here and someone's working to get me out, da-da-da.' Then you're given your cell. And they start knocking on the bars at six in the morning to wake you up. All the other prisoners started dropping bits of tobacco through for me, cause in any jail tobacco is the currency. Some of them were really great. Some of them were in for life. Shoving papers under the floor to roll it up with. The first thing you do automatically when you wake up is drag the chair to the window and look up to see what you can see out of the window. It's an automatic reaction. That one little square of sky, trying to reach it. It's amazing. I was going to have to make these little Christmas trees that go on cakes. And sewing up mailbags.

"Then there's the hour walk when you have to keep moving round in a courtyard. Cats coming up behind me, it's amazing, they can talk without moving their mouths, 'Want some hash? Want some acid?' Take acid? In here?

"Most of the prisoners were really great. 'What you doin' in here? Bastards. They just wanted to get you.' They filled me in. 'They been waitin' for you in here for ages,' they said. So I said, 'I ain't gonna be in here very long, baby, don't worry about that.'

"And that afternoon, they had the radio playing, this fucking Stones record comes on. And the whole prison started, 'Rayyy!' Going like mad. Banging on the bars. They knew I was in and they wanted to let me know.

"They took all the new prisoners to have their photographs taken sitting on a swivel stool, looked like an execution chamber. Really hard. Face and profile. Those are the sort of things they'll do automatically if they pick you up in America, you get finger dabs and photographs. In England it's a much heavier scene. You don't get photographed and fingerprinted until you've been convicted.

"Then they take you down to the padre and the chapel and the library, you're allowed one book and they show you where you're going to work and that's it. That afternoon I'm lying in my cell, wondering what the fuck was going on and suddenly someone yelled, 'You're out, man, you're out. It's just been on the news.' So I started kicking the shit out of the door. I said, 'You let me out, you bastards, I got bail.'"

Marianne Faithfull

I VISITED MICK at Brixton Prison the morning after his imprisonment. He was terribly frightened and very, very upset, in fact, freaked out. Of course, I wasn't surprised. Although I wasn't in jail, I knew how he felt, because it really was like the whole of the establishment was out to get us. The sentence imposed on Mick was terribly unjust and for what? Four amphetamine tablets. That's what he was busted for. To sentence him to prison for such possession was incredibly harsh and absolutely unjust. Nobody expected that, and it made him feel very desperate—and me too. I also felt a terrible guilt because he was really sacrificing himself for me since those were my amphetamine tablets. I don't think he had any inkling when he took the blame that it would turn out as bad as it did. I don't think he ever expected to wind up in jail. So when I went to see him in jail, he sat with me and I held him and he wept in his frustration—he was really, really freaked out. But I think that was a great thing for him, to be able to let go like that, to rebut his whole attitude of staying cool no matter what. This was a real feeling, and he was showing it, crying, and why the hell shouldn't he?

Jagger's conviction set off a fire storm of approval and disapproval, and it thrust Mick into a controversial role that made him a symbol, on the one hand, of how his generation was in the grasp of drugs, and on the other hand, a symbol of how young people were being unfairly persecuted by hidebound authorities. With this arrest and conviction, Mick's name became the rallying cry for the youth of the sixties—the Jagger Generation, it began to be called—and over the ensuing months and years, as the authorities continued their assault on Mick and the Stones and their girl friends, the Stones were infused with an aura of martyrdom.

Even the staid and conservative London *Times* abandoned its usual endorsement of righteousness and came out in Jagger's defense with an editorial by its chief editor, William Rees-Mogg, entitled: "Who Breaks a Butterfly on a Wheel?"

Mr. Jagger has been sentenced to imprisonment for three months. He is appealing against conviction and sentence, and has been granted bail until the hearing of the appeal later in the year. In the meantime, the sentence of imprisonment is bound to be widely discussed by the public. And the circumstances are sufficiently unusual to warrant such discussion in the public interest.

Mr. Jagger was charged with being in possession of four tablets containing amphetamine sulphate and methyl amphetamine hydrochloride; these tablets had been bought, perfectly legally, in

Italy, and brought back to this country. They are not a highly dangerous drug, or in proper dosage a dangerous drug at all. They are of the benzedrine type and the Italian manufacturers recommend them both as a stimulant and as a remedy for travel sickness.

In Britain it is an offence to possess these drugs without a doctor's prescription. Mr. Jagger's doctor says that he knew and had authorised their use, but he did not give a prescription for them as indeed they had already been purchased. His evidence was not challenged. This was therefore an offence of a technical character, which before this case drew the point to public attention any honest man might have been liable to commit.

If after his visit to the Pope, the Archbishop of Canterbury had bought proprietary airsickness pills in Rome airport, and imported the unused tablets into Britain on his return, he would have risked committing precisely the same offence. No one who has ever travelled and bought proprietary drugs abroad can be sure that he has not broken the law.

Judge Block directed the jury that the approval of a doctor was not a defence in law to the charge of possessing drugs without a prescription, and the jury convicted. Mr. Jagger was not charged with complicity in any other drug offence that occurred in the same house.

They were separate cases, and no evidence was produced to suggest that he knew Mr. Fraser had heroin tablets or that the vanishing Mr. Sneidermann [sic] had cannabis resin. It is indeed no offence to be in the same building or the same company as people possessing or even using drugs, nor could it reasonably be made an offence.

In any case Mr. Jagger's career is obviously one that does involve great personal strain and exhaustion; his doctor says that he approved the occasional use of these drugs, and it seems likely that similar drugs would have been prescribed if there was a need for them. Millions of similar drugs are prescribed in Britain every year, and for a variety of conditions.

One has to ask, therefore, how it is that this technical offence, divorced as it must be from other people's offences, was thought to deserve the penalty of imprisonment. In the courts at large it is most uncommon for imprisonment to be imposed on first offenders where the drugs are not major drugs of addiction and there is no question of drug traffic.

The normal penalty is probation, and the purpose of probation is to encourage the offender to develop his career and to avoid the drug risks in the future. It is surprising therefore that Judge Block should have decided to sentence Mr. Jagger to imprisonment and particularly surprising as Mr. Jagger's is about as mild a drug case as can ever have been brought before the Courts.

It would be wrong to speculate on the Judge's reasons, which we do not know. It is, however, possible to consider the public reaction. There are many people who take a primitive view of the matter, what one might call a pre-legal view of the matter. They consider that Mr. Jagger has 'got what was coming to him.' They resent the anarchic quality of the Rolling Stones' performance, dislike their songs, dislike their influence on teen-agers and broadly suspect them of decadence, a word used by Miss Monica Furlong in the *Daily Mail.*

As a sociological concern this may be reasonable enough, and at an emotional level it is very understandable, but it has nothing to do with the case. One has to ask a different question: has Mr. Jagger received the same treatment as he would have received if he had not been a famous figure, with all the criticism and resentment his celebrity has aroused? If a promising undergraduate had come back from a summer visit to Italy with four pep pills in his pocket would it have been thought right to ruin his career by sending him to prison for three months? Would it also have been thought necessary to display him handcuffed to the public?

If we are going to make any case a symbol of the conflict between the sound traditional values of Britain and the new hedonism, then we must be sure that the sound traditional values include those of tolerance and equity.

It should be the particular quality of British justice to ensure that Mr. Jagger is treated exactly the same as anyone else, no better and no worse.

There must remain a suspicion in this case that Mr. Jagger received a more severe sentence than would have been thought proper for any purely anonymous young man.

Marianne Faithfull

TO ME, THE whole thing about the court case and the bust and Mick being in prison never seemed real. I felt that it was only a temporary thing. And then that editorial came out in the *Times* by Rees-Mogg which changed the whole thing around. I must confess that I wasn't surprised. I had expected it, somehow. But on the other hand, I wasn't the one in prison. I wasn't going through it. But I knew it wasn't a game when we got busted, when we realized what had happened. The newspaper tapping the phones, and all that stuff. But I always felt an incredible sort of optimism. I felt also that the establishment was made up of people in institutions who were much older and tireder than we were. And I also felt how stupid it was what they were trying to do. To try and stop something so big, something all over Britain, by putting these two guys in jail for something so inconsequential. I knew what it was, it was definitely ridiculous victimization. It did look bad for a while, but I always felt it would be overturned somehow. But it must have frightened Mick a lot, I know. The irony was that Mick had never been into drugs very much. And this was just a planned trip to the country to Keith's house to take LSD, and we were so naive that it didn't occur to us we were being set up. We were like children, obviously. And the guy there, called David Schneidermann, who had this briefcase full of drugs which they didn't search or look at—he must have been part of the setup. Or else, why didn't the cops open up his briefcase? And afterwards, he mysteriously disappeared, never to be heard from again. Not even at the trial. No arrest. Nothing. Gone with the wind.

☐ ☐ ☐

Mick and Keith were both let out on seven thousand pounds bail pending their appeal.

Lord Michael Havers

THE PROSECUTING ATTORNEY called me in and told me that filing an appeal would be a waste of time and money because the appellate court never overturned criminal convictions of this nature, but I went ahead anyway. It was imperative that I get those convictions overturned or else Mick and Keith, with drug convictions on their records, would not be able to enter the United States to perform their concerts.

The appeals took two weeks or so to be heard and Mick's anxiety during this period was intense. I tried to allay his fears all I could, but as the prosecuting attorney had said, overturning drug convictions was very difficult.

On the appointed day, Mick arrived at the austere Appeals

Court in a dark suit with proper shirt and tie, but Keith had contracted chicken pox and was unable to attend. The spectators' gallery was chock-full of young squealing girls, all there to catch sight of Mick. Before the judges appeared, the bailiff announced that the court would not convene unless there was order in the gallery. But the girls continued to serenade Mick with their chorus of chirps, gasps, squeals and God knows what. "Mick," I said, "what can we do?" "Leave it to me, Uncle Mike," he replied, whereupon he stood up, faced the gallery and raised his arms in a quieting gesture, like Moses parting the waters. The girls immediately fell silent, allowing the judges to enter.

Although the conviction was upheld, the Chief Justice indicated they found it preposterous to convict Jagger on the basis of four pep pills and ruled that three months was excessive. Mick was given a one-year conditional discharge.

Then, consulting my appellate brief and the trial record, the Chief Justice said there was no evidence that Keith Richards knew that cannabis was being used or permitted it to be used on his premises. The judge also pointed out that the prosecutor couldn't even get the odor correct, one witness saying it was a sweet smell, and another that it was acrid. The judge then summarily quashed Keith's conviction and set him free.

The girls could no longer restrain themselves and burst out with spontaneous approval, prompting Mick to stand up, unbutton his proper jacket, thereby revealing that on the lower portion of his necktie, previously unseen, was a large painted figure of a naked lady.

□ □ □

"Why did they want to throw me and Mick in jail?" Keith Richards has said. "First they don't like young kids with a lot of money. But as long as you don't bother them, that's cool. But we bothered them because of the way we looked, the way we'd act. Because we never showed any reverence for them whatsoever. Whereas the Beatles had. They'd gone along with it so far, with the MBEs and shaking hands. Whenever we were asked about things like that we'd say, 'Fuck it. Don't want to know about things like that. Bollocks. Don't need it.' That riled 'em somewhat.

"But when our cases got up to the Appeals Court, they just threw it out in ten minutes. That trial judge had just blown it. I mean, he said things to me while I was up there that if I'd caught him by himself I'd have wrung his neck. When he gave me the year sentence he called me 'scum' and 'filth,' and 'People like this shouldn't be. . . .' "

"That's what got us off," Jagger said at the time, "Judge Block calling Keith and me 'scum' and 'filth'—he really blew it. Got thrown out of his club, the Garrick Club, a London club for barristers. They invited me to join. I may, too. They have very nice lunches. It's a very cool place. Anyway, they threw him out of the Garrick Club. I don't know whether you know what that means, but for them that's quite a bad scene. It's a very heavy number. For those people to be thrown out of their club—that their fathers belonged to, and it goes back and back—it's really a very heavy number, because in England 'my club' is a whole social thing, like being in the Roman Catholic Church and being excommunicated.

"But the harassment took its toll on Brian, it really did. He was just too sensitive. Some people might say too weak, but I mean he wasn't a criminal. Here was a guy, he was just a fucking musician, man—you've got to be tough to be a criminal. If you choose to be a criminal, you've got to rob people, pick pockets, you gotta be tough, take what's coming to you and all that. This guy's a musician and he just wants to get on playing his music and he's being harassed all the time and he just can't take it. And that's it, man.

"It just made me understand what people are like. Actually, I'd never thought about it until then. Before, I'd always believed that the police were nice and helpful, but now I know. It really opened my eyes and now I know exactly what they're like. You grow up and learn.

"I came quite close to doing six months, and a friend actually did six months. It was all so disgraceful and very stupid and so English. It brought Brian down. Granted, he made a lot of wrong moves. But Brian wasn't doing anyone any harm. He was followed all the time, but then we all were. It was a systematic campaign of harassment. The thing is they destroyed Brian in the process.

"I don't know what I feel about the busts. It's very difficult to put into perspective because I'm still being harassed. They were really nasty and mean. I mean all that—handcuffs—on four pep pill charges. It's just daft. The more I think about it—I hardly ever do—but it was just so absurd, they tried to blow it up into a whole thing that was like . . . that's the way the establishment works, particularly the police, y'know. I'm not saying the judges, but the police like to make it more than it ever is and is ever gonna be. They don't think they've got anything else going unless they've got the kitchen sink thrown in. Oh God.

"It was about four or five days. That was enough. Enough to put me off wanting to go, I can tell you. It was horrible. It was really weird. A strange existence. You just don't want to get involved if you can avoid it. I remember asking the guard if I could go out for exercise because it was the exercise period. And the guard said, 'You don't want to go out there with all those criminals, do you?' "

Ian Stewart

I VISITED MICK at Brixton Prison and what a sewer that place was! Mick was very grateful that I came to see him. I had never seen him in a state like that—thoroughly cowed, white with fear. I tried to bolster him up, but no use, he was a nervous wreck, his eyes tearing up, hands unsteady.

I can only say thank God that the Court of Appeals wiped out Keith's sentence and put Mick on a year's probation. They were damn fools for fooling around with dope in a group like that and I hoped it would teach them a lesson—especially Keith who was into hard stuff. But unfortunately this experience had no effect at all, and Keith went right on doing dope as he always had. So I knew there'd be a lot more bad news down the line.

But the one I really worried about was Brian. Once the narcs got their boots on the back of his neck, they never let him up. I don't think people realized then how corrupt the narc cops were all through the sixties. There was one detective who made a practice of keeping tabs on Brian and putting the bite on him for a payoff with a threat of collaring him if he didn't pay up. Brian told me about it. The narc always demanded the same amount—one thousand pounds to stay out of the slammer. The guy didn't even search Brian's pad. I guess he would have planted some hash if Brian hadn't come across with the bribe. Three, four times Brian paid him off.

But then Scotland Yard moved in on Brian and there was no payoff that time. This was in May of 1967. A whole narc squad from the Yard came busting in one afternoon when Brian was at home with Stash—Prince Stanislas Klossowski. The narcs found a jar with a dollop of coke in it—Brian never used coke and told them so, but he and Stash were hauled in and booked for possessing hash.

Rather weird that a whole squad from the Yard were laid on for a little bust like this. But you could tell from this what the big boys were up to—make an example of Brian as a way of squelching the rebellious Stones. Brian with all his fears and hang-ups was an easy mark, easy to destroy, and the authorities didn't give a shit about what they were doing to his life.

□ □ □

Brian was already close to the edge before that drug bust, so one can imagine the state he was in while he waited five months for his trial to come up. They had let him out on two hundred fifty pounds bail, but as the days passed, Brian got more and more paranoid about what they were going to do to him. There was no way to calm his fears. The narc raids simply underscored his conviction that everyone was against him, that no one liked him, that he was alone in the world, but not for long—Brian was convinced he was going to die soon, and he often alluded to his imminent death. What kept him from going under was a psychiatrist, Dr. Leonard Henry, whom he went to see quite regularly. He tried to alleviate the extreme stress Brian was under because of the drug arrest and impending trial, but despite Dr. Henry's best efforts, Brian suffered a rather severe nervous breakdown.

Dr. Henry arranged for Brian to get admitted to the Priory Nursing Home for treatment. During his stay there, Brian discussed his problems with the staff psychiatrists: that Mick had taken the band away from his leadership, that Mick and Keith got all the credit for the songs and all the royalties, that Brian felt he had some great music in him that had never been tapped, that the music the band now played rejected the pure R and B that had got them where they were. It was a crushing load that Brian carried on his back.

Chris Jagger

A GROUP OF us went to the courtroom on October 31, 1967, when Brian's case came before the judge. We were there because we knew that what Brian had gone through, his breakdown and all that, he needed a show of support. Brian entered a guilty plea to the charge of having smoked cannabis and having allowed his flat to be used for smoking. We thought he'd get probation but the authorities were determined to make an example of him, and the judge sentenced him severely—nine months in Wormwood Scrubs Prison, Brian to start serving his term immediately. I knew what a terrible dump Wormwood was because Keith had been sent there and described it. It sounded like a medieval dungeon from the days of the Borgias.

There were eight of us in the courtroom, and while they were handcuffing Brian to take him away, we took up a position outside the courthouse and began to chant a protest at Brian's sentence. The police warned us to disperse, we wouldn't, so we were all arrested and carted off, charged with abusive behavior and damaging a police van.

The following day, Brian got sprung on seven hundred fifty pounds bail, pending an appeal that his lawyer, Michael Havers, had filed. Our feeling was that Brian didn't have much chance of winning a reversal because the powers that be wanted to make an example of him. But someone like Brian, as sensitive and ego-frail as he was, nine months in prison was like a death sentence.

Dr. Walter Neustatter, an expert in forensic psychiatry, was appointed by the Court of Appeals to examine Brian and report his findings to the court. Dr. Neustatter had four sessions with Brian and this report was based on those interviews:

Brian Jones's IQ is 133. Intellectual functioning shows assets in his range of general knowledge, abstract reasoning capacity, social awareness and vocabulary. He does not reveal signs of formal thought disorder or psychotic disturbance of thought processes. However, Mr. Jones's thought processes do reveal some weakening of his reality ties as a result of intense free-floating anxiety. He currently tends to feel very threatened by the world about him as a result of his increasingly inadequate control of aggressive instinctual impulses. This repressive control seems to be breaking down and he often resorts to conspicuous denial of the threat created by the breakthrough of these impulses into consciousness. At times he projects these aggressive feelings so that he feels a victim of his environment; at others he introjects them, resulting in significant depressive tendencies and associated suicidal risk. Mr. Jones's sexual problems are closely interrelated to his difficulties of aggression—that is, he experiences very intense anxiety surrounding phallic and sadistic sexuality because of the implicit aggressive strivings. However, these phallic strivings are also in conflict with his gross passive dependency needs. This conflict prevents any mature heterosexual adjustment—indeed, he withdraws from any genuine heterosexual involvement. These sexual difficulties reinforce Mr. Jones's considerable emotional immaturity and effect gross confusion and identification. He vacillates between a passive, dependent child with a confused image of an adult on the one hand, and an idol of pop culture on the other. He is still very involved with Oedipal fixations. He is very confused about the maternal and paternal role in these. Part of his confusion would seem to be the very strong resentment he experiences toward his dominant and controlling mother who rejected him and blatantly favored his sister. In conclusion, it is my considered opinion that Mr. Jones is, at present, in an extremely precarious state of emotional adjustment as a result of his unresolved problems with aggressive impulses and sexual identification. His grasp on reality is fragile because of the debilitating effect of intense anxiety and conflicts surrounding these problems. Much of his anxiety is currently localized onto his potential imprisonment but its underlying sources are more deeply rooted. He thus urgently needs psychotherapy to assist in mustering his considerable personality resources and capacity for insight to contain his anxiety. Otherwise, his prognosis is very poor. Indeed, it is very likely that his imprisonment could precipitate a complete break with reality, a psychotic breakdown and significantly increase the suicidal risk for this man.

At the Court of Appeals hearing, two psychiatrists from the Priory Nursing Home painted a grim picture of what would happen to Brian if he were imprisoned. Their testimony, plus Dr. Neustatter's report, resulted in the Lord Chief Justice's vacating Brian's nine-month prison sentence and replacing it with a fine of one thousand pounds and three years probation. The only Stone who came to the courtroom to lend Brian his support was, surprisingly, Mick Jagger.

While Brian's drug problems were going on, Mick and Keith were simultaneously in trouble because of the Redlands bust. It really looked like the Stones were about to go under from all the pressure. In fact, Brian suffered another nervous breakdown and had no sooner recovered from that when, only five months after his last arrest, he was again arrested and charged with possessing cannabis. This time he was bailed for two thousand pounds, and on pleading guilty was leniently fined fifty pounds and one hundred five pounds court costs.

Brian was psychologically crushed by all this harassment. He even began to suspect that Mick and Keith were behind these police busts, with the intention of getting rid of him all the more quickly.

"It didn't hit me for months because I hadn't seen Brian a lot," Keith Richards has said. "The only time we'd see him was down at the courthouse, at one of his trials. They really roughed him up, man. He wasn't a cat that could stand that kind of shit, and they really went for him like when hound dogs smell blood. 'There's one that'll break if we keep on.' And they busted him and busted him. That cat got so paranoid at the end, like they did to Lenny Bruce, the same tactics. Break him down. Maybe with Mick and me they felt, well, they're just old lads.'"

A year after Brian had survived his last trial for possession of cannabis by getting off with a fine and probation, he had been arrested and tried before the same judge who had sentenced him before. This time Brian's situation was more precarious because of his previous conviction, and he faced the possibility of a ten-year prison sentence if the jury of ten men and two women found him guilty.

The task of defending Brian was again handled by Michael Havers.

Lord Michael Havers

THE ODDS THIS time were certainly not in our favor because the success of Brian's defense rested on his credibility in denying knowledge of the cannabis the police found in his dresser drawer. Considering his prior conviction and Brian's state of nervousness—he was near collapse—I knew my task in convincing a jury of his innocence was not going to be easy despite the fact that the prosecution had to prove that Brian was knowingly in possession of the hashish. The word "knowingly" was the key to my defense.

The prosecution began its case by putting Detective Sergeant Robin Constable on the stand who testified that, accompanied by three police officers and armed with a search warrant, he had rung Brian Jones's bell and knocked on his door for ten minutes, during which time he also yelled "Police!" through the letter opening in the door, but that there had been no response. The detective said he finally gained entrance into the flat by going through the refuse chute and unlocking the door for his fellows. He then testified that on searching the flat he found Brian Jones sitting on the floor beside his bed dressed in a caftan and holding a telephone on his lap. Constable said that Brian told him that he was about to phone his solicitor. Constable asked him why he had not come to the door. Brian's answer was, "You know the scene, man, why do I always get bugged?"

The detective testified that he was in the process of searching Brian's bedroom when one of the other detectives, named Prentice, called to him from the living room, and when he and Brian entered the room he found Prentice standing beside an open bureau drawer with a ball of wool in his hand, which, he said, he had just found in the drawer. Constable testified that Brian blurted out, "Oh, no, this can't happen again, just when I'm getting on my feet." Whereupon, Prentice put his fingers into the ball of wool and extracted a small piece of cannabis resin.

The prosecutor, Roger Frisby, asked: "Jones spoke, then, before he had seen what the wool contained?"

"Yes, sir," the detective answered. I asked Jones if the wool was his and he said, "It could be." His only other words were, "Why do you have to pick on me? I have been working all day and night, trying to promote our new record, and now this has to happen. I never take the stuff because it makes me so paranoid." Mr. Frisby had no more questions and turned the witness over to me for cross-examination.

☐ ☐ ☐

HAVERS: Detective Sergeant Constable, you remarked that Mr. Jones was sitting, when you entered his room, on the floor beside the bed. Was there anything sinister in that? A man may sit where he wishes, in his own room, may he not?

CONSTABLE: There was nothing sinister.

HAVERS: When Detective Prentice called to you from the living room, what was his manner? Was he excited, would you say?

CONSTABLE: I suppose so.

HAVERS: He was excited. When you and Mr. Jones came in, Prentice was standing at the bureau, holding the wool. Was there anything else in the bureau?

CONSTABLE: There were a woman's stocking and a man's sock. In the top drawer with the wool there was a Rolling Stones record.

HAVERS: Do you know who lived in the flat before Mr. Jones?

CONSTABLE: Miss Joanna Pettet, the actress. She had lived there about six months.

HAVERS: Is she an American?

CONSTABLE: She is English, married to an American.

HAVERS: Has she to your knowledge ever been involved with drugs?

CONSTABLE: No, sir. We investigated her at Scotland Yard, and at our request she was investigated in Los Angeles by the FBI. She has no drug record.

HAVERS: Did she say the wool was hers?

CONSTABLE: She said it might be. She had no knowledge of the cannabis.

HAVERS: Let's see, when you came in, Prentice was holding the wool?

CONSTABLE: He was.

HAVERS: And he did not show what was inside it?

CONSTABLE: No, sir.

HAVERS: What did you think it contained?

CONSTABLE: I . . . didn't know.

HAVERS: Certainly you didn't, but what did you think? You had come to search for drugs. Prentice called you excitedly. Surely you did not think it had nothing to do with drugs.

CONSTABLE: No, sir.

JUDGE SEATON: The point, as I see it, is that when Prentice called, it was obvious to you that it had something to do with drugs. So it should have been obvious to the accused as well.

HAVERS: No more questions.

Lord Michael Havers

THE PROSECUTION PUT Detectives Prentice and Wagstaff in the witness box to confirm Constable's testimony, after which the Crown rested its case and I addressed the jury. I told them that I would put Brian Jones on the stand so that they could judge for themselves what kind of man he was. I admitted to them that Brian had been previously arrested and convicted on drug charges and sentenced to prison but that the Court of Appeals had amended his punishment to a fine and probation. I also told them that since that last arrest, Brian had been regularly visiting a court-appointed doctor.

"I tell you all this," I said, "because it really is an important part of this case. To have spent months in all the worry and anxiety of court trials and litigation, with the threat of prison hanging over one—to have passed through all that and to be working and co-operating with the police and the parole board—and then suddenly to find oneself again, through no fault of one's own, in the same predicament—ladies and gentlemen of the jury, I ask that you listen with sympathy to the testimony of this young man—he has been under a great strain."

Of course, I was trying to soften them up, and at the same time I wanted to defuse the Crown's cross-examination as much as I could. Brian was very pale and nervous as he took the stand. He testified that he had been seeing a doctor on a regular basis since his last sentencing and that he had not used cannabis in all that time. He also testified that he was wary of the drug because when he had taken it the effect was to make him more unhappy. In response to my questions, he said he had moved into the flat only a few hours after Joanna Pettet had vacated it. Yes, he had looked into that bureau drawer but he only recalled seeing stockings and a bottle of ink, although the wool could have been there and the shock of this arrest could have affected his memory.

JONES: I was asleep when I heard this loud banging at the door. I did not immediately become aware of what it was. A minute might have passed before I knew it was somebody very intent on entering the flat. I put on a caftan—kimono sort of thing—went to the door and looked through the spy hole.

HAVERS: What did you see?

JONES: I remember seeing . . . three large gentlemen . . . of a sort I don't usually *see* . . . through the spy hole of my door.

HAVERS: Who did you think they were?

JONES: Police, perhaps, or, agents . . . I was afraid—

HAVERS: Of the police?

JONES: Yes, since last year I seem to have had an inborn fear of the police.

FRISBY: If it please the court, *inborn* means you've had it all your life.

JONES: Ah, an acquired fear. I went back to the bedroom on tiptoe. I couldn't make up my mind whether to call my secretary or my solicitor. I was very worried.

HAVERS: The police have said that ten minutes passed before they came into the flat. Do you agree with this estimate?

JONES: I can't agree or disagree. Some time passed. Certainly long enough to dispose of anything I shouldn't have had.

HAVERS: How did you feel when they showed you the resin?

JONES: I couldn't believe it. I was absolutely shattered.

HAVERS: When Constable asked if the wool were yours, did you say, "it might be"?

JONES: I might have said anything.

HAVERS: Was the wool yours?

JONES: I never had a ball of wool in my life. I don't darn socks. I don't have a girl friend who darns socks.

HAVERS: Later, when you were at the police station, you said that you never take cannabis because it makes you so paranoid. What did you mean?

JONES: That refers back to the events of last year. The effect of the drug for me was a heightening of experience that I found most unpleasant. That made me very frightened of it.

HAVERS: Were you advised what would be the consequences of breaking probation by using drugs?

JONES: Yes, sir. I have taken no chances.

HAVERS: Had you the slightest knowledge that the resin was in that wool?

JONES: No, absolutely not.

Lord Michael Havers

THAT CONCLUDED MY interrogation and I turned Brian over to Prosecutor Frisby for cross-examination, not at all sure that Brian wouldn't crack under the stress of hostile questioning.

☐ ☐ ☐

FRISBY: Mr. Jones, you have said that when the police arrived at the flat your conscience was clear—

JONES: Yes, entirely.

FRISBY: —so why did you not open the door?

JONES: Because I saw the three large gentlemen, as I mentioned before. I was afraid.

FRISBY: *Why* were you afraid?

JONES: Well, the events of last year, and there had been so many drug raids in the Chelsea area—I was just worried, I wanted advice.

FRISBY: Surely you knew what that would be. You would have to let the police in eventually. If you were innocent, there was nothing to fear. Yet you deliberately kept them out for as long as you could. And it's no good, you know, saying you could have got rid of anything in that time—for do not the windows of the flat open onto the King's Road, where there might have been police stationed outside, watching?

JONES: I expect there might be other ways to dispose of it—

FRISBY: Could one way have been to hide it in the wool?

JONES: It *could* have been.

FRISBY: Mr. Jones, please tell the court who, if not you, put the cannabis in the bureau.

JONES: A lot of people had come and gone while I was living in the flat but I have no reason to suspect any one person. I have no idea how cannabis got there and I've denied it ever since cannabis has been found.

FRISBY: Denied what?

JONES: Knowing about the cannabis.

FRISBY: You didn't say that.

JONES: Of course, I did.

FRISBY: Your counsel has cross-examined the police officers, they said nothing about your denying it.

JONES: I did deny it. I said, "You can't do this to me again."

FRISBY: Have you used the bureau where the cannabis had been?

JONES: No.

FRISBY: And you have no explanation for its being there. The whole thing, I take it, is a complete mystery to you?

JONES: Yes, a mystery.

FRISBY: And so, it must remain to us, unless we accept the only explanation that will accommodate the facts. What I am suggesting, you see, is that the cannabis was yours, that you knew it was there all along, and that you are now lying to us.

JONES: I am not guilty, sir. I believe that my whole conduct while the police were in the flat points to a denial.

Lord Michael Havers

IN HIS SUMMATION to the jury, Frisby concentrated on the fact that Brian had not opened the door because he was afraid of the police. On the contrary, if he had not known about the cannabis he would have been glad to invite them in because this time he could gloat over his innocence. But did Mr. Jones do that? No, just the opposite. He behaved like a man caught red-handed.

In my summation I contended that if indeed Brian had known about the cannabis he would surely have disposed of it while the police waited outside. I said that although I had not seen the flat I felt secure in presuming there was a bathroom with a toilet in it that was capable of flushing away a small lump of cannabis. If Brian had known about the cannabis, he certainly would have got rid of it. I asked the jury: "What if one of our sons brought home a friend who left cannabis in the house and later the police came and found it? What could your son say except, 'I did not know it was there'?"

Judge Seaton charged the jury with remembering that the burden of proof rested on the police, not on Brian, and that their case was entirely circumstantial. There had not been a shred of evidence that cannabis had been used in Jones's flat. There was no residue of it having been smoked, no ashes, no butt ends, and it was up to the jury to determine if it could have been disposed of in the ten minutes before the police entered. If you think the prosecutor proved without a doubt that the defendant knew the cannabis was in his flat, you must find him guilty. Otherwise, he is innocent.

With that summation and charge by the judge, it appeared certain that the jury would return with a verdict of not guilty. But when the jury did return, after an hour's deliberation, the foreman rose and addressed the court: "Your Honor, we find the defendant guilty."

A guard took Brian's arm and led him up to the bench for sentencing. "Mr. Jones," the judge said, "you have been found guilty. I am going to treat you as I would any other young man before this court. I am going to fine you, and I will fine you relatively, according to your means. Fifty pounds and one hundred guineas court costs. You will have one week to get up the money. Your probation order will not be changed. But you really must watch your step, and stay clear of this stuff."

The verdict meant that the judge had repudiated the jury's verdict, had refused to jail Brian and had allowed him to leave, a free man.

When I left the court with Brian, now smiling for the first time, he was serenaded by a group of girls gathered on the courthouse steps.

□ □ □

Tony Bramwell, who handled press relations for the Beatles and was their song plugger, gave me his recollection of that period when Brian and Keith had their fingers on the self-destruct button all the time. "You used to bump into them in town and you'd think, God, what wrecks," Bramwell told me. "They were both such good-looking boys when we first saw them in Richmond. And then you see these wrecks. Brian was a brilliant musician. But you'd bump into them in town and they'd be totally under the influence of everything. And they'd look like they were sixty—Brian, Keith, and I'll include Pete Townshend of the Who. They were old men in their twenties."

CHAPTER FOURTEEN

Anita Pallenberg:
Exchanging Allegiances

*Mick Jagger is a scared little boy who is about as
sexy as a pissing toad. He moves like a parody
between a majorette girl and Fred Astaire.*

TRUMAN CAPOTE

After the drug bust that had landed him in prison, and in
the interim until his appeal was decided, Jagger went
into seclusion for a while to try to deal with the after-
shocks of what had been, for his psyche, a painful bat-
tering. His role as young lord of the rock world had induced him
to believe that his status was inviolate, above the mundane rules by
which lesser mortals lived, a man of privilege, wealth and style, to
whom both men and women were attracted. But that moment
when he was pronounced guilty in open court, then fingerprinted,
photographed with a number across his chest, handcuffed and
put in a police van with a bunch of common criminals, that night
he had spent in a small cell, sleeping behind bars, had devastated
his self-image.

So while Mick anxiously awaited the outcome of his appeal, he
brooded and experienced a rare period of depression. He felt it
was time he became more decisive about what was happening in
his life. He had acted decisively in ridding himself of Allen Klein
and replacing him with Marshall Chess, and in hiring Prince Rupert to take charge of the Stones' finances—that was the way, Mick
was convinced, he now had to resolve other negative situations
that he was tolerating but that were eating away at him. He must
have felt he had tolerated Brian Jones for much too long. Brian

266

had become increasingly affected by all the drugs he took and it was no wonder that with Brian and Keith so heavily into dope, the cops had moved in on all of them. Whereas Keith's ability to function both as a performer and songwriter was unfazed by his drug use, Brian was affected by drugs to the point of uselessness—more than that, his drugged, unpredictable presence was often a hindrance. So, Jagger decided, the time had come to convince the other Stones that Brian must be forced out of the band. The other band members—Charlie Watts, Ian Stewart, Bill Wyman—weren't into drugs; they were simple, uncomplicated personalities, easy to get along with, came to rehearsals on time, never got into trouble on tours, perfectly content to stay out of the limelight, just do their jobs, pack up their gear and go home to their wives and kids. Mick probably thought, Now if only Brian, crazy Brian, could be replaced by someone like Charlie or Bill, someone talented who could quietly do his part and stay out of trouble . . .

There was another thing that Jagger brooded about—whether he shouldn't be planning some alternative role to being a rock performer. For some time now, he had been thinking about becoming an actor; watching Marianne Faithfull perform on stage had been an inspiration and had made him jealous of her success. If he could become a movie star, he could elevate himself, become disassociated from the stigmata of the rock world.

Another concern was Marianne. He felt her emanations of discontent, worried about her increasing drug use, was aware that she was less intimate and doing more and more things on her own without him, without even consulting him. He desperately needed to keep Marianne in his life and he brooded about how to do that. He knew that she yearned for a house in the country, for flowers, shrubs, grass, a running brook, a life away from the enticements and pressures of the rock world, and Mick seriously considered dropping out for a while and joining the nomad life of his friend, Sir Mark Palmer, the young aristocrat who had renounced his upper-class life. Perhaps that would assuage Marianne's restlessness. And his own. So Mick and Marianne packed a duffle and joined Mark Palmer in the south of England, where he was leading a caravan of horse-drawn wagons across the countryside.

Sir Mark had been a page boy at the coronation, and his mother is one of the queen's ladies-in-waiting. He was one of the most glamorous figures of the sixties, a handsome, well-bred aristocrat who renounced his heritage and became the quintessential rebel hippie. Today he retains his elegant handsomeness. When I met with him, he was wearing a black, loosely fitting suit, black shirt, pencil-thin bright red necktie, red pocket handkerchief, bright red socks, black shoes. Despite this potentially tacky getup, Sir Mark wore it with such sophisticated bearing that he made it look stylish. He had found all the components of his wardrobe in thrift shops, but nothing about his appearance gave any hint of his clothes' humble origins.

Sir Mark Palmer

THERE WAS THIS whole group of us from "better" homes and titles and all that, who had told our families to fuck off. Terrible rows with them. Disinherited, all that. We were very communal in those days and we shared everything—joints and acid included. We were into powerful stuff like DMT so we needed the peace and greenery of the countryside to counteract it. Mick and Marianne fitted in with us rather nicely. We were laid-back, about our drugs, our sex lives, whatever. Actually when people took a lot of drugs, they didn't get into that much sex. But equally they dismissed the sort of pathetic notion that it was disgraceful for you to sleep with whoever you fancied. Obviously, if you fancied somebody and they fancied you, you'd go to bed with them, whoever they were. But you were completely high and sort of rapping, you'd probably pass out with the rest of your friends. Or you're listening to some music you were into, or playing it if you were a musician. Sex wasn't uppermost in our minds, which also contributed to the fact that people didn't really care about it all that much. If it happened, it happened. And there were no sort of conventions about it. It was like anything else, it was very spontaneous.

I think that the straight world had this idea that all these people in the sixties were having all these love-ins all the time and that everybody slept with everybody and screwed around all the time, as if it were one big orgy. But it wasn't like that at all. That was a complete load of rubbish. In fact, if you had a girl friend, you slept with her and she didn't mind too much about losing her virginity, the way she would have a generation before, unless you married her or something. That's about all the difference there was. Certainly the drugs didn't make you more randy. They might have made it more interesting or less interesting, equally. Of course, speed does have a definite negative effect on male sexual performance. But with acid, sex is very good. Acid is wonderful. But terribly truthful. I guess you could say that acid was a sort of truth drug, in a way. It showed people what they were really like. The casualties were the people who saw themselves face-to-face and couldn't take it, I suppose. It showed you up. And it kept on showing you the truth, which was fine if you were going to be laid-back and accept it and say, "I want to learn, I want to know." But if you were going to fight it, and say, "No, I can't stand it, I can't take it," then you were in for a bad time. But if you were prepared to accept it and learn, it was fine.

Of course, drugs for a rock star like Jagger were something else. I think the pressures of being a rock star are terrible, or they certainly were then. They had a certain quality to maintain, in concerts, on television, in recording sessions. If you've got a million followers, you know that an awful lot is expected of you. You've got to show them and open their minds and blow their minds. And that's pressure. But I don't think drugs help the rock star perform. In fact, just the opposite.

In furtherance of his desire to placate Marianne, Mick bought a big, old Gothic Victorian mansion called Stargroves that was located outside Newbury, Berkshire. It was a dilapidated place, run-down, but there were vestiges of its one-time grandeur; actually being in possession of even a seedy country house was enough to set Marianne to dreaming about flower gardens and gazebos and restoring the mansion to its original glory.

Sir Mark Palmer

IN REALITY, IT was a grim place, and Mick really never intended to fix it up proper and move in. It did have big stables and all that sort of thing, so when winter came and we couldn't graze the horses any more, we all moved into Stargroves. We did that for a couple of winters. Mick and Marianne stayed for a bit but before long they took off. But they continued to come down for brief visits. So did Brian Jones. And Keith and Anita. But the thing about Marianne, she was into heroin by then, so were Keith and Anita, and Marianne really had to be in London to stay close to her supply. But the times he was there, Mick really liked the laid-back, communal life of our group at Stargroves.

I'm very fond of Mick, I like him a lot, but rock stars are very hard to be with in a lot of ways. Socially they're very neurotic. Well, you can imagine, they're surrounded by these toadies and all that sort of thing. It's a bit like the royal family. The same sort of thing. You've got to get through all that flak and shit. What Mick liked was that with us, he was just one of our family, not a big-shot rock star.

As soon as the grass got green enough for the horses to have a bit of a pick, we resumed our meandering. When we left Stargroves with our fifteen wagons, there were loads of people driving them, and there were three caravans, three or four trollies, two other carts, horses tied on the back, dogs, goats—everything about our caravan was haphazard, unplanned, living life for that day, a microcosm of life as it was lived in the sixties. There was usually some chick who reckoned herself to be a good cook. She got a lot of flak from everyone else. Of course, by then we were very much into being macrobiotic vegetarians. It was rice and veg and Mars Bars, as you can imagine. A lot of sugar lack so we needed the Mars Bars because we'd taken so much dope. We were on so much dope that we were convinced that we were probably poisoning our systems, so we ate simple foods like rice and veggies to clean up our bodies. And also it was cheap. All we needed was a sack of rice and we pilfered the veggies. Potato fields and kale and that stuff, we just lifted it out of the fields. And we had poaching dogs as well, sort of like greyhound mongrels, we call them lurchers over here. And they were catching rabbits and hares, and sometimes they'd nab a pheasant. You aim them at something, preferably. If you let them go on their own, they might go in the wrong direction. They're fairly thick in the head, but very fast. And they're meant to be cleverer than greyhounds. If you slip them on a hare, you catch that hare. They're deadly.

We always had enough dope to smoke. We could always go into a town to score or somebody would bring it down from London. We just smoked dope, and we weren't into any of the other stuff. So we had this great benign feeling, everybody loving everybody.

And great masses of people were coming down from London to join us. And all of them were dead welcome. We had communal eating, and at night we listened to some music together and smoked some dope. While looking up at the stars, people touching, arms around, some sex, not much, life as it should be lived. I'm not sure Jagger was as comfortable with all this as he pretended to be; Marianne was.

In matter of fact, to get his mind off his prison sentence, Mick needed a much stronger distraction than Mark Palmer's nomadic caravan. Keith and Brian were equally nervous about the outcome of their appeals, so it was decided that a week in Morocco would be just the thing to keep from brooding about their possible incarcerations.

The waiting period was especially hard on Brian, whose trial ordeal seemed to heighten his insecurity about his position with the band and his relationship with Anita. By now Brian was both very dependent upon Anita and resentful of that dependency, and this head-on conflict produced a rage in him not unlike the collision of hot air and cold air that causes a tornado.

Anita Pallenberg

AT THE TIME we all decided on the Morocco junket, Brian and I were living in a flat in Chelsea, and Keith, who had no girl friend right then, had been living with us. During that time, naturally, I got to know Keith quite well and I was intrigued with his laid-back, taciturn nature, so different from Brian's aggressive personality. Nothing occurred between Keith and me but we got to like one another. He was disturbed by Brian's outbursts against me, especially when Brian would physically attack me.

Keith wanted to drive the two thousand miles to Marrakesh in his new Bentley and we thought it might be a lark. Keith arranged for his driver, Tom Keylock, to come along and share the driving. We went across the English Channel by boat, and then across France toward Spain. When we got to the South of France, however, Brian became ill, developed a high fever, and by the time we reached Toulon he had come down with pneumonia and had to be hospitalized. It was Brian who suggested that we drive on without him to Tangier where we should wait for him at the Hotel Minzah.

That meant that Keith and I would be alone in the backseat of the Bentley while Tom drove. By the time we reached Valencia we could no longer resist each other and Keith spent the night in my room. In the morning I realized, as did Keith, that we were creating an unmanageable situation because, after all, Brian and Keith had to perform together, so we pulled back as best we could during the rest of the journey that took us from Malaga, by ferry to Tangier.

When we checked into the Minzah, there were several cables from Brian waiting for me, along with phone messages, demanding that I return to Toulon to get him and accompany him on the flight to Marrakesh. Mick and Marianne had also arrived in Tangier on their way to Marrakesh. At Keith's urging, I agreed to fly to Toulon to get Brian, and Marianne volunteered to keep me company while Keith, Mick and Tom drove on to Marrakesh.

From the moment I arrived in Toulon, Brian treated me horribly, disapproving of everything about me, using abusive language, obviously sensing that something might be going on between Keith and me but not discussing it in so many words.

□ □ □

Marianne Faithfull

BEFORE WE GOT on the plane, we had taken some acid to make the trip easier. During the flight I took out a book of the works of Oscar Wilde that I had brought with me—we were sitting three seats across—and I could feel that there was a terrible amount of tension between Anita and Brian, so I suggested that the three of us read *Salomé*. I assigned Brian to be Herod, Anita to be Salomé, and I would be Herodias. So we did. And that took our minds off everything until the plane landed in Gibraltar. I don't know why we stopped there, either something happened to the plane or we had to change planes or something like that.

We were on the Rock of Gibraltar for about two hours, I think, but we didn't want to stay in the airport because we were tripping. So we went for a ride in a taxicab. Brian had with him a tape recorder that contained a tape of the music he had just composed for a movie Anita was about to perform in. About the only thing to do on the Rock of Gibraltar was to go up to where the famous monkeys were and watch them at play. So that's what we decided to do. And when the monkeys came and clustered around us, Brian decided to play them his music. He turned on the tape recorder and after a few bars the monkeys, with a collective shriek, ran pell-mell away, tearing off into the distance. Brian took it as a terrible rejection. He screamed at the monkeys, trying to get them to come back, and then when they wouldn't, he began to revile them in terrible language. It was awful. And then he began to weep. A kind of madness, shouting, "The monkeys don't like my music! Fuck the monkeys! Fuck the monkeys!" I tried to comfort him, but there was no way of stopping his outburst. There were a lot of tourists around and they were appalled. Anita was watching Brian with an aghast expression on her face, and I knew right then and there that this was going to be a fatal week because all that day Anita had been asking about Keith, how I felt about him, comparing him to Brian.

☐ ☐ ☐

When the trio got to Marrakesh, they found that Mick, Keith and Tom had been joined by the art dealer Robert Fraser and by Michael Cooper, the photographer; a day later, the painter Brion Gysin came up from where he lived in Tangier.

Anita Pallenberg

THE NIGHT BRIAN and I arrived in Marrakesh, we had no sooner checked into our room than Brian began to berate me and attack me physically, beating me with a kind of sobbing frustration. I looked a pretty sight when we all went out to dinner that night. All through dinner, Brian kept staring at Keith but everyone was having too good a time drinking, smoking dope and eating couscous to pay any attention to him. But I could sense the rage building up.

☐ ☐ ☐

The following day, the elegant Sir Cecil Beaton, renowned for his photographic portraits, arrived at the hotel, not knowing that Mick and company were staying there. Sir Cecil later wrote about meeting them: "I arrived late and, to my surprise, discovered Mick Jagger and a sleepy-looking band of gypsies, sitting in the hotel lobby. Robert Fraser, one of their company, wearing a huge, black felt hat and a bright emerald brocade coat, was coughing by the swimming pool. He had swallowed something the wrong way. He recovered and invited me to join them all for a drink.

"It was a strange group. The three Stones: Brian Jones, with his girl friend, beatnik-dressed Anita Pallenberg—dirty white face, dirty blackened eyes, dirty canary drops of hair, barbaric jewelry; Keith Richards in eighteenth-century suit, long black velvet coat and the tightest pants; and, of course, Mick Jagger, together with Marianne Faithfull, hangers-on, chauffeurs, and Americans.

"I didn't want to give the impression that I was only interested in Mick, but it happened that we sat next to one another as he drank a vodka collins and smoked with pointed finger held high. His skin is chicken-breast white and of a fine quality. He has an inborn elegance. He talked of native music; he had heard a local tribe play pipes like those used in Hungary and Scotland. He liked Indian music, too. He said he would like to go to Kashmir and to Afghanistan, in fact, to get right away from England, which he considered had become a police state, with harassment and interference. Recently twenty policemen had invaded the house of his drummer [sic] in the country looking for dope. The newspapers had published completely false accounts. He was going to sue the *News of the World*. He maintained that he had done nothing to deprave the youth of the country. Here in Morocco people were not curious or bad-mannered. He liked people that were permissive.

"By degrees the shy aloofness of the gang broke down. We got into two cars; the Bentley I was in had been driven from Brian Jones's house in Swiss Cottage to here, and the driver was a bit tired. The car was filled with pop-art cushions, scarlet fur rugs, and sex magazines. Immediately the most tremendous volume of pop music boomed in the region of the back of my neck. Mick and Brian responded rhythmically and Anita leaned forward and screamed in whispers that she had just played a murderess in a film that was to be shown at the Cannes Festival.

"We went to a Moroccan restaurant—tiles, banquettes, women dancers. Mick considered the style of decoration gave little opportunity of expression to the artist. He is very gentle and with perfect manners. He indicated that I should follow his example and eat the chicken in my fingers. It was tender and good. He has much appreciation, and his small, albino-fringed eyes notice everything. 'How different and more real this place is to Tangier—the women more rustic, heavy, lumpy, but their music very Spanish and their dancing, too.' He has an analytical slant and compares everything he is seeing here with earlier impressions in other countries.

" 'What marvelous authority she has,' he said, listening to a colored singer. 'She follows through.' He sent his arms jerking about him. I was fascinated with the thin concave lines of his body, legs and arms. The mouth is almost too large; he is beautiful and ugly, feminine and masculine: a rare phenomenon.

"I was not disappointed and as the evening wore on found him easier to talk with. He asked: 'Have you ever taken LSD? Oh, I should. It would mean so much to you; you'd never forget the colors. For a painter it is a great experience. One's brain works not on four cylinders but on four thousand. You see everything aglow. You see yourself beautiful and ugly, and other people as if for the first time. Oh yes, you should take it in the country, surrounded by all those flowers. You'd have no bad effects. It's only people who hate themselves who suffer.' He had great assurance. 'If you enjoyed the bhang in India, this is a thousand times better: so much stronger—good stuff. Oh no, they can't stamp it out. It's like the atom bomb. Once it's been discovered, it can never be forgotten, and it's too easy to make.'

"We walked through the deserted, midnight streets. Mick admired the Giacometti-like doorways, was sad at the sleeping bundles of humanity, and had not seen such poverty since Singapore. He loved the old town with its mysterious alleyways.

"By the time we reached the hotel it was three o'clock and my bedtime, but they were quite happy to go on. Never a yawn and they had been up since five o'clock this morning.

"It is a way of life very different from mine and I enjoyed being jerked out of myself. Mick listened to pop records for a couple of hours and was then so tired that he went to sleep without taking off his clothes. He woke at eight, undressed and got into bed to sleep for another couple of hours.

"At eleven o'clock he appeared at the swimming pool. I could not believe it was the same person walking toward us. The very strong sun, reflected from the white ground, made his face look a white, podgy, shapeless mess; eyes very small, nose very pink and spreading, hair sandy dark. His figure, his hands and arms were incredibly feminine.

"None of them was willing to talk except in spasms. No one could make up their minds what to do, or when.

"I took Mick through the trees to an open space to photograph him in the midday sun. I gave his face the shadows it needed. The lips were of a fantastic roundness, the body almost hairless and yet, surprisingly, I made him look like a Tarzan by Piero di Cosimo. He is sexy, yet completely sexless. He could nearly be a eunuch. As a model he is a natural.

"Their wardrobe is extensive. Mick showed me the rows of brocade coats. Everything is shoddy, poorly made, the seams burst. Keith himself had sewn his trousers, lavender and dull rose, with a band of badly stitched leather dividing the two colors.

"Brian, at the pool, appears in white pants with a huge black square applied on to the back. It is very smart, in spite of the fact that the seams are giving away. But with such marvelously flat, tight, compact figures as they have, with no buttocks or stomach, almost anything looks well on them."

The next day, with LSD going the rounds, the group listened to music, ate copiously, drank and, in general, enjoyed their carefree ecstatic state, liberated by the acid. But as night fell and the day's euphoria faded along with the LSD, Brian reverted to his tirade against Anita, who had finally had enough of his abuse and locked herself in their bedroom. This infuriated Brian all the more, and, for revenge, he went into Marrakesh and found two local, unkempt whores, their braided hair reddened with henna, exotic tattoos, favored by Moroccan men, covering their bodies. It was Brian's intention to make Anita join the three of them in an orgy but Anita resisted, despite Brian's threat.

Anita Pallenberg

MY REFUSAL CAUSED Brian to go totally out of control. He overturned a tray full of sandwiches and cold cuts, spilling them all over the carpet, and then he began to pick things up and throw them at me. He grabbed me and beat me, screaming senselessly, a tornado of violence. When Keith saw what Brian had done to me, he got me aside and tried to console me. "I can't watch Brian do this shit to you any more," he said. "I'm going to take you back to London."

"What about Brian?" I asked. "He won't let me leave—he'll kill me first." Keith had already thought of something: He knew Brian was fascinated with the music played by musicians in the ancient town of Joujouka, and Keith arranged for Brion Gysin, who was an authority on Joujoukan music, to take Brian there to record their simple melodies, which they played on instruments passed along generation to generation for hundreds of years. It was Brian's intention to learn how to play Joujoukan music like the natives, and then adapt it to the Stones' recordings.

As soon as Brian left, Keith and I packed up and went off together. I was terrified but exhilarated to be freeing myself from Brian's tyranny. At the same time, there was the good side of Brian that still intrigued me, the way he was when he wasn't being paranoid. But I was more than ready to give that up, especially since I was now almost in love with Keith.

□ □ □

Marianne Faithfull

WHEN BRIAN GOT to the point where he didn't know what to do, how to handle a difficult situation, he hit out. He was a small man and that's the way it is with many small men. They compensate for their lack of size by using their fists. Of course, Brian had experienced that kind of brutality himself, because in the early days when the Stones were first appearing in dance halls, Brian would often get beat up by guys who had been watching him on the bandstand and waylaid him when he left. It was partly because of the way he looked, his rather feminine costumes, but it was also because he had a sort of transsexual appeal. And I think, too, that of all the Stones, Brian was the one that the girls in the audience fancied.

But later on, it was Brian's way to beat up people who couldn't hit back. He was full of anger and rage and fear. I think it was his fear of the women he was with that made him punch them out. At one time there was a woman named Zou Zou, a French woman whom Brian got involved with. Brian couldn't speak a word of

277

French and Zou Zou knew no English. Zou Zou said that Brian was very scared of her, that he always said that she scared him to death.

Although I was sad when Anita ran off from Brian and set up her liaison with Keith, I knew it would be better for her because there was something very sick about Brian and Anita when they lived together. Whereas Anita with Keith presented a much more acceptable relationship. I think if they hadn't got so heavily into drugs they would have been very happy. And I think part of the reason that they submerged themselves into drugs was because they were trying to punish themselves, more than anyone else could have, for what they had done to Brian. After all, they were in constant contact with Brian since he was still a member of the group and it isn't as if they could have got away from him and forgotten him. I think the fact that Keith, a member of Brian's own group, took Anita away from him, poisoned any possibility for the group ever to function the way it had before. That was the beginning of the end. It dragged on for a long time, but it tainted everything and there was really no chance for Brian to survive in the group after that.

Keith Richards had his own assessment of Brian: "Brian, in many ways, was a right cunt. He was a bastard. Mean, generous, anything. You want to say one thing, give it the opposite, too. But more so than most people, you know. Up to a point, you could put up with it. When you were put under the pressures of the road, either you took it seriously or you took it as a joke. Which meant that eventually—it was a very slow process, and it shifted and changed, and it is so impossible to describe—but in the last year or so, when Brian was almost totally incapacitated all of the time, he became a joke to the band. It was the only way we could deal with it without getting mad at him. So then it became that very cruel, piss-taking thing behind his back all the time. It all came to a head when . . . he was with Anita at the time, and he started beating her up and kicking her around. And I said, 'Come on, darlin', you don't need this. Let's go. I'll just take you away.' I didn't give a shit. I wasn't involved in it at the time. Just, 'Let's go, I'll take you out of *this*, at least, then you can do what you want.' So we split. It was very romantic in Marrakesh, tramping through the desert and all that crap. I mean, Brian was ludicrous in some ways and such a nice guy in some ways. It was like they used to say about Stan Getz: 'He's a nice buncha guys.' You just never knew which one you were going to meet."

Marianne Faithfull

I HAD HOPED that after losing Anita, Brian would find another woman to take her place, but that simply didn't happen. He just became increasingly unhappy and paranoid and screwed up. I was his friend, but I wasn't his girl friend. I saw him often, but Brian was too proud and too cool to discuss his inner turmoil. He just wasn't that kind of person. He kept it in. I would have liked to have talked to him, but I wouldn't pry into someone's life if they didn't want me to. There were times when, feeling comfortable with Brian, I would have liked to confide some of my problems with Mick. But since I was part of the group that was slowly pushing Brian away, I suppose it would have been regarded as sort of treachery for me to have taken Brian into my confidence. And knowing Brian, it's quite possible he would have turned such confidence against me by using my revelations to get at Mick.

Naturally, after Anita ran off with Keith, Brian got much more heavily into drugs. That was to be expected. And it was the absolute wrong time to become unhinged because Mick and Keith were writing their best songs then. They were in that period where they were really consolidating their work as musicians, and they were very disciplined about everything. I had a feeling that they knew they were about to pass over this sort of threshold of pop stars to become great rock stars and they knew it—like you do if you are an artist, you do know those moments where you really must keep yourself together or you're going to blow it. So they really didn't let themselves go at all. They kept themselves as healthy as possible and on top of everything. Which, of course, was contrary to everything that was being fed to the public in the way of publicity. But the fact is that the only way that one can deal with that kind of superstardom, especially at first, before it palls, is to keep yourself in very good shape. Later on, I suppose, when you take it for granted and get used to it or bored with it, then you might sink into drinking too much or taking too many drugs or something like that. But *this* moment when Brian decided to go into an orbit of excess with his drugs and his drinking, that was

279

the absolute wrong moment to do that. Not if you wanted to be part of the Rolling Stones.

The inevitable result of the downward spiral that Brian was on was that he would eventually be forced out of the group. But it was almost like he wanted to be ousted but didn't have the guts to walk straight out. If he really had been sensible about it all, had had his wits about him, had not been as neurotic and paranoid as he was, then the minute all this happened, the minute that Keith Richards, a brother member of his own band, ran off with his girl, he would have said, "Okay, that's it, I'm leaving. Get on without me." And then he would have avoided this awful, humiliating, drawn-out ouster. But I think Brian was very, very scared. And I don't think he realized how ruthless Mick Jagger was.

There is another factor that did him in: He always thought he was cleverer than the others and that they would never be able to put one over on him. The trouble was that he didn't see what I saw, and that was the change from being really rather ordinary working-class boys into being great stars. I saw the whole thing happening, and I'm amazed that Brian didn't see it. It was a stunning metamorphosis, when somebody changes from being young and unsure of himself to suddenly becoming a kind of young prince with all the power and privilege of royalty. What fooled Brian was that Mick and Keith made the transition very smoothly, just as if everything that was happening to them, no matter how enormous and quickly, was rather normal. Brian didn't pick up on that; he didn't notice. But I feel strongly, since I believe in predestination, that all three of them were playing out pre-plotted roles, that they were behaving just as they had been ordained to behave.

Mick and Keith realized that they were on the verge of breaking through into something incredibly exciting, musically, and although they made a few really bad records before they came up with the good ones, they seemed to know where they were headed. Brian didn't want to make those couple of records that were bad, hated them, and, of course, was right about them, but Brian's protest, the way he did it, his churlishness, was offensive to Mick and Keith. It just wasn't acceptable to have one of the group hitting on all the others, saying that what they were doing was terrible—even if it was. At this time in their lives, this formative stage, loyalty was very important. Brian was urging them not to change their style of music, that what they were doing was really imitation Beatles, and it was important that they keep true to themselves.

But the rest of the band was saying, "We have a right to try it and see what happens," but Brian insisted that it wasn't going to work, that it was going to be terrible, that it was going to be imitation Beatles, and that they would be beat up in the marketplace. Of course, he was right and they were wrong, but all that did was heighten the alienation from him, the resentment of him. What Brian didn't understand was that, in the process of artistic development, it is often necessary to try some things that don't work. What Brian couldn't comprehend was that the other members of the band felt that they had to change in some way, even if it was only for a little while, so that eventually they could come back to what they were really good at, stronger than before. Sometimes you have to do that. You have to try other new forms. Even if it's just to fail at it. That way, you get to know what your limitations are. If you never try out something else, then you never know, you wonder whether perhaps you might be better at that. They needed that lesson at failure. It was very important for them.

But Brian couldn't pick up on any of that. The other thing that bothered Brian was they never used any of his songs in any of their recording sessions. But then again he never really submitted a song that was ready to be recorded. Bill Wyman did, and he had accomplished the unheard of by getting them to record one of his songs on the album *Satanic Majesties*. And that showed that if Brian hadn't been so paranoid about their having ganged up against him as far as composing was concerned, and if Brian had actually presented them with a good song, they would have recorded it as they did Bill's. So much of Brian's resentment of Keith and Mick was in Brian's head and not in actual fact. What Brian said was, "I can't play them my songs, because they'll never, never record them, so I won't play any for them," thus avoiding the humiliation of rejection. Of course, that was pure paranoia.

□ □ □

"There was always something between Brian, Mick and myself that didn't quite make it somewhere," Keith Richards observed.

"Always something. I've often thought, tried to figure it out. It was in Brian, somewhere; there was something . . . he still felt alone somewhere . . . he was either completely into Mick at the expense of me, like in the early days nicking my bread to go and have a drink. Like when I was zonked out, taking the only pound I had in me pocket. He'd do something like that. Or he'd be completely in with me trying to work something against Mick. Brian was a very weird cat. He was a little insecure. He wouldn't be able to make it with two other guys at one time and really get along well.

"I don't think it was a sexual thing. He was always so open with his chicks. It was something else I've never been able to figure out. You can read Jung. I still can't figure it out. Maybe it was in the stars. He was a Pisces. I don't know. I'm Sag and Mick's Leo. Maybe those three can't ever connect completely all together at the same time for very long. There were periods when we had a ball together.

"As we became more and more well-known and eventually grew into that giant sort of thing, that in Brian also became blown up until it became very difficult to work with him and very difficult for him to be with us. Mick and I were more and more put together because we wrote together, and Brian would become uptight about that because he couldn't write. He couldn't even ask if he could come and try to write something with us. Where earlier on Brian and I would sit for hours trying to write songs and say, 'Aw, fuck it, we can't write songs.'

"But man, when he wanted to play, Brian could play his ass off, that cat! But to get him to do it, especially later on, was another thing. In the studio, for instance, to try and get Brian to play was such a hassle that eventually on a lot of those records that people think are the Stones, it's me overdubbing three guitars and Brian zonked out on the floor.

"It became very difficult because we were working nonstop . . . I'm skipping a lot of time now . . . when we were doing those American tours in '64, '65, '66. When things were getting really difficult, Brian would go out and meet a lot of people, before we did, because Mick and I spent most of our time writing. He'd go out and get high somewhere, get smashed. We'd say, 'Look, we got a session tomorrow, man, got to keep it together.' He'd arrive completely out of his head and zonk out on the floor with his guitar over him. So we started overdubbing, which was a drag 'cause it meant the whole band wasn't playing."

Brian's close friend, Ronni Money, thinks that whatever hope there was for Brian disappeared when he got involved with Anita Pallenberg.

Ronni Money

SHE DIDN'T LOOK after him, she didn't care about him—she couldn't even look after herself. Look what she did to him and how she did it—running off with a member of Brian's band, a guy Brian had to work with. Is there a worse humiliation than that? Brian rang me from Marrakesh, where he had gone with Anita for a holiday, along with Keith and some others. Brian was in a terrible steam. He said, "She's taken all my money and my camera and my credit cards, and she's gone off with Keith." It's four in the morning, and Brian's pleading with me, "Can you come over?" I said, "Look, don't be stupid, Brian, this is getting silly. You've got to get hold of yourself." I didn't tell him this, of course, but Anita did him a favor running off like that because the way she liked drugs, she was his downfall.

You see, there are people who actually enjoy doing drugs. I'm not talking about addiction—it's something else. My husband was forced to tell me, after numerous cures, "Well, I like it." He liked the whole culture of it. Because he didn't want to be touched by anything. It doesn't let you get touched by anything. It cuts out a lot of things that you normally would wake up worrying about. You really just have to care about your drugs. That is your whole day.

There always has been a certain amount of mystique about musicians who "boldly go where no man has"—all that kind of shit. Well, a musician can follow that road for as long as he can, but eventually he comes to the end of the road and that's it—he either takes one drug too many or he gets fortunate enough to have someone who is stronger than he is and who represents a real life. Sometimes it can be children, sometimes it can be a woman. But the tragedy is when the man gets involved with a woman who likes doing drugs and gives him companionship. Anita was one of those women and it was her drug support that wrecked Brian. That is the killer, when you get a partner who likes drugs as much as you do—then you're never going to get away from it. I tried to turn Brian off by telling him in detail what happened to my husband. But by the time Anita got through with him, he was too far gone. Mick was relentless in his pressure to get Brian out of the band. He played on all of Brian's weaknesses, his paranoiac insecurity, his alcohol and drug dependency, his fears and his self-destructive impulses.

□ □ □

Marianne Faithfull

IN AN EFFORT to try to patch things up, on one occasion I made Mick go to visit Brian, who was staying at Keith's house in the country. I thought they could talk things out and be friends again, but it was a disaster. The reason I frantically urged Mick to go was because I had read the *I Ching* and it was so awful about Brian. Death by water, terrible, and I got so nervous, I said, "You must go and see Brian right now." And we did. But after we got there, it was awful. Mick was so rude and Brian was so defensive.

Brian invited us to dinner, which was being prepared by Brian's cook. But Mick is very fussy about his food and hated the thought of having to eat the cook's food. And with absolutely no grace at all, he just said, "Well, Marianne and I are going to eat in the hotel in town, and afterwards we'll come back." That really offended Brian, of course. The result was they had a terrible row. Everything boiled up. They shouted the most awful things at each other. Such terrible hatred. They pushed each other around, and then Brian pulled a knife on Mick, and I think he would have stabbed him if Mick hadn't gotten it away from him. But then Brian ran out into the garden and jumped into the moat. The moat was only about two feet deep, but Mick jumped in after Brian and they thrashed around in the water and I thought they'd drown. But I didn't intervene. I was too appalled and, besides, I didn't think it was so bad that they had this row, actually. I thought anything's better than not talking to each other. And when they finally staggered out and coughed up water, they did start to talk a bit. But it was hopeless, it was hopeless, it was all hopeless. Everything was wrong.

In one way, I think, Yeah, Mick and Keith must've done everything on purpose to fuck Brian up. Then again, maybe it was just thoughtless and spiteful, but not planned, really. But what's the difference?

Brian definitely felt very, very persecuted. And in a way they did persecute him. The reason for that was because when they started the band—and this seems ridiculous, but little, tiny things like this caused the most awful, awful rows later on when they'd found out—Brian went behind everyone else's backs and arranged that since he was the leader of the band the manager should give him a secret five pounds more than the others. And he didn't tell the others that. When the Stones found that out, they never forgave him. And I think that was something that festered in Mick and Keith all those years.

Also, Keith and Mick were the only ones to write songs; Brian seemed not to have their facility to do that. For that reason, I think Andrew became more involved with Mick and Keith than with Brian. They were more malleable. Brian was more developed as a person. And more intractable. He had very definite ideas about what he wanted this Rolling Stones music to be. If he'd shown himself to be a good writer, they couldn't have done anything about it. But he was very paranoid, anyway. And he was demanding this role of leadership in the band over and above everyone else. The five pounds shows it precisely. And the question is, what was he really doing to get that kind of privilege more than anyone else? Since he wasn't the writer of the band, why should he have that position of privilege?

I think Mick wanted to get rid of Brian early on, but he couldn't make a move as long as Brian and Keith were so close. What Mick needed, really, for any ambitions he had was the total involvement of, and loyalty of, Keith. And of course, when Keith ran off with Anita, that really fixed it. Because Keith was then too embarrassed to be friendly with Brian.

And I added to it because I was with Mick, and it turned into a natural foursome. With Brian on the outside.

Brian's response to this isolation was to buy the A. A. Milne Pooh house and try to devise for himself an entirely new kind of existence, tranquil, domesticated, the life of a country squire. He busied himself planning extensive reparations to the house and grounds and furnishing the cottage with antique furniture, tapestries and paintings.

Now in mortal fear of the prison from which he had barely escaped, he virtually eliminated drugs and amphetamines and tried to restrict his drinking to white wine. He also tried to improve his physical condition by swimming regularly in the pool. And he brought into his life a young Swedish beauty named Anna Wohlin whose easygoing temperament complemented his new existence.

Mick, however, was not interested in Brian's attempt at rehabilitation. He summoned the other members of the band, and for the first time openly suggested that they excommunicate Brian for their common good.

Ian Stewart

MICK WAS VERY forceful about Brian. He said it was imperative that we get rid of Brian and replace him with someone who could perform. So we talked it over, and it was decided that Mick, Keith and Charlie would go see Brian at Cotchford Farm and tell him that we were planning a new U.S. tour but that Brian might have trouble getting in because of his drug busts. It was Mick's idea to put it to him this way, hoping that Brian would then decide to quit. Keith suggested they tell Brian that Mick Taylor was already lined up to replace him. Of course, we didn't have Taylor on tap—he was still with the Bluesbreakers—but we thought it would put more pressure on Brian to back off and not harbor any notions about rejoining the band. As a financial settlement, Mick proposed one hundred thousand pounds.

The meeting turned out pretty much as planned. Brian said he couldn't go back on the road again, those one-nighters were just too hard on him, and Keith suggested that perhaps the best way to handle it was to say that Brian was resigning because of musical differences with the band. Brian approved.

When the press got hold of Brian after his resignation hit the newsstands, Brian went along with the account that the Stones' press office had released. Brian said that he had left the Stones because he wanted to play his own style of music and that his departure was on a friendly basis.

What I heard was that after Mick, Keith and Charlie had left that afternoon, Brian had broken down, weeping.

☐ ☐ ☐

John Dunbar IT WAS A really terrible thing they did to Brian. They had a lot of other options than to sack him as cruelly as that. That took away whatever last reserves Brian had. It was Mick being the Godfather.

☐ ☐ ☐

Jim Carter-Fea ran the Revolution Club, a popular London night spot in the sixties, and was friendly with Brian.

Jim Carter-Fea I SAW BRIAN quite a lot over the years, right up to the time he died. I was very fond of him, and it was easy for me to forgive him his faults, which were many. I spent a couple of weeks with him after Mick pushed him out. It was very painful for Brian, the way they did it. I drove with him once in his silver Bentley and we parked in front of the building where the Stones were recording a new album. He had no interest in going inside, just wanted to sit there for a while. He said, "They're in there, making music, and they don't want me." There was nothing I could say. We just sat there in silence, sat there in his Bentley parked at the curb, for twenty or thirty minutes before he started up the engine and drove off.

What hurt Brian doubly about Mick walking out on him was the fact that Brian's girl friend, Suki Poitier, did the same thing at about the same time. Suki was a stunning blonde who came into Brian's life soon after Anita Pallenberg's brutal rejection of him. Suki looked quite a bit like Anita, and with Suki as his constant companion, Brian's spirits seemed to be restoring themselves. Before Brian, Suki had had an affair with Tara Browne, who was a Guinness heir, an extremely rich young man. They had been in a violent car accident that killed Tara. John Lennon's song "A Day in the Life" was about Tara. Suki once told me that she was con-

287

vinced that three more men who were in close proximity to her would die. After Tara, Suki had lived with Jimi Hendrix, and after his death she had taken up with Brian. She eventually left him at Cotchford Farm, a few weeks before his death. It was Anna Wohlin whom Brian had installed as Suki's replacement

Brian's relationship with Suki was tempestuous, to say the least. Brian returned to Morocco with Suki, for the first time since the tragic episode with Anita. Brian was excited at the prospect of hearing the native music, especially the Joujoukan pipers, but during the course of their stay, Brian beat up Suki so badly she had to be taken to the hospital by ambulance.

At Brian's funeral, Suki told me how shocked she had been to discover that all of Brian's valuable possessions had disappeared from his house. "I went there the day after," she said, "and the interior of the house had been ransacked. That lovely William Morris tapestry, all covered with fairies and elves, was gone from the wall. I would have liked to have had it as a memento of Brian."

□ □ □

Following Brian, Suki became involved with the wealthy son of a notorious Chinese gambler, whom she married and had children with. But when he told her that he planned to divorce her, she was extremely upset at the prospect of coming back to England alone with her two children. Apparently, this disturbed her so much that, while driving with her husband in her car, she drove off a cliff, killing both of them. Her prophecy had come true—Jimi Hendrix, Brian Jones and her Chinese husband.

CHAPTER FIFTEEN

Who Killed Brian Jones?

Please don't judge me too harshly.

BRIAN JONES

ick Jagger, Keith Richards and other members of the Rolling Stones band were in the Olympic Studios in London, working through the night on a new album, when they got the news about Brian's drowning. From what Marianne Faithfull told me, it's easy to imagine how they reacted. For a long beat there was uncomprehending, immobile silence, underscored by the hum of the high-powered amps in their headphones. Keith Richards slowly removed his headphones and his guitar strap from around his neck and placed the guitar on its stand. Jagger had been holding a tambourine, which he now let fall to the ground with a rattly clank as he pushed his headset down around his neck. Charlie Watts, the drummer, bent his head and dug his fingers into his eyes. Bill Wyman, the bass player, had not yet arrived, and Ian Stewart, who sometimes played piano or keyboard, was not scheduled for this session. Mick made a gesture to the console engineer behind the glass of the control room, who shut down the tape and cut the amps. The fourth Rolling Stone in the studio, Mick Taylor, was a newcomer who had just replaced Brian Jones, whom he had never met, and this was to be his first session with the band.

This replacement must have been what Jagger was turning over in his mind as he dealt with his emotions. Mick felt a surge of guilt, according to Marianne, as he recalled his recent confrontation with Brian at Cotchford Farm—in fact, they had sat on deck chairs around the very pool where Brian had now drowned, as Mick had told Brian that the time had come for him to leave the Stones, the band that Brian had formed and named.

Mick probably wondered, as he sat there on a high-legged stool, his shoulders hunched forward, his chin bowed against his chest, whether Brian's death was suicidal. He knew Brian was an excellent swimmer. He also knew that Brian had become pathologically afraid of being busted again and put in jail and that that fear had finally throttled Brian's drug habits. So it was unlikely Brian had drowned because of an overdose.

Mick's mind must have moved relentlessly over glimpses of their early times together, when they were struggling, in fact starving, continually discouraged and rebuffed, many times ready to give up, but rallied by Brian's tenacity. Brian had discovered them, one by one; Brian had named them the Rolling Stones. Brian had given their music its identity, and now as his reward, they had excommunicated him, demoralized him and perhaps contributed to his death.

Quite likely Keith Richards was also thinking about that last confrontation with Brian, the way they pretended it was just a temporary parting, only for the sake of the U.S. tour, that they would be back together, Mick faking friendliness, almost affection for Brian. Of course, the truth was that Keith and Mick had been plotting this excommunication for more than a year, and there was no possibility in their minds that he would ever be a Rolling Stone again. Brian went along with their charade, but he knew as well as they did that this parting was terminal.

Keith probably thought about all those agonizing times that Brian, filled with dope and booze, had obstructed their recording sessions, sometimes passing out on the floor of the studio, sometimes playing music unrelated to theirs. And yet, there was no denying his brilliance on the guitar and the harmonica and his mastery of the dozens of other instruments that he had learned to play.

Keith lit up a cigarette, the match illuminating his pale, wasted face. This news about Brian had hit him very hard, and not just because they had driven Brian out of the band. Keith certainly must have felt awful about Brian. All those rotten early times when Mick, Brian and he had lived in that squalid, cold, filthy Edith Grove flat, the hunger, the disappointments, the rejections, only seven years ago—how could so much have happened in seven years? Brian and his crazy clothes, Brian and his notorious sex life, Brian discovering the underworld of drugs, Brian cutting through the traditional bonds of music.

And Keith was undoubtedly thinking about Anita Pallenberg, the love of Brian's life, the only woman of all those he had had who truly mattered to him. They lived together now, Keith and Anita, but Brian had never completely given up on her, hoping that one day she would return to him. That's what Keith was likely thinking about now, how much Brian had suffered, how much he had wanted Anita. For a long time Brian wouldn't speak to Keith, on tour or in the studio, and this heavy awkwardness somewhat impaired their performances. After a while the intensity of Brian's resentment abated, but the underlying wistfulness about losing Anita was always there.

Charlie Watts was crying.

Although Keith had no way of knowing exactly what had happened at Cotchford the night Brian died, he nevertheless immediately suspected that Brian's drowning was not, as the coroner reported, the result of swimming under "the influence of drugs and alcohol." Keith knew from his own experience with drugs and alcohol that anyone who swam as well as Brian would not suddenly lose his ability to stay afloat and sink to the bottom of a pool.

"Some very weird things happened that night," Keith has said. "There were people there that suddenly disappeared. We had these chauffeurs working for us, and we tried to find out. Some of them had a weird hold over Brian. There were a lot of chicks there and there was a whole thing going on, they were having a party. I don't know, man, I just don't know what happened to Brian that night.

"There was no one there that'd want to murder him. Somebody didn't take care of him. And they should have because he had somebody there who was supposed to take care of him. Everyone knew what Brian was like, especially at a party. Maybe he did just go in for a swim and have an asthma attack. I'd never seen Brian have an attack. I know that he was asthmatic, I know that he was hung up with his spray, but I've never seen him have an attack.

"He was really easing back from the whole drug thing. He wasn't hitting 'em like he had been; he wasn't hitting anything like he had. Maybe the combination of things. It's one of those things I just can't find out. You know, who do you ask?

"Such a beautiful cat, man. He was one of those people who are so beautiful in one way and such an asshole in another. 'Brian, how could you do that to me, man?' It was like that.

"We were completely shocked about his death. I got straight into it and wanted to know who was there and couldn't find out. The only cat I could ask was the one I think who got rid of everybody and did the whole disappearing trick so when the cops arrived, it was just an accident. Maybe it was. Maybe the cat just wanted to get everyone out of the way so it wasn't all names involved, et cetera. Maybe he did the right thing, but I don't know. I don't even know who was there that night and trying to find out is impossible.

"Maybe he tried to pull one of his deep-diving stunts and was too loaded and hit his chest and that was it. But I've seen Brian swim in terrible conditions, in the sea with breakers up to here. I've been underwater with Brian in Fiji. He was all right then. He was a goddamn good swimmer, and it's very hard to believe he could have died in a swimming pool.

"But goddamnit, to find out is impossible. And especially with him not being officially one of the Stones then, none of our people were in direct contact so it was trying to find out who was around Brian at that moment, who he had there. It's the same feeling with who killed Kennedy. You can't get to the bottom of it.

"He was surrounded by the wrong kind of people. Jimi Hendrix was the same way. He just couldn't suss the assholes from the good people. He wouldn't kick out somebody that was a shit. He'd let them sit there, and maybe they'd be thinking how to sell off his possessions. He'd give 'em booze and he'd feed 'em, and they'd be thinking, Oh, that's worth two hundred fifty quid and I can roll that up and take it away. I don't know."

Ronni Money

I HEARD THERE was big party going on at Brian's house the night he drowned. Those construction guys who were working on his house were there with their girls. All those months they'd been really sucking Brian dry. They'd all been living off him, fake bills, not doing their work, drinking his booze, all that stuff. People who suck off you don't like you, they hate you really, because that's what makes it easy for them to suck. Brian was foppish, he was rich, he lived luxuriously with beautiful young women, a chauffeur drove him about in a Rolls-Royce, and these construction workers resented him for that, sneered at him.

Brian was terrified of dying. There's no way he would have

drowned himself or not fought desperately to stay afloat if he had experienced trouble. He was a great swimmer and strong, so there had to be dirty work at Cotchford Farm that night.

I believe in ultimate evil now. I do, I've seen it, and I believe in it. And I don't think it's got anything to do with horned people, it's to do with people who can actually loathe you to death.

Tony Sanchez was the self-avowed drug-provider for the Stones, Marianne Faithfull, Anita Pallenberg, all of them. He visited Brian Jones at Cotchford Farm shortly before his death and gave this account in his book entitled *Up and Down with the Rolling Stones*: "We had a few more glasses of wine, and then Brian leaned across to me conspiratorially. 'Want to work for me, Tony?' he whispered. 'That bastard' Keith gave me is taking outrageous liberties. I mean he cooks for me all right and everything, but he treats me as though he's my boss. I sent him out to buy some furniture a few weeks ago, and I only discovered quite by accident that he had bought two sets of everything—one for his house, one for mine. But when I mentioned it to him, he just told me not to be so fucking petty. Everyone seems to think I'm a millionaire or something, but I'm not. Mick and Keith get all the money for writing the songs, and they take a larger share of the profits from the records and concerts as well. They're not going to pay me that first hundred grand [$240,000]until next year, and I'm really worried about how I'm going to pay for everything until then. And I don't trust anybody. I know it sounds as though I'm getting paranoid again, but I'm not. It's just that there are a lot of people around who seem to think I'm still so out of my skull that I just don't know what's going on. But I'm not blind. I've got a pretty good idea who's ripping me off and how much they are ripping me off for.' "

When Sanchez told Keith about the incident of the duplicate furniture, Keith said, "I warned him not to do that to Brian. That bastard tried the same stunt with me, and that's why I had to get rid of him."

In my attempt to piece together what really took place at Cotchford Farm on that fatal night, I went back to speak with Brian's boyhood friend, Richard Hattrell, who had been forced to leave the squalid Edith Grove flat when he developed severe peritonitis.

I asked him if he had seen Brian in the intervening years, during which time he had become a bartender.

| Richard Hattrell |

I ONCE SAW Brian not long before he left the Stones. I found a great change had come over him. In fact, the Stones were playing a concert in Cheltenham, on tour, and I searched all over town for him and eventually found him in a club frequented by musicians called the Waikiki. He was literally hiding in a dark corner of the club. Didn't want anybody to see him, which I thought was very, very sad.

But he put his arm around me and said, "Great to see you, man," all that, but I sensed a change in him physically—he was beginning to be a wreck. I can't say that he was mentally ill, but he was certainly beginning to show a rather odd mental behavior, paranoiac, afraid that there were people after him, pursuing him, out to get him. I said, "Brian, what the hell are you doing to yourself?" He said, "That's the way it goes, man," or something to that effect. Very sad.

But later on, after he and the Stones broke up, I went to visit him at A. A. Milne's cottage, Cotchford Farm, and he seemed to have pulled himself back together. The house was stuffed with priceless antiques, a beautiful Elizabethan house that Brian was having restored. Brian did complain about the workmen doing the restoration, charging him for work that was not done. He also said that he was paying for food and drinks for the large group of workers.

Brian had also restored all the little stone statues around the pool that Milne had had fashioned after the characters in his book. Brian loved that house because *Winnie-the-Pooh* had been one of his favorite books and he used to read passages from it out loud. Brian seemed in pretty good spirits the last time I saw him there.

So his death was really a blow because he had been pretty much up when I saw him, and I knew him to be a keen swimmer. But a couple of months after his funeral I was hit even harder by something that happened one night in the hotel where I was bartending. It was a place called the Chase Hotel in Ross-on-Wye. A fellow came up to the bar for a drink and we recognized one another—it was one of the Walker Brothers, another rock group. [They weren't really brothers, they just used that name.] We got to chatting, and we were reminiscing about Brian, who had been a pal of his, when out came a truly startling revelation.

He said that on the evening of the night that Brian drowned, he called Brian to tell him that he and his friend were nearby and could they get together. Brian said that there was a party going on around the pool and invited them to join, which they did. The fellow said he did not know any of the people at the party, and that it was a rough party. He said that he and his friend both felt that some of the men at the party seemed to be hostile toward Brian—I think he used the word "jealousy" to describe the feeling in the air. He said these guys were baiting Brian, poking fun at him, taunting him, and at some point he saw that one man was holding Brian down in the pool. Another was clearly discernible standing on Brian's head, the fellow said, to keep him from getting out of the water. The light wasn't all that good, he said, but there was no doubt about what he saw.

I asked him if he thought they were trying to drown him or just to scare him and simply went too far. He said there was no way for him to tell and that he and his friend left the party right away to avoid involvement. After Brian died, all those beautiful antiques disappeared from the house. The whole place was stripped down.

Hattrell has been carrying this account around with him all these years, as have these two fellows. Almost twenty years have passed now, so, according to Hattrell, there's no way to go back and find out what really happened. He believes that the fellows probably did not want to get involved with the inquest because it was a time when everybody was dumping on "junkie rock stars," so everone just took it for granted that Brian died from an overdose.

Jim Carter-Fea

I WAS A close friend of both Brian Jones and his girl friend, Anna Wohlin, the young Swedish beauty who was with him at Cotchford Farm the night he drowned. I knew Anna before she met Brian.

Anna telephoned me early in the morning after Brian died. She said that someone had insisted that Anna and Linda Lawrence leave England immediately. Linda was Anna's best friend, and Anna had probably phoned her that night. But before she hung up, Anna told me that Brian had not been doing drugs that evening, that he had had a couple of drinks but that he wasn't at all drunk or anything like that, and that he had been in a very good, up mood because he was happy with his music at the time.

Anna said that she had gone to sleep and at some point came downstairs. She found two people standing by the pool looking down at Brian in the water. Anna said she dived in and tried to fish Brian out. The others just stood there watching. Perhaps someone wanted to get her out of the country so that this story couldn't come out.

I was so upset about all this that I went to see a man I know in Parliament, but he said that I was just pitching my head against a brick wall.

□ □ □

Nicholas Fitzgerald, a member of the Guinness family, was a long-time friend of Brian Jones's, and has written a book about him, *Brian Jones: The Inside Story of the Original Rolling Stone,* in which he gives an account of his visit to Cotchford Farm on the night Brian drowned.

Fitzgerald and his friend Richard Cadbury had run into Brian earlier at a pub in Hartfield. "He looked vulnerable, wretched," Fitzgerald wrote, and he was in the company of a guy whom Brian described as "one of the bunch hanging out at the farm. . . . Some days they hide my motorcycle. When I'm on the phone, the line will suddenly go dead. Then when I get the engineers in, they say there's nothing wrong. They're always leaping up to answer the phone and then they tell me it was a wrong number. I just can't trust anybody. I know you think I'm paranoid. Maybe I am, but not about this. I know they're up to something.' "

Whether he was paranoid or not, Brian did seem to have good prospects ahead. He was enthusiastic about his band plans. According to Fitzgerald, he had talked to Jimi Hendrix and John Lennon and both were seriously considering joining up with him.

On the afternoon of July 2, Brian told Fitzgerald that there was a girl named Luciana who was supposed to be waiting for him in the village, and he asked Fitzgerald to pick her up. Fitzgerald and

Cadbury spent the evening in the village pub, drinking and having dinner, but they never did find the girl. At about ten, Fitzgerald decided to ring Brian and check to see whether the girl had turned up there. He used the public phone in the inn.

"A girl's voice said, 'Hello?' I asked to speak to Brian. There was no answer. In the background I could hear a lot of noise and loud music, as if a party was going on. This struck me as odd. Brian hadn't mentioned any party and there had hardly been anyone about when we had left. Could Luciana have arrived with a bunch of friends?

"I said 'Hello?' There was still no reply, only the sound of revelry. After no one had answered about three minutes later, someone put the phone down at the other end. What the hell was going on? I hadn't recognized the girl's voice on the telephone. It hadn't sounded foreign. Why had she refused to answer after that first hello? Had someone taken the handset from her? I looked at my watch. It was five to ten."

Fitzgerald went back to the bar, but after a short while his concern got the better of him, and he suggested they drive back to Brian's to have a look. It was around eleven when they pulled onto Cotchford Lane. The lane ran through thick hedges. As they came into it, they were blinded. Two powerful headlights on high beam glared into the windshield. They stopped and set off toward the headlights. "Fifty yards away, blocking the drive to the house, was a foreign car, left-hand drive. The driver's door was open. The car was empty. I walked around the back of it and into the opening of the drive. I saw lights from the house dancing in the leaves of the trees. There was silence. Richard hung back. 'Not that way,' he called in an urgent whisper, 'there's something going on. Let's go through the trees.'

"We went back to my car where there was a gap in the hedge leading into Bluebell Wood. We clumsily groped through the trees and emerged behind the beamed stone wall of the summerhouse in shadow, where we heard muffled voices. We skirted the summerhouse, came around to its side and saw the full glare of the lights now over the pool and in the windows of the house. We had a clear view of the pool and of what was going on there. And what the hell *was* going on?

"At the far right-hand corner of the swimming pool three men were standing. They were dressed in sweaters and jeans. Their clothes gave the impression they were workmen. The power of the spotlights blotted out their features and made their faces look like white blobs. At the very moment I became aware of them, the middle one dropped to his knees, reached into the water and pushed down on the top of a head that looked white.

"At the opposite corner of the pool—far left—stood two other people, a man and a woman, gazing down into the pool where the kneeling man was pushing down on the head, keeping it under. The man to the right of the kneeling man said something. It sounded like a command, and I caught the words, '. . . do something.' At that, the third man on that side jumped into the water the way an animal might jump, arms outstretched, knees bent. He landed on the back of the struggling swimmer. The man who snapped out the command seemed to be preparing himself also to jump in. I looked at the man and woman. She was standing a little in his shadow and I couldn't see her face. Why didn't they move?

"Out of the bushes right next to us stepped a burly man wearing glasses. He pushed Richard out of the way. He grabbed my shoulder. His other hand made a fist, which he put in my face menacingly. 'Get the hell out of here, Fitzgerald, or you'll be the next.' It was a cockney accent. I was terrified. He meant it. He turned me around and pushed me hard in the back into the woods. I went stumbling into the darkness under the trees. Ahead of me I heard the rustle and swish as Cadbury went struggling away. I followed this sound. And now I saw the lights of the parked car. Richard was slumped over the steering wheel, groaning. 'Richard,' I was almost shrieking, 'get this bloody thing out of here.'

"I have replayed that scene at the pool in my mind over and over again, trying to recall any more details, trying to identify any of those people. I am sure I never before saw that man who surprised us in the woods. Yet, he knew my name. I was on the lookout for him around London but never ran into him. And, peculiarly, Richard Cadbury and I got separated that night when we ran out of gas, and later when I tried to contact him, I was told he had moved with no forwarding address. I never saw him again.

"I considered going to the police and telling my story, but frankly I was too terrified of that man in the woods and what might happen to me. Brian was dead. I couldn't rectify that and I might be putting my own life in danger. So I let it pass, but that scene hasn't passed from my mind and even to this day it troubles me very much."

Using the foregoing information as leads, I went to the villages surrounding Cotchford Farm to see if anyone was still around who might have been involved in the construction activity at Cotchford back in 1969. Two of the men who had worked at Cotchford were located, but one said it was too long ago to remember and the other simply refused to discuss what had happened that night. However, a chain of information finally led to a man, now living in London, who, with urging and the payment of two hundred pounds, consented to talk.

Marty is a short man with long sideburns; Marty is not his name—he has been assured that his identity will not be revealed because reaction to any inquiry relating to the July 2nd events at Cotchford Farm is still very volatile. Example: While I was living in London, my editorial assistant, Electra May, arranged an interview with Justin de Villeneuve, who was the mentor of the sixties celebrity model Twiggy, and a sixties character in his own right. A couple of days before the meeting with de Villeneuve (his real name was Nigel Davies) I took a train to Eastbourne to meet with the coroner, Mr. E. N. Grace, who kindly provided me with all the police and medical reports relative to Brian's death, and a transcript of the inquest. A few days later, Electra phoned de Villeneuve to confirm the interview for that day. "There is no interview," de Villeneuve's assistant said. Electra asked why. "Because Hotchner has been to see the coroner, hasn't he? We didn't know he was opening that can of worms. That's why."

Electra was quite shaken by this response since other than myself, she thought she was the only person who knew about my meeting with coroner Grace. Also, de Villeneuve's attitude was baffling for there was no indication that he was in any way involved with the circumstances surrounding Brian's death. "There was something ominous about the way de Villeneuve's guy said the interview was canceled," Electra said. "His voice had a threatening quality to it, quite scary."

When I saw the man I call Marty, he was in London looking for work. We met in a back corner of the Duke of York pub, and he held a copy of the *Observer* to identify himself. He drank pints of shandygaffs, which is a drink that combines beer and ginger ale.

"Marty"	WE'RE TALKING ALMOST twenty years back, when I was an apprentice on the job, I won't say doing exactly what, but the lot of us was fixing up this old

place where Brian Jones lived. Hadn't been tended to in years. We was taking our time, fucking off, running up hours. Anyway, what you want to know about is that night Brian drowned. We was there, some of us who was working on the house. Came back after work with girls, wives. I meself was there alone. It was, you know, drinks, some eats, some guys had joints.

There was two guys in particular had it in for Brian. Been on his back for weeks, I mean, always making remarks, the rich fag, all that kinda stuff. They used to pinch stuff off Brian all the time—leave work with a bottle or a coupla towels under their shirts, some shit like that. Anyway, this night Brian was swimming a lot. He could swim good, bounce off the diving board, lots better than any of us lads, and the girls was watching him, also because he was a celebrity they sort of gave him attention. These two guys got pissed about that—they was drinking pretty good by then—it was kind of like, when it started, kind of like teasing. Sort of grabbing Brian by the leg and pulling him down, meanwhile saying bitchy things, just horsing around, but kind of rough. Sort of interfering with his swimming.

I wasn't paying much attention at first, just that they were poking at Brian and roughing him up in the water, and a coupla the girls began to say, "Aw, let him alone, will ya?"—like that, but that just sort of made these lads pester Brian all the more, and then Brian tried to get out the pool and they wouldn't let him, kept pushing him back and pulling him under, and then it started to get rough and these lads really got worked up at Brian the more he resisted, I mean, really bad-mouthing him now and ducking him and then sort of holding him under water and keeping him under and then letting him up for a coupla seconds and he was gasping and then down again. I guess they were just wanting to throw a scare into him, I don't know, but they seemed to get more steamed about Brian the more they pushed him down, and I could tell it was turning ugly as hell.

Finally, one lad wanted to get Brian out, but the other wouldn't let him and they was kind of tugging on him. It got real crazy and then the next thing I heard was somebody say, "He's drowned." That's the first we knew what these guys had done, and someone said, "Let's get the hell out of here," and we all ran for it. Got to our cars in one hell of a hurry and cleared out. But if you ask me, those guys got carried away and I wouldn't say what happened was an accident. They knew he was taking in water but they got themselves so worked up they got kinda crazed, if you know what I mean. They hated him for being rich and doing nothing and having beautiful women around and wearing all those super-fancy clothes of his, and then having to work for Brian, laboring for small money and he looking down on them, treating them like shit. He could be snotty sometimes and walk right by you and not say hello or look at you.

I always thought he was okay, but there were those who he rubbed the wrong way and it all just seemed to get out of hand that night. Everything was handled okay, and nobody got burned but it was a damn shame about Brian. They shoulda just scared the shit out of him and let it go at that.

□ □ □

"Everybody was around Brian's grave," Bill Wyman remembers. "All his family and relatives were tranquilized. As the coffin was being lowered into the ground, the press was terrible—cameras poking into the grave, everyone asking questions. There was no respect. But when we drove away through Cheltenham, there were thousands of mourners, men with their hats off and women crying. I'd never seen anything like it."

Long before Brian's death, the Stones had scheduled a free concert in Hyde Park for July 5th; Richard Hattrell told me that Brian had asked him whether he thought it was proper for him to attend, even though he was no longer a Stone and would just be there as a spectator. They discussed it and decided to go together.

Brian drowned on July 2nd, three days before the event, and that prompted Mick to do a fast shuffle and declare that the Hyde Park concert was being given as a memorial to Brian. A giant color picture of Brian was put up at the back of the stage and Mick sent out an SOS for boxes of butterflies.

Richard Hattrell

I THOUGHT THIS opportunistic memorial was rather tacky. I would say that only a fraction of the two hundred fifty thousand who crowded the park were aware before they came that this was meant to be a tribute to Brian.

Mick came on stage wearing the goddamndest costume I ever saw. First of all, he was wearing heavy makeup—lipstick, eye shadow, rouge, mascara—like a tart. And his costume was a white, lacy affair that was cut like a dress, with pants and a vest underneath, and he wore a necklace that was a brass-studded leather choker. Hanging from his neck was an outsize wood crucifix. His hair was parted in the middle and hung to his shoulders. With his long hair and dolly dress, it was hard to tell, if you were in that crowd, whether it was Mick on stage or some chick from a boutique on King's Road.

□ □ □

Ian Stewart

THAT PERFORMANCE IN Hyde Park was one of the worst, if not *the* worst concert we ever gave. First of all, Mick came on stage alone and announced that he would read a poem by Shelley, which he said would tell how the Stones felt about Brian's unexpected packing off. Then came this long, boring poem that started, "Peace, peace! He is not dead, he doth not sleep—He hath awakened from the dream of life—" and so on and on and on. An endless poem. Now I admire Mick for a lot of things but one thing he ain't is a reader of epic poems. So everybody got restless while he droned on.

Then when he was finished, for dramatic effect, those cardboard boxes were opened to let the white butterflies fill the air, but they had been in the sun so long that most of them were dead in the boxes, and those that weren't sort of struggled around and most of them lit near the stage.

I guess by then Mick realized that he had to pump some life into the proceedings, so the band jumped into "Honky Tonk Women" but the problem was that this was the first time we had given a performance in over a year, we hadn't rehearsed, so we were ragged and rusty, and besides, Keith had shown up in terrible condition, off some kind of dope binge, looking like a derelict, and since as Keith played so went the band, the musical results that day were pretty ragged.

Mick's performance got increasingly frantic as he tried to over-compensate for the band's sluggishness, with the result that he really went overboard. He stripped off his dolly tunic and was leaping around in his vest and pants when he suddenly went to his knees, stuck his mike on his crotch and put his mouth over it, leaving nothing to the imagination as to what he was mimicking.

A rather tacky way to commemorate Brian's death.

CHAPTER SIXTEEN

The Degradation of Marianne Faithfull

I don't think people mind if I'm conceited. Every rock and roll star in the world is conceited. . . . If God wants me to become a woman, then a woman I will become.

MICK JAGGER

A few days after Brian's death, and before his funeral, Mick and Marianne flew to Australia, where they were to star in a film called *Ned Kelly*. Mick had involved himself in this project as a means, at last, of establishing himself as a movie actor and also to get Marianne away from her heroin suppliers in London. The title role that Jagger would play was of an Australian bandit hero of the nineteenth century, with Marianne playing his girl friend. According to her, Mick felt relieved to be far away from the aftermath of Brian's death and the guilt feelings it engendered in him. And he hoped that this joint acting venture would help restore his relationship with Marianne, who had become increasingly remote.

It didn't work out that way. The movie was ill-advised because Jagger's attempt to portray a nineteenth-century rogue-adventurer was ludicrous, and bringing Marianne to Australia proved as ill-advised as his movie role.

Marianne Faithfull

WHEN WE REACHED Sydney, Mick went right to bed to counteract his jet lag, but I found myself thinking about Brian, who had not yet been buried, and the more I thought of him drowned and wasted, the more I began to identify with him and think of myself as also drowned and wasted. It would have helped ease me over the panicky feelings I began to develop if I had had some acid or smack with me, but Mick had insisted that we enter Australia clean; I was already feeling intense withdrawal anxiety since I had been on heroin rather regularly for many months. I took several Mandrax tablets to try to ease off. If only I could have gone to sleep, I might have been able to get through this withdrawal period.

I phoned room service and had them send up some hot chocolate, which I slowly drank while swallowing some of my sodium amytal sleeping pills. It was a new prescription so there were about one hundred fifty pills in the bottle. When I started to take them I only intended to take a few, enough to get me to sleep, but watching myself in the mirror of the vanity table, sipping the hot chocolate and carefully placing each pill on my tongue before swallowing it, I somehow couldn't restrain myself, and I kept putting pill after pill on my tongue. I saw Brian appear in the mirror looking directly at me, and I became Ophelia, the part I'd been playing at the Royal Court Theatre. As the number of pills I swallowed mounted, my desire, as Ophelia, to commit suicide as I had in the play, increased.

When the bottle was empty, I got in bed next to Mick, closed my eyes and found myself in a huge, gray expanse, very still, no sun or clouds or temperature, a void, and Brian came to greet me. He was very happy that I had come. He told me how lonesome he had been, wandering around this strange terrifying place where he didn't know anyone. He kept saying, "Oh, thank God you're here, Marianne, thank God you're here!"

We began to glide along together, Brian and I, our feet not touching the ground, not touching each other, just these long looping glides, like skating on ice, and Brian was talking like he always did. "Man, what a jolt I had waking up here, no pills, no smokes, no Valium, a real drag, but then it came to me that I was dead, and that was another jolt, but man, I can adjust, you tell Mick, I can adjust . . ."

We kept gliding along until we came to a place where the terrain jogged away and Brian said I couldn't go any further and he'd have to go the rest of the way without me. I wanted to go with him but my mother and my son, Nicholas, were calling me back, and then I heard another voice and I recognized it as Mick's.

Mick told me that he had awakened and called for help as soon as he found he couldn't wake me. The fact that Mick had awakened me when he did and that the ambulance came very quickly saved my life because the amount of sodium amytal I had taken could have killed me three times over. As it was, I was in a coma for six days, most of the time with Mick at my bedside.

My understudy replaced me in the film, and during the two months it took to shoot it, I slowly convalesced. But I realized that if I was to avoid a second try at this I had to get away from Mick as soon as I could or the next time it might be suicide by suffocation.

□ □ □

After the debacle of *Ned Kelly*, Jagger made another attempt to make a successful motion picture, this time playing a part well-suited to him—an eccentric rock star.

Ian Stewart

I DON'T THINK he really would have made a film if it hadn't been for the fact that Marianne was scoring big on the stage. Mick had a broad streak of envy in him, jealousy, and I think it got to him that Marianne had received such terrific notices for her performance in the Chekhov play *Three Sisters*. Mick didn't like to be overshadowed by anyone, especially the women in his life.

So I think that's why he got involved with the movie *Performance*. It was a pretty weird picture, in which Mick was to play a wacky rock star. For the part of his girl friend, both Marianne and Anita were considered, the part finally going to Anita when Marianne discovered she was pregnant and the start of the movie was only six months away. I thought the movie might have a chance when that good actor, James Fox, was cast in the other male lead, and Nicolas Roeg signed on as director. But it was a weird flick from day one. Since it was being shot in London, mostly in a spooky house in Powis Square, I went on the set a few times and it was fucking scary, all gloom and sinister, you expected bats and worse to come down on you.

Keith was not at all pleased about Anita being in the film. He had read the script and he knew she had to perform some sex

306

scenes with Mick. Marianne also knew about these scenes but she had gone to Ireland to live in peace and quiet during her pregnancy. So she was not around London during the filming, but Keith was, and when I'd see him I could tell he was on edge. Anita was playing her shitty game with him, teasing him about how finally she was going to get it on with Mick, just as once she had teased Brian about her lust for Keith.

Keith refused to go into the Powis Square house and often parked outside and sent messages in to Anita. As for Anita and Mick, I always felt there was no love lost there; they always seemed to be a bit wary of each other, but when the big sex scene of the movie was filmed, instead of simulating sex they really got into each other, and although what wound up in the picture was a lot of vague, tumbling bodies in the sheets, nothing explicit, there was a lot of very explicit footage of Mick and Anita really screwing, steamy, lusty stuff, and that was edited into a separate X-rated short feature that was shown all around and actually copped an award at some X-rated film festival in Amsterdam.

Of course, Keith got hold of this and was pissed at what he saw. For a while things were strained between him and Mick, and of course things were pretty rough with Anita. For all I know, that may have been one of the causes of their eventual bust-up.

□ □ □

Although *Performance* had an interesting offbeat quality, it didn't find an audience and quickly passed into movie oblivion. On the heels of that disappointment, Jagger, who had been eagerly awaiting the birth of his child with Marianne, suffered a much more painful disappointment.

Marianne Faithfull

I THINK MICK and I could have overcome all our problems if I hadn't had a miscarriage in my seventh month and the baby hadn't died. If I'd had that baby, I think we would have stayed together, and I believe I might have pulled myself together. I wasn't far from becoming a real person at that point. I hadn't yet attained that status, however, and I was still very much under Mick's thumb and still a nasty, resentful, jealous little girl, full of anger and hostility, all of which I kept bottled up inside. But when I became pregnant, I began to have feelings that I think would have liberated and removed all those negative elements. I think with the baby I might have been able to make a fresh start. But what happened with that baby was a tragedy. After you have a baby, you are meant to do exercises to make sure that your uterus goes back into the right shape for the muscles. I didn't. So when this baby I had with Mick got heavy, the water broke and the baby burst out of it. That's what happened. Besides that, I like horses, I'm a good rider, and I rode a lot during my pregnancy. I had had Nicholas so easily, and I was so healthy and strong that I spent a lot of time riding. As a matter of fact, there are only three things that I do well: ride, cook, and fuck.

What really hurt me terribly was that I was told that I had lost the baby because of drugs, because I was a junkie. The doctor who attended me was the same doctor who had taken care of me when I was pregnant with Nicholas. But then, you see, I had been living a four-square life with my husband, John Dunbar, and I was a proper mother. Now I had run away with the bad man of rock and roll. I simply accepted the fact that the drugs had caused me to miscarry, although I was not taking any heavy drugs. The worst thing of all was that I was actually denounced from the pulpit of Westminster Abbey. It's a terrible feeling. You have no forum. You have no way to answer back. Mick commiserated with me a little, but I don't think he realized how bad I felt. But he was very attentive and sweet after my miscarriage.

But then, once it was over, he hardened toward me, and I felt it had a significant negative effect on him. He really wanted that baby. And so the miscarriage did both of us in.

But even if I had had the baby, I might have left Mick, because I was destroying myself. I had to get out, I had to grow up. I really had to. I couldn't stay in that life and in a funny way, I know this sounds absurd, but in a way, he loved me almost too much. He spoiled me to death. He did everything I wanted. It was terribly bad for me. I'm the sort of person who reacts very well to not having everything I want, to resistance. I like to go against the grain. And then when everything is made too easy for me, I really have nothing to do. My spirit wilts, I have nothing to fight against, no struggle.

So the only way I knew to deal with my relationship with Mick was to go off with another man. I could never have sat down and explained to Mick why I had to. It was my way, that I simply had to remove myself. Mario Schifano was his name. He was absolutely the opposite to Mick in temperament. He was much more like John Dunbar. He was a wealthy, Italian intellectual, an artist, a serious man—I still had a residue of my cultural snobbery in me. I ran off to Rome with him while Mick was away in America on tour. When he got back to London and the press confronted him with my defection, Mick reacted with resentment and fury. He came to Rome on Christmas Eve, looking for me. I suppose that his motivations were not so much to get me back but to overcome his public humiliation. He had to do it to preserve his personal machismo.

It was an awful encounter, something that made me cringe because Mario loved me, too. But I must admit that I was frightfully glad to see Mick when he showed up, although I had a much better physical relationship with Mario. The truth is that I felt more comfortable with Mick than with anyone else.

Mick and Mario got into a violent argument over me. They were on the verge of physically attacking each other. It was a startling experience for me. I could have made a choice and stopped them in their tracks, but I truthfully didn't know who I favored. Mario was an unknown quantity, Mick was a quantity that I knew only too well. I decided that the best thing was to withdraw and let them fight it out, let them make the decision for me.

I went to the bedroom, took my usual sleeping pills, and fell into a deep sleep. When I awoke in the morning, there was Mick sleeping beside me. Mario had spent the night on the couch in the living room and left early in the morning. I felt happy that Mick cared about me enough to wage this fight for me, but I knew in my heart that the real purpose of this confrontation was to restore his ego and that once back in London we would settle back into that deadly routine that was slowly killing me. Which is exactly what happened.

I stayed for another six months, until I found someone else to run away with. Actually, I think that was a mistake—if I had it to do over again, I wouldn't do it like that. I would have stayed and I would have said to Mick, "I'm staying in this house, you go. You're going to France anyway to make a new album, so you go. I've given you five years of my life, I'll take the house and I'll take an allowance, too, thank you." It was insane that I went off the way I did. I just left that house with all the furniture that I had not only picked, but some of it I had paid for with money I had earned from my performing. But I left with Nicholas under one arm and a Persian rug under the other. And that was it. I didn't take my jewelry. I didn't take anything. Out of pride. But in a way it's a good thing, because it gives me an edge on Mick, now, because he really feels that women are a terrible sort of grasping, feral creatures. But he can never accuse me of that because of the way I left. Mick, you see, likes to sneer at women. He even does it with Jerry Hall, whom he's with now, despite the sweet, pliant nature that Jerry has.

I think that by the time I left Mick, he had begun to give up on his dreams. When he was with me, he had great ambitions and great ideas. One of his ambitions was to be a gentleman. He may think he's done that, of course. But I don't think he's made it. And I don't think he's really fulfilled any of the things he wanted to be. I think he's given up and settled for what he is. Part of it is because of the women he's been with, the sort of women he has chosen. These are women who are adequate but that's all, rather than women who could really stretch him and help him in the sense of challenging himself. For example, after he got interested in the whole idea of acting, he took on a role in the movie *Performance*. I worked very hard with him on that part. I worked out a way for him to do it that was really very good, and in my opinion he was excellent in the part. I had the idea that he should make himself into an amalgamation of himself, Brian Jones and Keith Richards, physically as well as in portraying the personality of the character. It was my idea that he should dye his hair dark like Keith's and wear it like Brian's, but it was much more than physical, it was an attitude toward the part that suited him very well.

I think the reason that Mick didn't have a further movie career after his role in *Performance* was that we split up and he didn't have anyone to goad him into overcoming his fears about acting again. That was one of the things that we could talk about—one of the only things—our ideas. Once I had decided to dedicate myself to his talent and to help him realize himself, my method was to question everything he did. When he played me a song, I would question it, or if he gave me an idea, I would discuss it with him, not criticize it as such, but discuss it and try to enlarge it, put more flesh on its bones. And he started to rely on me to do that. The fact that he let me write the words to "Sister Morphine" showed that he had recognized my creative ability. I couldn't see him ever letting Bianca help him write a song. Or Jerry. But he did let me do that, and that illustrates his regard for my ability.

There was another thing that happened after I lost our baby that hastened the deterioration of our relationship. I suppose out of his disappointment at the loss of our baby, Mick had drifted into an affair with a beautiful black actress named Marsha Hunt, with whom he had a child, Karis, and Marsha told me that one of the reasons that she had Karis was that Mick was so unhappy about losing me and everything falling apart, he wanted a baby, that he felt that might give him some sense of solidity again. And that is why she had the child—yes, she told me that herself.

It was a fact that Mick had always been quite brutal toward the women he had lived with. Before me there was Chrissie Shrimpton, who was gorgeous and very much in love with Mick, but while he was living with her, he began to have his affair with me, and toward the end of his time with Chrissie he began to write those awful songs about her. The song "Yesterday's Papers" was really a horrible public humiliation for her. "Under My Thumb" was also about Chrissie. You see, when he got her where he wanted her, he didn't want her any more. And I often think that if he'd ever got me where he wanted me, he probably would have been the same, but he never got me to that point.

Mick couldn't talk in an ordinary way with the people he was involved with, but he used his songs to express his feelings. He also tried to explain things to me through his songs. "You Can't Always Get What You Want" was one of those songs. He wrote "Wild Horses" when we were breaking up—he didn't want to break up, and he wrote that to try and prevent it. When he played it for me—with its recurring refrain, "Wild, wild horses couldn't drag me away"—I burst into tears. I was terribly moved, "Oh, God, no, no! I'll never leave you." It was a very effective way to accomplish what he wanted. Much more effective than if he had sat down and had a long talk about it.

After I went back to living with Mick following my brief escapade with Mario Schifano, Mick had become heavily engaged in business matters that took up most of his time, and when he did have a spare evening, he'd most often go to St. John's Wood, where Marsha Hunt, who was performing in *Hair*, was living. I was very unhappy and had gone back heavily on heroin, so where

311

Mick was and what he was doing was not a lot of concern to me, and I realized that if I didn't get out quickly that Mick was going to get even with me for running away with Mario by finding somebody to take my place and get rid of me. I didn't want him to do to me what I had done to him.

But it was difficult for me to organize myself enough to act upon what my mind told me to do. The heroin kept me off balance, and I often did weird things I tried not to do. There were times in restaurants when I would pass out in the middle of dinner, my head in my food. I knew Mick was with Marsha Hunt and others, but I didn't care. I didn't care about anything except maintaining my heroin supply.

I went to live with my mother—I guess she could tell I was on something, but the days passed for me in a satisfactory haze. Mick continued to phone every day, and I could tell he was on the verge of coming to get me, to induce me to go back to him. My mind being in the shape it was, I knew I couldn't resist him intellectually, but it occurred to me that physically I knew a way to turn him off. The shape of a woman's body was of extreme importance to Mick, as was his own, so I stuffed myself with gobs of fattening food, and on the day that Mick finally showed up and saw this fat thing that had once been the lovely Marianne Faithfull, he left abruptly, as I knew he would. And that was finally the end of my long affair with Mick.

□ □ □

Gered Mankowitz I SAW MARIANNE in London some time after she had broken up with Mick. She was living in the flat of one of her friends, recovering from one of her terrible blows. I went to see her to try and cheer her up. She was lying on a couch, looking very romantic and sort of Byronish. She grabbed my hand and put it on her crotch, and she started rubbing herself. And I said, "Marianne, this is me. What the hell are you doing?"

Sir Mark Palmer

I VIVIDLY REMEMBER what drugs did to Marianne Faithfull. She came to do a concert gig near us, a sort of a rock festival. She had become quite a junkie by then, Marianne, and her performances relied very much on the tension she created by her possible inability to perform, that she may not be able to even open her mouth, that she may have lost her voice. She was a total wreck, and there was a good chance she wouldn't be able to perform. This tension held the audience. And she had that sort of secondhand glamour anyway. I was helping organize this rock concert in a valley down a rough track, miles from any roads, and the valley was filled with tents, with campfires burning, and Marianne was the highlight of the evening. But the organizers were worried—"Marianne's on in five minutes," they said, "and she seems unable to make an appearance, can you help her get it together?" So I said, "Come on, Marianne," but she said, "I can't, I've got to go back to your place." So I got her back to my place and then she sort of did what was necessary in the way of dope; I don't know what it was exactly because my friends never do smack in front of me because I'm not into smack and they know it. And then we drove back and we were late, but not too late. Marianne was pouring sweat; she was a livid, yellow-green color, and, frankly, she looked like she was dying. She said, "There's no way I can sing tonight, no way I can go on. I think you'd better call an ambulance." She tried to shape up a bit by taking a little bit of this and a little bit of that. But it got worse and worse. Her blood seemed to be seeping out of her. But when the time came to go on stage, she was spot on. Absolutely spot on. I've never seen anything like it. She was just brilliant. All these people had come down from the hillsides into this valley, and now they surged up to the stage and she just held them there in her cracked, old voice. And she started off, "I feel guilt." An absolute ace performance. But she knows her drugs, you see. And I didn't, I was a greenhorn. I had thought, Oh, fuck, I'm never going to get her on, this is hopeless. But her performance was the best thing I'd ever heard.

Of course, there were many performers who were not able to handle drugs as well as Marianne, and they paid the price. Janis Joplin, Jimi Hendrix, Jim Morrison and that lot, but if it hadn't been drugs it would have been something else, I suspect. There

313

are those who are doomed and those who aren't. I reckon if they're going to blow it, they'll probably blow it anyway, one way or another. I think you must always think of the person rather than the drug or the stimuli or whatever it is. We've taken a lot of acid. Hundreds of people were taking acid all the time. And there weren't all these casualties. I used to slug bottles of it back and so did loads of other hippies in the sixties. And they're all perfectly all right—well, most of them. Pretty good, really. I think there are great survivors from that period. But they weren't into smack. That's the bad stuff. But everybody always knew that. It's a more negative thing, and the sixties were very positive and optimistic.

□ □ □

Marianne Faithfull

AFTER I SPLIT up with Mick, it was very difficult to learn to be an ordinary person. I'm terribly proud of that. I think that's one of the most important things I've ever done—to learn to be poor. My fears and phobias still followed me around a bit, but I had to learn to survive in the normal world without lots of money and attention and get through it. I don't think Mick could manage that if he ever had to.

Thinking about why society turned on us, I think they must've sensed our arrogance. Our "You're so boring, and we're so great." That kind of thing. They knew that. People always do. They pick up on it. And they don't accept that kind of arrogance. It makes the public determined to show people like us where God lives. But, still a lot of people had affection for us as a couple, and I think they hold that against me in England, that I really should not have broken up with Mick. I was supposed to continue with him till I dropped over. But it would have killed me, eventually, staying with Mick. Really.

CHAPTER SEVENTEEN

The Long, Ugly Shadow
of Altamont

*When I think about that kid getting murdered at
Altamont, I think, It could have been me.*

MICK JAGGER

Despite the severe traumas of 1969—Brian's death, the movie debacle, Marianne's defection—Jagger embarked on the Stones' U.S. tour in late 1969 with optimism. The band figured to be a sellout everywhere, their new album *Let It Bleed* was at the top of the charts, and Jagger's personal popularity was at an all-time high. What's more, the kids now had a cause on which to focus their rebellion—the Vietnam War—and their concerted opposition would give a powerful unity to the Stones' rock audiences.

Although at the start the tour gave every sign of living up to Jagger's expectancy, before it was over it was to become a calamity from which Jagger and the Stones would never recover—the bloody Altamont concert at Livermore, California, during which the Hell's Angels beat and maimed kids in the audience, knifed one young man to death, contributed to the deaths of three others and intimidated Mick and the other Stones to the point of sniveling impotency.

Ossie Clark, who designed Mick's costumes, accompanied the Stones on the tour.

Ossie Clark

I FLEW WITH the Stones to their first date, which was at the Forum in Los Angeles. I remember vividly that from the moment I set foot in that plane, before it took off from London, I felt a kind of oppressive fear. There was a negative electric charge in the atmosphere, compared to the tours I had gone on before that. The flight over was a nightmare, truly scary. The way the Stones were toward each other, toward me, an insistent, brooding, uncontrolled intimidation. In Los Angeles we were put up in a big house, and the evil vibes intensified. The Stones were taking all kinds of horrible drugs, primarily a new kind of potent acid that they had gotten hold of.

But it was more than that. They had been getting deeper and deeper into black magic. Led by Anita Pallenberg, Keith and Mick had developed a kind of Satanic identification, as if they were openly dealing with the devil. I suppose it was all bound up with the music they were doing, Satanic songs like "Jumpin' Jack Flash" and "Sympathy for the Devil," but that didn't make it any the less frightening.

I had once spent three weeks with them in the South of France. Keith had rented a house that had been built by an English admiral who eventually threw himself into the sea off the window ledge. The house still contained strong vibes from that. But on top of that ghostliness was the Satanic thing that was going on. I spent most of the time smoking opium with Anita, who was definitely the high priestess in control of the black magic that was pervasive. She had pushed Keith far into it, and I shied away from him. Her bible was *The Master and Margarita*, which deals with Satanic fantasy. In the late night, while they smoked dope, she'd read frightening passages to Keith and Mick, and when she really got herself worked into it, she did have the aspect of a witch, and they were right into it with her. It scared the hell out of me.

There was another time when Keith and Anita were living in the house in Cheyne Walk. I remember going there one night, and Anita came up to me with this pin, a golden pin with a skull on the head. It had an emerald for one eye and a ruby for the other. She thrust it at me menacingly: "Don't you think it's beautiful?" she demanded.

"I think it's rather macabre," I said.

She said, "I think it would be nice to stick it in your neck." She

316

lunged at me and I had to grab her arm or she would certainly have plunged it into my neck. That was Anita—no wonder she was able to destroy Brian Jones. Keith got away from her just in time.

One night I was at Mick's house in London—I was designing the costumes for this 1969 tour. The principal costume I made for him was dominated by a black and red shirt with streamers—half black and half red with one black streamer and one red streamer, set off by a red, white and blue Uncle Sam top hat. The way Mick worked with me, he'd phone and say, "Come on over tonight and let's do costumes." He'd put on a tape of the music that would be played on the tour and he'd dance around and say, "I'd like to do this and that," and we kind of evolved our costume ideas together. But for this trip, our costume night was different. Mick danced around with great intensity and he was telling me in a stream of what seemed subconscious feelings, somewhat incoherent, what he wanted to convey. It was more than just describing costumes or anything like that, it was as if he had become Satan and was announcing his evil intentions. He was reveling in this role. Frightening, truly frightening. I always knew that Mick had several clearly defined personas—talk about a split personality! But this was a side of Mick never revealed before. He was rejoicing in being Lucifer.

There was a time I saw another side of his persona, when anger overcame him and he became like a man possessed. It happened at a party the Stones gave when they decided to become tax exiles, a going-away party that they gave themselves. They threw this party in a place in Maidenhead. John Lennon was there, and a lot of their other musician friends. At four o'clock in the morning, the owner said, "That's it, no more drinks." Mick was incensed, absolutely furious because the party had thinned and there was a nice lot of his favorite people who were left and Mick wanted to go on partying with them. But the owner just told Mick to fuck off and left, after padlocking the bar. Mick went out of control, smashing things all over the room. Finally he picked up a chair and threw it through the big glass window, spraying glass all over the place. Then he dashed out and disappeared into the night. I had gone to the party with him but he left without me, ranting and raving.

That night in Los Angeles, November 7, 1969, when the Stones appeared before those eighteen thousand young people at the Forum for their concert, the atmosphere was very tense. I clearly recall my feelings when we were backstage watching the preliminaries. Ike and Tina Turner and the Ikettes, who were on the bill with the Stones, were warming up with Mick and Keith, and there was a strange look on Mick's face, a kind of sneer, and I thought, Oh, my God, we're in for it tonight.

We went out and took our seats, the Stones appeared, the first note was played and the whole place erupted like a tiger roaring. I almost blacked out. This was not the wave of adulation I was accustomed to hearing, no, this was like a mob being exhorted by a dictator. And then when Mick went into his Lucifer routine with the black and red streamers flying, the audience seemed to spit out its defiance.

He introduced himself as "a man of wealth and taste" who had been around a long time, had taken men's souls, and achieved a catalogue of Satanic triumphs.

I was trembling I was so frightened. And the more the audience's reaction intensified, the more Mick baited them. I expected a riot, an explosion. I escaped before the concert ended, went back to the house, packed my bag and immediately left for New York. Even when I got to New York I couldn't shake off the scary, ominous feelings of that night. It stayed with me. For a week or more after that, I'd wake in the night in a heavy sweat.

Then, just a few weeks later, when their tour took them to the Altamont Speedway outside San Francisco, the disaster I had anticipated happened. It seemed to me inevitable. Perhaps it was a backlash, all those kids with changing emotions, the Hell's Angels thugs, the murdered black youth, the beatings, the pathetic nude girls, as if Lucifer was being chased back to his lair.

I never designed another costume for Mick. That was the end of my association with the Stones. And to my mind that was the end of the Stones. They had clearly gone beyond where I wanted to go.

☐ ☐ ☐

After the Maysles brothers had finished editing their Altamont footage, they decided to gamble and bring it to London to show to the Stones. The gamble was that they planned to film the Stones while they were watching the movie, and there was no telling how the Stones would react when they saw how they had behaved at Altamont while the Hell's Angels' brutality was occurring. Also it was in the Stones' power to refuse to allow the Maysles brothers to release the film if they didn't like it.

David and Albert Maysles

WE WENT TO London and set up the film in an editing room, with Jagger, Richards, Charlie Watts, Bill Wyman and Mick Taylor in attendance—nobody else. They watched the footage of Altamont, the rampaging Hell's Angels, Mick's ineffectual appeals for order, the killing, the repulsive destructiveness that followed. They watched the screen intently and our cameras recorded their faces, which were expressionless, especially Mick's. When the film ended, there was a long silence, then Mick asked us to show it again, which we did. Again, Mick showed no expression on his blank face. He didn't say a word to anyone. He didn't look at Keith or anyone else, and he said nothing to us about the film itself. He just got up and walked out. So did the others.

We titled the film *Gimme Shelter*, after one of the Stones' songs with its ominous rumbling that war was "just a shot away." We knew we had something special, that it was a unique and exciting film, but to our surprise and dismay, no distributor wanted to take it on. Too downbeat, they said. We screened it for the producer, Joe Levine, who viewed it with his top assistant. When it ended, Levine turned to his assistant and said, "Who is Mick Jagger, anyway?" His assistant replied that he was a great rock and roll star. "Well," said Joe Levine, "he's no Sammy Davis," and walked out.

□ □ □

The Maysles eventually were able to get the film distributed, having raised most of the money themselves, and it was an unqualified success both critically and at the box office. After viewing the film, detectives were able to identify the Hell's Angel who knifed Meredith Hunter. His name was Alan Passaro and they found him in jail doing time for drug possession. When he was brought to trial, his defense was that Hunter had pointed a loaded gun at him and that Passaro had knifed him in self-defense. The jury acquitted him.

No one else was ever brought to account for the carnage at Altamont. But years later it was revealed that the Hell's Angels had planned a murderous vendetta against the Stones.

NEW YORK *DAILY NEWS*, MARCH 14, 1983
ANGELS OUT TO KILL STONES, PANEL TOLD

Washington (AP) The Hell's Angels have an "open contract" against Mick Jagger and the Rolling Stones and have tried at least twice to kill the British rock group, a former member of the motorcycle gang said yesterday.

A witness identified only as Butch told the Senate Judiciary Committee the vendetta dated back to the slaying of a spectator at a 1969 Stones concert in Altamont, California, that was captured in the film *Gimme Shelter*.

Authorities said the gun-toting spectator was stabbed in a scuffle with Hell's Angels hired to provide security at the outdoor festival attended by 300,000 people.

Butch, whose real name was not revealed under a federal witness-protection program, said the Angels still were angry because they felt the Rolling Stones "did not back them" in the subsequent furor and prosecution of a gang member.

"There's always been an open contract on the band," said Butch, a convicted murderer who testified behind a screen. "There's been two attempts to kill them that I know about. They will someday. They swear they will still do it."

He said the first attempt had occurred in the mid-1970's.

"They sent a member with a gun and a silencer" to a hotel in an unidentified city where the Angels believed the Stones were staying, Butch said. "He staked out the hotel, but they never showed up."

Butch said that in 1979 members of the Angels' New York City chapter planned an assault by boat against a house in which the Stones were staying.

"They were going to put a bomb in the house and blow everybody up and kill everybody at the party," he said. The plot died, Butch said, when the Angels, moving in on a rubber raft, lost their plastic explosives overboard.

He said that killing the rock band was an obsession with the Angels, reported by law officials to have more than 500 hard-core members in 33 chapters in the United States and 18 in other countries.

After the screening of *Gimme Shelter*, Keith Richards had this rather feisty disclaimer as to his responsibility for what had happened: "The underground suddenly leaps up in a horrified shriek when some spade hippie gets done, which is a terrible thing, but they never get uptight if some cop gets crushed at a pop concert. For all the control you have over an audience, it doesn't mean you can control the murders. You can't make someone's knife disappear just by looking at him, you can't be God, you can't ever pretend to play at being God. You don't shoulder any responsibilities when you pick up a guitar or sing a song because it's not a position of responsibility.

"What is evil? I don't know how much people think of Mick as the Devil or as just a good rock performer. There are black musicians who think we are acting as unknown agents of Lucifer and others who think we are Lucifer. Everybody's Lucifer."

Ian Stewart

THE ALTAMONT CATASTROPHE took place in December of 1969, appropriately as the sixties decade came to an end. As far as I was concerned, Altamont was the death knell for all those things that we thought would last forever. I personally felt like the sixties had been an extravagant stage show and I had been a spectator in the audience. Altamont had rung down the curtain to no applause.

Altamont cast its ominous shadow over the ensuing decade. Although the Stones toured Europe and the United States to full houses, their concerts progressively lost vitality and so did the responses of the audiences. The songs had become tamer, the lyrics more garbled, the albums banal, the use of drugs accelerated.

In 1971, when Richard Schickel of *Life* was assessing the fallout from the Altamont tragedy, he wrote:

Jagger has cast himself in a role not unlike the one played in letters by Jean Genet, that of the outlaw saint. His music never charms, it only overwhelms. His personal style is deliberately unappetizing by conventional standards. And so to the undiscriminating he becomes something more than the most interesting musical figure to emerge from the pop ferment, something more than a phenomenon on the order of Presley or the Beatles. He becomes an existential hero.

He is at least dimly aware of this new and potentially dangerous factor in his celebrity. But, needless to say, he lacks the intelligence—social, philosophical, moral—to deal with it. He also—thank God—lacks the forcefulness of personality to mobilize his followers in support of anything except adoration of Mick Jagger, as his rather pathetic attempts to control the Altamont crowd demonstrate. And so, finally, he appears sometimes to be just another scared boy riding a tiger and hanging on for dear life, rather happy, it seems, behind his wall of Hell's Angels, free as a result of their presence from all those feverishly clutching, adolescent female hands. Finally, one imagines, he will withdraw physically, as he already has psychologically, from his public.

In the spring of 1971, Jagger unexpectedly married a Nicaraguan socialite model, Bianca Perez Morena de Macias, who was four months pregnant. Bianca and Mick had been having an affair for the past year, but no one had expected them to marry and, in fact, Keith and Anita lobbied intensively to get Mick to change his mind. But with only two days' notice, Mick announced that the wedding would take place in St. Tropez, and he chartered a jet to transport a load of his friends from London.

Bianca cleverly disguised her burgeoning pregnancy by wearing a low-cut dress that partially exposed her ample breasts, thereby directing attention away from her midriff. There was a crush of paparazzi at the wedding such as St. Tropez had rarely experienced.

Before the ceremony commenced, and with Paul McCartney, Keith Moon, Ringo Starr, Ossie Clark, Eric Clapton, and other such London luminaries assembling, Mick and Bianca engaged in a rather heated argument over their prenuptial agreement. French law stipulates that the groom must list all assets that the bride is entitled to share in the event of a divorce; Mick wanted Bianca to declare that she was not to share in any of his property, but she resisted to the point of suggesting that they cancel the wedding. In the end, Mick prevailed and Bianca gave up any claim to his possessions.

Although the marriage to Bianca lasted until 1980, from the outset Mick was peculiarly detached from it, almost as if it had not been consummated. That it lasted that long is probably attributable to Mick's devotion to their daughter, Jade, on whom he doted. But after only a few years of his marriage to Bianca, Mick became openly involved with other women, notably a Texan named Jerry Hall who, from the mid-seventies on, became his rather constant companion.

Mick was officially divorced from Bianca in 1980; after a well-publicized attempt by Bianca's divorce lawyer, the notorious Marvin Mitchelson, to collect thirteen million dollars plus a hefty monthly allowance, the eventual settlement amounted to one million dollars.

The Stones' performances in the seventies increasingly depended, for their drive and energy, upon the adrenalin that drugs provided. Sally Arnold, who managed many of those tours, gave me this inside account of their day-to-day life while touring.

Sally Arnold

WE ALL TOOK a lot of drugs—mostly coke and speed to keep going at the breakneck pace that touring required, finishing a gig at two in the morning, then right on to another, one airport after another, crash for a few hours, then back on stage. When they had been on tour in the sixties, the Stones seemed to be able to handle this hectic routine, but by the time I was running the tours, in the seventies, they couldn't keep going and get "up" for performances without the help of dope. Every tour the promoters would be charged with a ten percent budget requirement credited to "miscellaneous"—it was common knowledge that that ten percent was to provide coke and speed for the crew.

The Stones had their own suppliers. I don't know where they came from or who contacted them. The suppliers simply knew that the Stones were coming to town and they'd turn up at the door. They'd tell the security guards they were a friend of Keith's, and the security guards would come to me and give me their names, and when I'd ask Keith he'd say, "Oh, yeah, yeah, let him in, he's our friend." I remember one instance, when we were playing in Berlin, and this dealer arrived and put on the table in front of me a mound of cocaine the size of a football, a mountain of coke. I had never seen anything like it. Using a piece of cardboard, I divided it up into approximately equal grams, and gave a cut to whoever wanted it—Keith, Woody [Ron Wood, Mick Taylor's replacement], Mick, practically the whole crew wanted some, including myself.

When I distributed coke I always kept track of the amount each person took, and I still have some of those lists. I remember once I kept track on a paper napkin, and their accounts would be charged with the cost: Keith, ten grams; Woody, eight grams; and so forth, and the accountants would charge their accounts with the cost of the amounts they had taken.

We also made coke and heroin available during the performances. There was one tour we had a walkway on each side of the stage, which Mick and Billy Preston would mount and then dance on the platform that connected them. It stretched the whole width of the stage. The entire structure was covered with drapes, and hidden underneath the drapes were the amps. The audience couldn't see behind these drapes or behind the amps. That's where we put lines of cocaine and heroin, right on top of these amps under the walkway, stripes of coke on one side of the stage, stripes of heroin on the other. Everybody working the show knew which side was the heroin and which side was the cocaine. The side with the heroin was Keith and Woody's side, and the side with the cocaine was everybody else's. While the show was going on, all of us would sneak back behind the drapes and have a quick line whenever we needed a fix, and that included Mick.

Also, Keith and Woody would smoke what we called "DCs"—dirty cigarettes, which consisted of an ordinary cigarette that had most of the tobacco removed, then they would suck up the heroin into the cigarette, light it and smoke it. For all intents and purposes it looked like an ordinary cigarette and they'd smoke them while performing. I myself wouldn't touch one of those because even the smell of it made me feel quite ill. It was a very acrid, sort of nasty, cloying smell, a smell like no other I can think of to compare it with. Mick used to help himself to coke during a performance but I never saw him doing heroin.

In 1971 or thereabouts, I was at Mick's—he was married to Bianca then and I was nanny to their infant daughter, Jade (this is before I became manager of their tours)—the Stones were all living in the South of France then to avoid paying British income tax. Bill and Astrid Wyman were present—they lived nearby—and some other people and we were having a dinner party. After dinner Mick decided to show some home movies, and what appeared on the screen was a group photo of the Stones all dressed in drag—wigs and all that—posed to make a picture to promote a new single that was called "Have You Seen Your Mother, Baby, Standing in the Shadow?"

After the photo session, Brian, who was dressed in an airline stewardess's costume, sits down on a chair, hikes up his skirt and starts masturbating, right on camera! He looks very proud of himself, as he merrily keeps wanking away. Well, needless to say, being quite young at the time, I was shocked and embarrassed—I mean, here I was this proper Norland Nanny watching Brian playing with himself while everyone was watching and laughing and joking, "Oh, isn't it enormous?" and "Oh, come on Brian, hurry up!"—all that kind of thing. Brian is loving all the attention, absolutely grinning away, quite pleased with himself, actually. I was blushing so fiercely I had to leave the room, so I didn't see the end of the film but I presume Brian obliged everyone with an orgasm. It seemed peculiar to me that Mick would show that film what with Brian long dead and buried.

When I was nannying for Mick and Bianca, Mick was most certainly taking cocaine and smoking grass. And I suspect they were taking amyl nitrite, Bianca and him, because the evidence was all over their bedroom. I saw needles on the road, which I supposed belonged to Keith and Anita. I don't think Woody ever injected—I think he just smoked and snorted heroin and coke. But I know for sure that Keith and Anita did because the police caught them on tour. I remember one night, while we were touring, Keith warned me that somebody would be bringing me a package for him. Of course, I knew right away what it would be. I was fast asleep when there was a knock on my door about four in the morning. There was a guy standing there who gave me a packet all bound up in gaffer tape that I just tucked under my pillow and went back to sleep. A few hours later Keith woke me up and asked for the packet.

Another time, Mick asked one of his friends to carry some hash through customs for him. The friend never used drugs, had never even been around drug people, so as he approached the customs police he got so worried that he swallowed the whole lot. He was deathly ill for days—he told me about that himself.

Sometimes on the night flights from concert to concert we were all so stoned nothing would have gotten a rise out of us. This one time, I recall, we were flying from Barcelona to Nice to do a concert there, all of us drugged out, and sitting right next to me were Keith and Anita; with no attempt to cover themselves, Anita apparently gave a blow job to Keith, completely oblivious to everything and everybody around them. I was so out of it I didn't notice a thing. Everybody was saying, "Didn't you notice it?"

And there was the occasion when we had given a concert in Leicestershire, a big horrible hall. It was a really stormy, rainy night but Keith decided not to stay at the hotel but to drive back to London. So he drove on the M1 in his Bentley with four or five other people and his little boy, Marlon, then about eight years old. We started out after midnight, Keith driving fast, missed a turn and crashed the car. No one was hurt, but just before the police arrived Keith chucked out the window all the drugs he had in his possession—probably heroin, cocaine, hash, pills, quite an assortment, just opened the window and pitched the whole lot into the tall grass. But on the back shelf of the car was this big silver necklace that had silver straws and spoons on it. The police found traces of heroin and cocaine in the straws, and as a result put Keith in jail for the night and didn't release him until the following evening.

Keith came back to London late that night and went straight to my flat and asked me to help him get some heroin, needles and syringes. I didn't know where to get things like that, but at the same time I didn't want him to have to use dirty needles because of the danger of hepatitis. So I phoned a lady doctor I knew who worked with addicts, and asked her advice. She said she could give me a syringe and some needles so Keith wouldn't have to go and get street things, but that she couldn't give Keith any drugs. So Keith and I turned up at her doorstep around three in the morning to collect these needles and syringes from her. And then he went to get the drugs elsewhere.

It was obvious to me that celebrities who got busted were given preferential treatment. When Keith and Anita were caught with heroin in their suitcases while traveling in the States, the only punishment they got was having to do a concert for charity. But in that same courtroom, a teenage boy who had been caught with dope on him was sentenced to three months in prison. So much for justice.

☐ ☐ ☐

On subsequent tours of the United States the Stones worked hard to overcome the stigma of Altamont but the temper of audiences had drastically changed and the Stones were hard put to deal with the undercurrent of belligerence they faced. Just as the use of drugs had escalated with the Stones, so, too, were audiences increasingly into coke and other drugs, and they often seemed disgruntled during performances to the point of throwing beer bottles and other objects at the Stones.

Anita and Keith had become confirmed heroin addicts but both were able to continue performing. Anita, however, had no illusions about her ability as a movie actress.

Anita Pallenberg

I WASN'T REALLY an actress, in the sense Marianne Faithfull was, doing Shakespeare and all that, no, my attitude was—it's only me, pay me a fee and you can borrow my face. But I gave up acting when I had a son in 1969. Keith and I took Marlon with us when the band traveled. As a toddler, he went to rehearsals and recordings, and during performances he even sat on a stool next to Keith while he played. Marlon was a true rock baby.

In '71 we all moved to the South of France to avoid the heavy British taxes. Keith and I tried to get clean of our heroin addiction before we left England. We both took cures, but twenty-four hours after we occupied the villa Keith had rented in Villefranche-sur-Mer, we were back injecting ourselves because a cure's no good when you live in the middle of pushers and users—God knows there was plenty of both on the Riviera.

The following year I gave birth to a daughter. We called her Dandelion at first, later changed her name to Angela. It should have been a good time but it was difficult having children and belonging to Keith's world. We were both still on heroin, and then he'd go off to perform and I'd have to stay there by myself still stuck on heroin but now I'd have to look after my own supply since Keith was not around to provide for the two of us. Being on heroin the way I was, I had the kids to take care of but I couldn't do a good job of it. I was more interested in getting my supply than I was in looking after them. People started to condemn me as a bad person, neglecting my kids, only interested in feeding my habit. Instead of getting them dinner, I'd go out and wander around and meet people and spend the night in the park looking for flying saucers. I used to enjoy feeling the glow of heroin and searching the sky for signs of flying saucers.

While Keith was away, I'd be starting to get off the heroin, really trying, but then he'd return and he'd get me on it just as bad as before. People who used to be friends began to get very bitchy toward me. Keith had this entourage of hangers-on who were always around the house, came for a weekend, stayed on for weeks and months, always a full house of freeloading sycophants, "Yes, Keith, yes, anything you say, Keith," no private life, no time to talk, the suppliers bringing us the heroin, but that's all we had in common. Then Keith started to have girl friends that I found out about, and I started to see other men. But things took a turn for us and got better when I had our third child, the son Keith always wanted with me. Keith announced that we were going to be married and began to make elaborate wedding plans. He was really happy when he took off on a European tour with the Stones, but while he was away the baby died, and, in a sense, we died, too.

☐ ☐ ☐

Sally Arnold told me that when Anita joined Keith on tour after she had the baby, some weird things were going on between them.

Sally Arnold

I'M NOT SAYING there were other men and women, because they were too high on smack to be involved sexually with anybody else. I doubt that Keith could get it up if his life depended on it because he was so smacked out all the time. But he was very violent toward her even though she had had the baby shortly before she joined the tour.

When she came on the tour, she showed us photographs of the infant. A couple of weeks into the tour, Anita got word that her baby son had died.

Keith took the baby's death very hard, and so did poor Anita, who had completely lost her looks. I have pictures of her at that time, and she looked terrible! Fat, bloated, flabby, her skin was yellow and drawn. I'm told this is very typical of women on heroin. It was sad because she had once been so beautiful, so stunning.

Anita Pallenberg

WE STAYED TOGETHER for a short while after the baby died, but then we got seriously busted going into Canada and our lawyer lectured us that we were a bad influence on one another and that if we were ever going to kick heroin and stay out of trouble we would have to separate. We took his advice and I went to live in Connecticut while Keith stayed with friends in New York. But then the last straw for Keith was that boy of seventeen who shot himself in my house. That really ended it for us, and although we occasionally saw each other after that for the sake of the children, it was the end of our personal relationship.

Marlon stayed with me, and we got along okay, but Angela was something else. I suffered a bad bout of depression after the baby died and I wasn't able to cope with Angela. We used to take her on the road with us but she'd wander off and pick up men and bring them back to meet us, like prizes. So we stopped taking her on the road but I still couldn't handle her, so I sent her to live with my mother in England. I guess if the baby had lived we would have been okay, Keith and me, but then again, maybe not. Perhaps the lawyer was right and it took that tragedy to convince us.

The malaise affecting the Stones was but a manifestation of a larger malaise which was wilting the spirit of the sixties generation. "By the end of 1968," Christopher Booker observes, "the image of youthful, irreverent vitality which had so dominated England in the mid-sixties had all but evaporated. Despite the continuing efforts of a determined avant-garde minority, the trend toward permissiveness in the arts, the mass media and social mores which, barely two years before, had still seemed to be holding out to its devotees such infinite promise, was beginning, with its very success, to take on a tired and even somewhat dated look. Even more revealing was the extent to which the activities of the pop avant-garde, the make-believe of the 'hippies' and 'flower children,' the light shows of the psychedelic 'underground,' seemed less and less to involve the rest of the nation, which observed them with increasing boredom and detachment as a sort of unreal raree-show.

"Indeed it was clearly noticeable in these years after 1966 that the flow of new figures and personalities who, between 1956 and 1965, had poured on to the national stage in successive waves, as the symbols and representatives of social upheaval, had virtually dried up. While in the attitudes of many people toward the drug scandals or the student protesters, and in the increasingly scornful use of such terms as 'trendy' and 'leftie,' there were signs for the first time in over twelve years of a fashionable drift back toward the right.

"By the closing years of the sixties, however, this changing climate in Britain was only a microcosm of a much wider process taking place in many countries. Particularly by the eventful year of 1968, this phase of exhaustion and loss of momentum, this 'fading into reality' of the collective dreams of the sixties, this rightward swing and the beginnings of transition to a different age, could be seen all over the world. In 1966–8, the world continued to be overshadowed by the peculiar horror of the war in Vietnam. The speed with which, in just a few years, the American Dream, the most powerful image of the twentieth century, had collapsed into nightmare, had left the world quite stunned. Only by the second half of 1968, in the wake of the assassinations of Martin Luther King and Robert Kennedy, in the mood of national introspection over such matters as the influence of television saturated with images of violence, in the comparative lull in rioting in the cities and the beginning of Vietnam peace talks, were there signs at last of a numbed quiescence in the previous apparently helpless drift toward disaster. With Richard Nixon's election victory on a tide of conservatism, recognition of the ending of an era, and of the desire for a fresh, less excitable start in American life became widespread. But it was clear that in the events of 1965–8, the innocence (if that had ever been the right word) of the American Dream had been lost forever."

CHAPTER EIGHTEEN

Requiem for the Jagger Generation

People have this obsession: They want you to be like you were in 1969. They want you to, because otherwise their youth goes with you, you know?

MICK JAGGER

As the seventies progressed, as the Vietnam War ended and Nixon resigned the presidency, the students' protests abated and with them what remained of the throb of the sixties. By the time the eighties decade began, there was little vestige of the glitter of King's Road, Haight-Ashbury, Carnaby Street and the other stages where the sixties' circus had performed. And just as they had mirrored the rise of the madcap sixties, so now the Stones were beholden to its fall. The glitter generation no longer glittered and the Glimmer Twins, Mick and Keith, no longer glimmered.

The last time I saw Ian Stewart, a few weeks before he died, I asked him how, in retrospect, he would evaluate the sixties scene.

Ian Stewart

THIS BUSINESS ABOUT London being the glamour city of the sixties, swinging London, all the famous hairdressers and fashion designers and pop artists and artsy-fartsy photographers—let me tell you, it's all bullshit. Phony London, that's what it was—tacky. All that hoopla, and the truth was that there were a couple of bands—the Beatles and the Stones

331

and a few others—and everything spun off them. If you sold a painting to a Beatle, you were overnight a hot artist. Or if you made a dress for a Beatle wife or a Stone girl friend, you were hot stuff in the world of fashion. If you went to the same clubs as Mick or Brian or McCartney and they said two words to you, you became "presto!" very big on the social scene. And that goes for young duchesses and Lady This and Lady That.

So the David Hockneys and Mary Quants and David Baileys and all the rest were just spin-offs from the only thing London was all about—the rock groups and the music they made. But as for any real *movement*, any real revolution, hell, there was no foundation. The whole pop thing was just a big balloon that could've gone bang at any time. The London scene was just a goulash of that silly drug, acid, silly clothes, silly people, silly discos, and the whole thing was very incestuous. I thought it was dreadful. Just a lot of commotion chasing its own tail and not something I wanted to be a part of— and I sure as hell wasn't. We set out to be a serious band, to play music seriously, and phony London disgusted me. But what kept me going was our studio sessions, because the guys in the Stones band were all damn good musicians and when we got it going it was *some* lift. And I enjoyed the tours. But not all that London bullshit. Some of those groups got by with murder. Like the Beatles. It beat hell out of me how they became as famous as they did. But that's the sixties for you—over the years, Liverpool never produced a decent musician and the Beatles were living proof of it.

In the seventies and into the eighties, the Stones were subjected to a continuation of persecutory drug busts; wives and girl friends were traded in for new models; the band was further depleted by resignation and death; the Stones' life-styles emphasized wayward opulence and their behavior remained unpredictable but self-indulged; their new albums continued to sell, but nevertheless a pall, a taint, a catheter of doubt drained something vital from both the Stones and their times, which, in turn, had lost their militant thrust with the end of the Vietnam War.

"It was really a reaction of society against what society itself had done," Marianne Faithfull has observed. "They had built us up too high and now they would tear us down."

That tearing down was brutal: the deadly assault on Brian

Jones; the killing and mayhem at Altamont; the nightmarish drug persecution and its residue, exemplified in the drug wrecks who once were the beauteous Marianne Faithfull and the exotic Anita Pallenberg; the death of Ian Stewart at age forty-seven; Mick Taylor's departure from the band, hopelessly addicted to heroin, replaced by Ron Wood, a veteran guitarist, no stranger to drugs himself. Bill Wyman, the old man of the group and its once steadying influence, scandalized Britain with the revelation of his affair with a thirteen-year-old virgin named Mandy Smith whom he recruited from the Holy Family of Enfield Convent in North London. Bill topped off his mid-life escapade by recently, at age fifty-three, marrying Mandy, now nineteen.

Despite Altamont and the drug busts, Mick Jagger was untouched, unscathed, unrepentant. He remained the epitome of the rock hero who produced this universally embraced music that sprang from the proletariat, as he himself did. Mick made no bones about the fact that his overriding motivation was money, and lots of it. And yet, he became a romantic outlaw, making no concessions to anyone, totally self-absorbed, embracing no causes, no commitments, no goals, although he had a vague yearning to succeed as a film star and as a certified, gilt-edged gentleman. A few years ago Mick accepted an advance of a couple million dollars from the publisher Lord Weidenfeld, to write his autobiography, but apparently Jagger's porous memory had let too many people, places and events slip through to oblivion, and he reluctantly returned the money. As far as his personal life is concerned, after his divorce from Bianca, a marriage that was meaningless, he appears to have settled down with the Texas model, Jerry Hall, with whom he has two children. But Jerry Hall is a truck driver's daughter and a far cry from the lady of social standing and means whom Mick always idealized.

He precipitated a rupture of his long relationship with Keith Richards when he rejected Richards's urging to mount a tour in 1986 after they produced an album called *Dirty Work*. Instead, Jagger recorded two albums that he wrote by himself, both failures, and his studio bands did not include a single member of the Rolling Stones. In retaliation, Richards recorded his own solo album, which was no more successful than Mick's. Their failures made them both realize eventually that they could not succeed apart from each other and the other Rolling Stones.

"I think of our differences as a family squabble," Keith said at the time. "If I shout and scream at him, it's because no one else has the guts to do it or else they're not paid to do it. At the same time I'd hope Mick realizes that I'm a friend who is just trying to bring him into line and do what needs to be done. Though rock and roll is over thirty years old, no one has really tried to make it grow up.

"Mick has a Peter Pan complex. He worries that the Rolling Stones are old-fashioned and thinks that he can do better on his own making high-tech records. I've reminded him that the Rolling Stones are in a unique position. We've been on top for twenty-five years and don't have to worry about suddenly coming to the end of the road. But Mick keeps looking back over his shoulder at Michael Jackson, Prince and George Michael. I've told him it's ludicrous to try to pretend you're twenty when you're forty-five."

At the time of their dispute, Mick was charitable toward Keith: "We're two men who've been friends for thirty-five years, but when you work with somebody every day, occasionally you want to strangle even the closest of friends. Keith knows he can rely on me. If the phone rang in the middle of the night and he was needing my help, I'd go straightaway. But, Keith never calls me. He never calls anybody."

Recently, during their 1989 tour, Keith summed up their relationship this way: "Mick and I are incredibly diverse people. We've known each other over forty years—ever since we were three or four years old. But while a certain part of our personalities is incredibly close, there's an awful lot which is very, very different. I'm his friend and he knows it. It's just, like, 'I love you, darling, but I can't live with you.' "

"Mick and I never hit it off," Anita Pallenberg told me. "He'd always put me down, make snide remarks about me, criticize the way I dressed. You know why? Because it was plain to see that he was in love with Keith. In many ways Keith was the man Mick wanted to be. Free and easy in his own skin, not uptight like Mick. Tough when he had to be, never backed down, had a good time, really enjoyed drinking, drugs and carousing, enjoyed sex—Mick wasn't into any of those things and he envied Keith and was jealous of me."

Mick's huge fortune provides him the luxury of total self-absorption, a boundless arrogance, and as one of the premier rock performers, if not *the* premier, he knows that his very presence on stage ensures the success of whatever fortunate group he chooses to anoint.

And yet he has a persistent uneasiness that, now, at age forty-seven, he has peaked and missed the opportunities that would have allowed him to succeed in areas he coveted beyond the rock stage. The 1989 U.S. tour was a huge ninety-million-dollar success, as were the tours of the Who, featuring a middle-aged, balding Pete Townshend, and the Grateful Dead, the over-the-hill potbellied gang headed by Jerry Garcia. But the audiences were not the vibrant, pulsating teenagers of the sixties, but predominantly middle-aged sixties refugees titillated by their twenty-year-old memories.

In fact, the barometer of success among rock groups—album sales—indicates that despite attendance at their concerts, the Stones have lost their dominance. Assessing album sales for 1989, *The New York Times* stated: "The Rolling Stones, Paul McCartney and the Who—all veteran rock acts that won headlines with their multi-million dollar tours—did not finish in the Top 50. Although the Rolling Stones' *Steel Wheels* album sold a respectable 1.5 million copies, that number is only one-fourth of the six-million-plus sales of Bobby Brown's album *Don't Be Cruel* and the New Kids on the Block album *Hangin' Tough*."

In a sense, the Stones and the other touring rock groups constitute today's vaudeville circuit. Just as Fred Allen, Eddie Cantor, Burns and Allen, Abbott and Costello and other vaudeville stars used to periodically bring their acts to the Palace and theaters on the RKO circuit, repeating their tried and true routines year in and year out, so, too, do the Stones dress up the stage with expensive scenery and lights and thrill their audiences with old favorites—"Satisfaction," "Let's Spend the Night Together," and "Honky Tonk Women," which they perform flanked by giant, lifelike inflatables of two wayward women. The few new songs on the program from their latest album, *Steel Wheels*, made little or no impact. Vaudeville always relied on the appeal of the star turn, and that's what the Stones deliver, replete with Mick—mirabile dictu!—still able to perform his whirling dervish struts, bumps, grinds, pivots, twists, twirls and mock striptease.

Jagger, himself, is realistic about how important touring their act has been to the Stones' success: "We have had our ups and downs. When we were a new band, our first record got in the Top

Forty. Our next record went in the Top Ten, and so I suppose in that way we were instantly successful. And from then on, we've always had hits of some kind. Success on the road—that's the reason we're still around. Because we've always been successful on the road after having downs and troughs in our lives. Why that is, I don't know. You could put it down to anything: luck, hard work, not giving up when things look bleak as it did on a couple of occasions toward the end of the sixties when we were all in and out of jail, and then again when Keith was in trouble in Canada. That was another drug-related problem. But you kind of put those things past you and carry on, as if nothing had happened."

Keith, Marianne and Anita have all three made remarkable recoveries from their heroin addictions, at least for the time being. Keith has readily admitted that he would have been better and have played better if he had not been on heroin. "The thing about smack is that you don't have any say in it. It's not your decision anymore. You need the dope, that's the only thing. 'Why? I like it.' It takes the decision off your shoulders. You'll go through all those incredible hassles to get it and think nothing of it. Because that is the number-one priority—first the dope, then you can get home and do anything else that needs doing, like living, if you can.

"It took me about two years to get addicted. The first two years, I played around with it. It's the greatest seduction in the world. The usual thing, snort it up, then 'What do you mean I'm hooked? I've taken it for two days and I feel all right. I haven't had any *all day*!' And then you think that's cool. And it draws you in, you know? I licked it loads of times. The problem is not how to get off of it, it's how to *stay* off of it. Yep, that's the one."

Keith has finally reached an accommodation with himself that has kept him off it as have Marianne and Anita. Anita is now studying fashion design and has blocked out both alcohol and drugs.

Marianne recently performed in New York at the Church of St. Ann and the Holy Trinity and although the songs she sings are dark and somber, she has a solid assurance in delivering them. Critics have lauded her "mature voice with its husky intonation and quality of ravaged sensuality" and feel that hers is an ideal voice for interpreting the acerbic songs of Brecht and Weill. "I used to worry," she says, "that if you took away all my neuroses, where would I be and what would I have? But after giving up drugs and drink and going through therapy, I find I didn't lose my feelings. If anything, I feel more poetic and exposed."

I asked Tony Palmer what effect he thought Jagger had on the sixties, and he replied, "If you accept that it was the Jagger Generation, then you are bound to accept the complete meaninglessness of it. If you take him as being, as it were, the revolutionary leader, and then you compare him with any other revolutionary leader at any point in any society throughout the whole of history, there ain't nothing there. It is simply not enough to pound up and down the stage, however good a stage performer you are (and he's a marvelous stage performer), pound up and down the stage saying, 'I can't get no satisfaction.' Tough luck. Satisfaction for what? He had these millions of kids out there all over the world, what was it that he was trying to say? Did he have anything to say? Or was the sum total pointless ass-twisting and phallic symbols?"

Phil May, the leader of the Pretty Things, disagrees with Palmer's complaint: "So many people now ask those of us who were well-known in the sixties—Mick, Pete Townshend, myself, other band leaders—'Why, when you had it in your hands, did you not use your power to bring the whole fucking lot down? You had the sway,' they say, 'so if you'd have said to go out and do it at the end of each concert, you could have caused great commotion.' And my response is we'd have created a power vacuum which we didn't have the wherewithal to fill. It's all right bringing something down if you can replace it. But to have no backup would be very irresponsible. It's all right saying, 'This, this and this sucks. Let's pull it down.' But if you haven't got something to replace it, if you're going to put up a tent afterward, what's the point?

"The American kids that disrupted their colleges and left them in a shambles, there wasn't an original thinker amongst the whole roll call. That's why in the end nothing came of it."

There is an unidentifiable mystique that enables one particular group of rock musicians, out of the hundreds who are struggling to "arrive," to scale the heights of the rock world. In the case of the Stones, there was, in the beginning, an exciting blend of Keith Richards's raunchiness, Brian Jones's neuroticism, Andrew Oldham's outrageousness, and Mick Jagger's showmanship. They matched the rebellious mood of the sixties, fell in step behind it and pushed, but certainly did not induce it. But the Stones were clever enough to ride the sixties' shirttails, and they get high marks for that. As Ossie Clark said about fashion, "The trick was to pick up on what the kids wanted and get it in the stores while they still wanted it." That was precisely the Stones' formula.

But in the seventies, signals from those uninhibited, free-associating kids of the sixties, now turning thirty, faded; and although the Stones continued to go through the motions, the emotions were no longer the same. What remained the same was the Stones' propensity for getting their names on police blotters around the world: Mick and Keith booked in Rhode Island for punching a photographer; Keith and Anita busted by French police for possessing large quantities of heroin, cocaine and hash-ish; Anita caught with marijuana and arrested in Jamaica; Keith nabbed by London police for possession of guns, Chinese heroin and Mandrax in his Cheyne Walk house; Keith's arrest in Arkansas for carrying an illegal knife, and again in Toronto where he and Anita had a cache of hashish and heroin in their suitcases; Ron Wood and a girl friend arrested in St. Martin when cocaine was found in their rented house.

Just before Mick's marriage to Bianca, Marsha Hunt gave birth to his daughter Karis; his daughter Jade was born shortly thereafter, so that Mick had two newborns at about the same time. It was ironic that Marsha waited until 1980, the precise time that Mick was divorcing Bianca, to file a paternity suit against him. Not long after that, Jerry Hall presented Jagger with his first son.

Although Keith Richards had announced plans to marry Anita Pallenberg, the death of their infant son drove Keith and Anita deeper into heroin, and the marriage never occurred. After they broke up, Keith met and married Patti Hansen, an American model with whom he produced two daughters.

Ron Wood was also producing children, divorcing and remarrying. The total effect of all this activity, which also included Bill Wyman's severance of his sixteen-year marriage, was to distract the Stones from the concentration required for composing, recording, touring and promoting as a bonded group. In retrospect, Brian, who in many ways was the soul of the Stones, was buffeted by inconsistencies: arrogance and insecurity, talent and unyielding stubbornness, vanity and self-debasement, sexuality and impotence, vitality and torpor, gaiety and remorse. The tragedy was that not one member of the Stones, seeing his mounting wretchedness, came to Brian's rescue, tried to help him or get help for him. They all turned their backs and abandoned him as he slipped farther and farther into degradation. Marianne Faithfull saw Brian's drowning graphically predicted in the *I Ching*, which she believed in explicitly, but she felt powerless to help him avoid what turned out to be a wretched fate.

John Lennon said of Brian: "At first Brian was the most interesting Stone, but he changed over the years as he disintegrated. He ended up the kind of guy that you dread when he would come on the phone because you knew it was trouble. He was really in a lot of pain. In the early days he was all right because he was young and confident. He was one of them guys that disintegrated in front of you. I think Mick disintegrated, also. I like 'Honky Tonk Women,' but I think Mick's a joke, with all that fag dancing, I always did."

"At first Mick's movements had a freshness and spontaneity to them," Marianne says, "but after a while, by sheer repetition, Mick began to become a caricature of himself, a cartoon, but I actually feel that if you really want to be successful in that kind of show business you have to caricature yourself. Dolly Parton is a caricature. All the people in 'Dynasty' are caricatures, and Tina Turner is a caricature, too. The trick is to caricature yourself and keep some kind of cool. And that's what Mick has done, although I think that by now he has gone over the top, so that now his performance has become rather weird. There is so much bottom-wiggling and all the rest of the vulgar stuff he does, you don't listen to his voice, and you can't even hear the music because his gyrations are so distracting. Everything is intensely rehearsed, every bump, every grind, and it robs the performance of the vitality it needs."

When Marshall Chess managed the Stones, his interaction with Keith and Mick gave him an intimate evaluation of them. "Mick is very smart," Marshall told me, "but to me Keith is the Rolling Stones. I always say, if the Stones finish tomorrow, Keith would still be Keith. He'll be the way he always was, he'll never change. He may have more money, more drugs, might drink more, whatever, but he'll always be Keith and his favorite meal will be bacon and eggs with brown sauce; he is the constant factor. Mick, he's trapped in his own image now, so he can't talk to anybody. If I pick up a phone and try to ring him, it's impossible. And we were good friends. I doubt he has friends now. That's what happens to some pop superstars. They wind up in a corner, singing to themselves."

Keith, on the other hand, has a very realistic attitude toward who he is and what he has accomplished. "When we started playing, people said that rock and roll was just another cha-cha-cha or Hula-Hoop. But there's no way that you can deny that it's a way of life. It's as much a part of the lives of most of the people in the world as eating and riding the bus. This kind of music that we play is part of kids' lives as they grow up. More important to me than the records and songs is the fact that so many people have listened to me for so many years, and all these kids are now trying to play like me. I remember when I would sit for hours, trying to play like Chuck Berry. So for me that's a kind of continuity. If I turned a few people on and passed a few licks on to some people, or got them doing something that maybe they would never have done otherwise, what a turn! That's great. That's what it's all about."

As for Jagger, by not committing himself to anything, not peace, politics, charity, the anti-drug movement, or any other social or political cause, he has been able to coat himself with an impenetrable shield. Not one of his songs has stood for anything significant. The closest he came was with "Street Fighting Man," but instead of coming down unequivocally on the side of the Vietnam protesters, he whimpered that all he could do was be a rock singer because London was no place for a fighter.

Even when feminists have attacked him for some of his more notorious assaults on the dignity of women, as with "Some Girls," "Under My Thumb" and the repugnant billboard for the album *Black and Blue,* which depicted a woman bruised, gagged and bound, accompanied by the slogan, "I'm black and blue with the Rolling Stones and I love it," Mick has never stood his ground and defended his lyrics but has always ducked the punches and ultimately run away from the fight. As a result, his contempt for women, who have been no more to him than objects of carnal interest, has not alienated the large contingent of uncritical women who regard him as a sexual icon. Both Chrissie Shrimpton and Marianne Faithfull attempted suicide while they were with him, but none of the fallout landed on him. By not reacting in any way to Altamont, by totally ignoring the ugly events over which he presided, the effect was as if some other band and some other rock star had been involved. By adroitly switching a free park concert into a memorial for Brian Jones, Jagger camouflaged the fact that he had treated Brian callously and had very recently booted him from the band Brian had started. Mick has also maintained an impenetrable curtain around his financial dealings, his wealth and the extensive investments Prince Rupert Loewenstein has made for him. He is quite probably the wealthiest of all rock multimillionaires. Recently, there has been some information forthcoming about a valuable art collection that Jagger has been secretly assembling.

In the spring of 1989, when the Stones were gearing up for their tour, Keith Richards had this perception of Jagger: "Ninety-nine percent of the male population of the Western world—and beyond—would give a *limb* to live the life of Jagger. To be *Mick Jagger*. And he's not happy being Mick Jagger. He's not living a happy life. To me, that's unacceptable. I've *got* to make him happy! To me, I've failed if I can't eventually get my mate to feel good about himself. Even though he's very autocratic and he can be a real asshole. But who can't be an asshole at times?

"The siege mentality kind of worries me about Mick. Nobody can get in there, even me, who's known him longer than anybody. What bothers me sometimes about him is not being able to get through to him. He's got his own vision about himself, which is not actually who he is. So he has to play a game; he has to act. He's not about to give you *anything*. He's not about to give *anything* away. He'll be flip.

"It's a very sad thing to me to have a friend in such a privileged position, who should be able to live one of the best lives ever—and not to be *happy*? What's so *hard* about being Mick Jagger? What's so tough? This exaggerated sense of who you are and what you should do and worrying about it so much. Why don't you just get on with it and stop trying to figure all the angles? That to me is a waste of time.

"The one thing you find out when you make a lot of money—and it always sounds *trite* when you say it, but it isn't—is that that's not the important thing. It doesn't add one iota to your happiness in life. It just means you have different problems to deal with. And it brings its own problems. Like 'Who are you going to put on retainer?'

"It's much better to be rich than poor, but not for the reasons that you would automatically think. I grew up with no bread at all. We just about made the rent. The luxuries were very, very few. I know what it's like down there. I remember it. There wasn't a lot of chances for someone, the way I grew up. My dad worked his butt off in order to just keep the rent paid and food for the family. To me, people are more important than anything else. Rock and roll, anything else, people are more important."

It must be acknowledged that Tefloning himself has enabled Jagger to outlast most of his contemporaries. By keeping the world at arm's length, and then some, Jagger has protected his performing ego. He has not allowed a voracious public to devour him, nor has he taken his high jinks in front of the band seriously. Mick is very realistic about his position in the rock world. "There's a time when a man has to do something else. I can't say what it'll definitely be. I don't want to be a rock and roll singer all my life. I couldn't bear to end up like Elvis Presley and sing in Las Vegas with all those women coming in with their handbags over their arms—it's really sick."

But until that day of judgment, Mick continues to be secluded, secretive, and paradoxical. Whoever named Jagger "King Bitch of Rock" had it right—a ruler with no queen, no jester, no kingdom, just an egocentric bitch king with a neon scepter sitting on a hollow throne.

Brian Jones's life was a metaphor of the sixties, a life goaded by a mysterious catalysis that also aroused the traditionally stodgy teenagers of Britain. As Brian struggled to free himself from the deadly torpor of Cheltenham, so too were David Hockney, Mary Quant, Joe Orton, David Bailey, Ossie Clark, Vidal Sassoon, and other talented teenagers pushing themselves to break the shackles of their confining environs. It is impossible to say whether the disciples of rock sparked the progenitors of pop art, clothes design, avant-garde theater and all the other innovators of the early sixties, but coming simultaneously as they did, they undoubtedly cross-pollinated to produce the spectacular days of the mid-sixties.

Brian Jones was a born nonconformist who couldn't accept any aspect of the world he was born into. He rebelled early on against the restraints of his home life, his school life, and the mores of his community. As a school boy, he violated the dress code, the drinking code, the sex code, the ethics code, and the parental code of his day, daring to defy the strictures rooted deep in his community. He had a basic musical talent that probably could have thrived within the bounds of the traditional world of music, but he was dedicated at all costs to defy tradition and follow his own uncharted path.

Despite the grim, discouraging circumstances that he faced when he left home and struck out on his own, he was determined, in fact *driven*, to succeed, and his belief and commitment carried the other tentative boys he had recruited—Mick, Keith, Dick, Ian and Charlie—along with him. Brian refused to change his tune to suit the ears of the rock impresarios but was determined to change their reluctance to accept the music of the group he had named the Rolling Stones. During this critical time of poverty and rebuff, more than likely the other Stones would have given up if Brian had not stubbornly held them together.

During those struggle years, the interplay among the boys was harmonious. They had a common mission, and the early manifestations of success bonded them even more. But when their popularity suddenly exploded and catapulted them into rock's upper reaches, they became a different group. Brian Jones rebelled at the very success he had created, not even able to conform to that. As the group's founder, he could have led them with his superior musicianship, but he abrogated that responsibility by wrecking the one thing that could have kept him in charge— himself. Even though Mick and Keith were composing the songs, that would not necessarily have deprived Brian of his authority. But as Brian's precipitous use of drugs and alcohol eroded his position, rendering him not only ineffective but a burden to the group, Mick, the consummate opportunist, grasped control. From the beginning, Mick's stated goal was the accumulation of money, and he smartly realized that control of the group meant control of the vast sums of money that suddenly appeared within reach.

In the climatic years of the sixties, Brian epitomized all the excesses of the rock superstar: the extravagant clothes, the profligate use of drugs, the succession of beautiful girls, the encounters with the police, the trials, the punishments, the assaults on women, the ostentatious living, the bastard children, the extraordinary talent, the constant, lavish publicity. As the decade wore on, the kids who at first admired and envied Brian began to resent him, to resent his Rolls-Royces and his elaborate clothes, his tabloid girl friends and his acid escapades, and that escalating resentment of the rich, young rock lord, more than anything else, accounts for Brian's brutal drowning. Brian probably did not die, as the world believed, from an excess of drugs and alcohol, if one is to accept a preponderance of the evidence: 1) the somewhat conflicting and rather curious statements given to the police by the three people who were at Cotchford Farm when Brian drowned, which reflect, among other things, time discrepancies and unaccounted-for time, and thus make me question the accounts; (2) the various medical reports which pathologists submitted to the coroner, none of which contained a medical reason for the drowning, i.e., heart attack, drug overdose, alcoholic excess, etc.; (3) the account by one of the Walker Brothers of what he personally observed at Cotchford Farm on the night Brian drowned; (4) Nicholas Fitzgerald's detailed account of what he observed at Brian's swimming pool the night of the drowning, an account which jibes with that of one of the Walker Brothers; (5) Marty's statement, which corroborates the other descriptions but with more direct detail. Even though I paid Marty for his disclosure and preserved his anonymity, I feel that credence should be given to his testimony, since, in my judgment, he was giving an honest account of what transpired that night.

When the sum total of all this evidence is considered, it is difficult to accept the coroner's finding of accidental drowning while swimming under the influence of drugs and alcohol; rather, the proper conclusion would seem to be that Brian drowned as a result of a brutal hazing that got out of control.

And a few months later, another outburst of brutal resentment, this time at Altamont, California, put the finishing touches on the decade, a decade that ushered in pervasive change. But for all those changes, what is left? How much of the sixties remains?

The Class System: Far from being threatened, as it seemed for a brief time, the British class system remains as entrenched as ever. Royalty remains in place, the privileged school system still flourishes, and rock stars are no longer referred to as "new royalty."

Schools: The revolutionary-minded students of the sixties, who occupied faculty offices and erected barricades in the streets, lost their steam with the end of the Vietnam War, and today campuses on both sides of the Atlantic are operating traditionally.

Drugs: What can only be thought of now as the "innocent" drugs of the sixties—marijuana, even acid since it was not addictive—have been overtaken by the deadlier drugs now sweeping the world—cocaine, crack, heroin, and ice.

Sex: The sexual revolution of the sixties, the communes, the love-ins, and the rest have given way to a retrenchment and a constrained era of safe sex as a result of the proliferation of AIDS.

Politics: The kids of the sixties had threatened to uproot entrenched politicians and shake up the political system, but, in reality, when it came time to vote, they rejected change and innovation and instead elected the staid, ultraconservative governments of Margaret Thatcher, Ronald Reagan, and George Bush.

Crime: The festive streets of the sixties, populated as they were by flower children, guitar-playing rock freaks, hippies, and other nomads, are now streets of fear, inhabited by drug dealers, muggers, and syndicate bosses.

Money: As avidly as the young people of the sixties renounced money and material things, so did they go after them once they graduated into the marketplace. Jerry Rubin traded his blue jeans for a three-piece suit and is now a Wall Street wheeler-dealer, as are many of his sixties' cohorts. Many a sixties' visionary traded his ideals for arbitrage and junk bonds, and his macrobiotic fare for junk food. Junk bonds, junk food, haircuts, and neckties are the order of the day. In sports, too, millionaires are commonplace, and comics and bubble gum have been replaced by *The Wall Street Journal* and vintage wine.

Morals: Keith Richards sounded the keynote of his day when he told the prosecutor at his drug trial, "We are not old men, worried about petty morals," but how times have changed. A few Robert Mapplethorpe photographs caused an uproar in Congress and police action in Cincinnati. The liberalism of the sixties has reverted to pre-sixties conservatism, and church affiliation and attendance have dramatically increased. And in this new climate, a woman's right to choose abortion is viciously opposed. A consortium of Roman Catholic bishops has, at a cost of several million dollars, even hired two slick Madison Avenue advertising agencies to promote its viewpoint.

There were lasting and important social contributions in the sixties, among them civil rights and the advancement of women's liberation, but, of course, the most universal contribution is the music. Nothing since has been produced that can compare with the body of work contributed by the Beatles, the Who, the Grateful Dead and the Stones; the songs they sang were known the world over, crossed into a new generation, and still find a wide audience on the radio and in concert arenas. Mick Jagger is doubtless the most electrifying of all the performers who cavorted across the rock stage, and even now, at age forty-seven, he has the verve and remarkable delivery of his youth.

Since Mick's attempts to perform on his own without the Stones were failures, it appears that he will never become a solo star, as did Diana Ross, for example, when she broke away from the Supremes. But as long as Mick has the Stones to back him, a chemistry results that fuels his unique performance. Perhaps Mick needs the reclusive, self-centered, opulent life he lives to feed the forces within him that motor his remarkable performances. The superego is certainly a common factor in the world of performers, and the better they are the more it is tolerated. Considering the impact of his performance, it would seem that Mick can go as far as he likes.

The Stones exemplify both the degradation and the celebration of the sixties. Two of the original Stones are dead and the others have subjected themselves to a hailstorm of abuses, but, remarkably, the survivors have emerged with their riches and their musical energies unimpaired. This is, perhaps, the most significant phenomenon of the sixties, that despite its dangerous excesses, most of the members of that generation have, like Jagger, emerged unscathed and have returned to a conforming society not unlike the one against which they rebelled twenty-five years ago.

References

There were a multitude of books, press articles, and published interviews used in the writing of this book. The most notable sources on the Rolling Stones and the sixties are:

Aftel, Mandy. *Death of a Rolling Stone*. Sidgwick & Jackson, 1982.

Aldridge, John. *Satisfaction*. Proteus Publishing, 1984.

Bailey, David, and Evans, Peter. *Goodbye Baby and Amen*. Condé Nast Publishing Ltd., 1969.

Balfour, Victoria. *Rock Wives*. William Morrow, 1986.

Blum, Richard H., et al. *The Dream Sellers: Perspectives on Drug Dealers*. Jossey-Bass, Inc., 1972.

Booker, Christopher. *The Neophiliacs*. Collins, 1969.

Briggs, Asa. *A Social History of England*. Weidenfeld & Nicolson, 1983.

Bulgakov, Mikhail. *The Master and Margarita*. Grove Press, 1967.

Charone, Barbara. *Keith Richards*. Futura Publications Ltd., 1979.

Crowley, Aleister. *The Diary of a Drug Fiend*. Samuel Weister, Inc., 1922.

Dalton, David. *The Rolling Stones*. Rogner & Bernhard, 1981.

Duncan, Robert. *The Noise*. Ticknor & Fields, 1984.

Eisen, Jonathan. *The Age of Rock*. Vintage Books, 1969.

Fitzgerald, Nicholas. *Brian Jones: The Inside Story of the Original Rolling Stone*. Putnam Publishing Group, 1985.

Flippo, Chet. *On the Road with the Rolling Stones*. Doubleday, 1985.

Frame, Pete. *Rock Family Trees*. Omnibus Press, 1980.

Gillett, Charlie. *The Sound of the City*. Pantheon, 1973.

Goodman, Pete. *The Rolling Stones*. Bantam Books, 1965.

Herr, Michael. *Dispatches*. Knopf, 1977.

Hoffmann, Dezo. *The Rolling Stones*. Vermilion & Co., 1984.

Hunt, Marsha. *Real Life*. Chatto & Windus, 1986.

Jahn, Mike. *Rock*. Quadrangle/The New York Times Book Co., 1973.

Jasper, Tony. *The Rolling Stones*. Octopus Books Ltd., 1976.

Lee, M. A., and Shlain, Bruce. *Acid Dreams*. Grove Press, 1985.

Legman, G. *The Fake Revolt*. Breaking Point Press, 1967.

Lewis, Peter. *The 50's*. William Heineman Ltd., 1978.

Mairowitz, David. *Some of It*. Knullar Ltd., 1969.

Mankowitz, Gered. *Satisfaction*. Sidgwick & Jackson, 1984.

Martin, Linda. *The Rolling Stones in Concert*. Crescent Books, 1982.

Melly, George. *Owning-Up*. Weidenfeld & Nicolson, 1965.

Miller, Jim, ed. *The Rolling Stone Illustrated History of Rock and Roll*. Rolling Stone Press/Random House, 1980.

Napier-Bell, Simon. *You Don't Have to Say You Love Me*. Nomis Books, 1982.

Norman, Philip. *The Life and Good Times of the Rolling Stones*. Harmony Books, 1989.

Norman, Philip. *Symphony for the Devil*. Linden Press/Simon and Schuster, 1984.

O'Neill, William. *An Oral History of America in the 60's*. Quadrangle Books, 1971.

Palmer, Robert. *The Rolling Stones*. Rolling Stone Press/Doubleday, 1983.

Rolling Stone magazine. "The Rolling Stones." Straight Arrow, 1975.

Rolling Stone magazine. *The Rolling Stone Interviews: The 1980s*. St. Martin's Press/Rolling Stone Press, 1989.

Rolling Stone magazine. *The Rolling Stone Interviews 1967–1980*. St. Martin's Press/Rolling Stone Press, 1981.

Sanchez, Tony. *Up and Down with the Rolling Stones*. William Morrow, 1979.

Schaffner, Nicholas. *The British Invasion*. McGraw-Hill, 1982.

Stevens, Jay. *Storming Heaven: LSD and the American Dream*. Atlantic Monthly Press, 1987.

Tobler, John, and Grundy, Stuart. *The Record Producers*. St. Martin's Press, 1983.

Turner, Tina, and Loder, Kurt. *I, Tina*. William Morrow, 1986.

Weiner, Sue, and Howard, Lisa. *The Rolling Stones A to Z*. Grove Press, 1983.

White, Timothy. *Rock Stars*. Stewart, Tabori & Chang, 1984.

Picture Credits

BLOWN AWAY · THE ROLLING STONE
ML 421 R64H65 1990

KEY TO RENAISSANCE ART

DATE DUE

AG 27 '92			
NO 16 '92			
JA 8 '93			
MY 23 '93			
AP 29 '94			
JY 14 '94			
AG 18 '94			
AP 7 '95			
DE 20 '96			
AP 27 '98			
JY 31 '00			
OC - 1 08			

DEMCO 38-296